MW01007722

Books by Arlene Rossen Cardozo

SEQUENCING
WOMAN AT HOME
JEWISH FAMILY CELEBRATIONS
THE LIBERATED COOK

SEQUENCING

SEQUENCING

ARLENE ROSSEN CARDOZO

COLLIER BOOKS
Macmillan Publishing Company
New York

Names and other identifying information about women who provided case histories and quotes have been changed to protect their privacy. Persons thanked on the acknowledgment pages, however, appear by name in the text.

Collier Books
Macmillan Publishing Company
866 Third Avenue, New York, N.Y. 10022
Collier Macmillan Canada, Inc.

Library of Congress Cataloging-in-Publication Data
Cardozo, Arlene.
    Sequencing / Arlene Rossen Cardozo.
        p.   cm.
    Bibliography: p.
    ISBN 0-02-042235-0
    1. Motherhood—United States.   2. Mothers—Employment—United
States.   3. Motherhood—United States—Psychological aspects.
4. Mother and child—United States.   I. Title.
    HQ759.C286   1989
306.8′743—dc19   88-38526   CIP

Macmillan books are available at special discounts for bulk purchases for sales promotions, premiums, fund-raising, or educational use. For details, contact:

Special Sales Director
Macmillan Publishing Company
866 Third Avenue
New York, N.Y. 10022

Design by Laura Rohrer

10 9 8 7 6 5 4 3 2 1

To Mother, with love
and thanks for staying home to give me a
wonderful, secure childhood.
And to Daddy, with love
and thanks for making it possible.

To Miriam, Rachel, and Rebecca, with love
and thanks for all of the pleasure
you have given me during the years I've been
privileged to be home with you.

And to Dick, with love
and thanks for making it possible.

Preface to the
Paperback Edition

Rarely does one have the opportunity to help provide a generation with new focus, perspective, and direction. It is my privilege to have been part of that process, through identifying, defining, and documenting *sequencing,* the new movement which has dramatically changed the way women are planning and living their lives.

At the time *Sequencing* was first published two years ago, millions of women were caught in conflict between their careers and their children. Fearing that if they left their work they would not only sacrifice income but never be able to return to their fields in a meaningful way, many continued in their careers, only to feel enormous sadness as they watched their children's lives all too quickly slipping past them.

Since the book's publication, many of these women have found a new solution to their dilemmas: the recognition that they can both have their careers and raise their children through sequencing their lives, rather than trying to do everything simultaneously. As more and more women begin sequencing, they join those trendsetters who are already doing so, and are redefining what "success," "career," and "family" mean in this society.

Preface

The Washington Post, The New York Times, and a host of other media are covering this phenomenon as sequencers set a new agenda through which they are leading women, children, and men into the new millennium.

Arlene Rossen Cardozo
January 1989

Preface

Sequencing is the story of trailblazing women who have wrested control over their lives from a society that seeks to make them Superwoman by imposing impossible dual roles upon them. Not only are women today expected to have full-time meaningful careers while raising families, but worse yet, they are told how to do it. The male career norm dictates that professions must be practiced nearly around the clock, and feminist theory maintains that children can be mothered in small scraps of time in early morning and late day. The result is that millions of mothers today work long hours away from their children while filled with guilt, doubt, and conflict about the benefits of doing so.

Sequencing details the ways an increasing number of courageous, imaginative, married mothers are breaking the Superwoman mold to *combine the best of modern feminism with the best of traditional mothering.* They do so first through having full-time careers, next through concentrating their energies on full-time raising of their children, and finally through carefully reintegrating their work into their lives so that it enhances rather than dominates their life-styles.

The book explores the reasons why women decide to leave the security of professional positions to mother their children; how they can and do enjoy full-time mothering to the fullest through recognizing and solving problems that frequently accompanied the role in previous generations; how, as their children grow, they are overturning long-held shibboleths about professionalism to innovate new and effective ways of combining mothering with challenging work in their chosen fields by creating meaningful part-time professional positions, flexiplace work arrangements, and entrepreneurial options.

This book is the result of more than a year of my in-depth interviews with over 200 women across the country and small group interviews with an additional 150 women, all of whom left a variety of professions for the same reason: to mother their children. All are married women with college or equivalent educations. Many have additional professional degrees. The majority of the women I interviewed worked from five to ten years before interrupting their careers, but some worked for as few as three years and others worked for more than fifteen. I particularly, though not exclusively, sought to interview women in previously male-dominated fields to learn why they, who are among the first generation of women to have entered those fields in any numbers, are leaving their work to care for their children.

I interviewed women in each of three critical life stages: (1) full-time careerwomen-mothers—both those who seemed to feel no conflict, and those who did feel conflict about working full time while raising their families and thus contemplated leaving their work for a period of time; (2) women who had recently decided to leave their careers, as well as those who had been mothering full time from one to ten or more years; and (3) women who have reintegrated careers into their lives after years away from their work.

From the first group I learned about the motivations, values, and attitudes of women who were simultaneously pursuing careers and raising families. From the second I learned about the conflicts inherent in the decision to leave their careers and about the lives of mothers who have made that decision. They told me about the difficulties they experience, the adjustments they have made, the rewards they have gained, the lifestyles they have created for themselves and their families—how they make full-time mothering work for them. From the third group I found out how they prepared to reincorporate careers into their lives, when they began to reemphasize their careers, why they chose a particular time, what difficulties they encountered, how much time they now spend on their careers, what those who have returned to organizations have done to accommodate their work to their lives, and how those who became entrepreneurs combine self-employment with mothering.

To ensure that I would talk with sequencing women from a variety of professions, backgrounds, experiences, and regions, I sought my leads from a variety of sources, including directors of college alumni associations; leaders of business and professional organizations, to whom the question, who is out mothering? is becoming more and more familiar; parent education faculty; pediatricians and obstetricians, who, though they are not free to give the names of their patients, frequently cooperated in giving my name to patients who then contacted me; personal contacts such as a former specialty book club director who recommended several of her own friends around the country who are also full-time mothering; a director of the national women's honorary, Mortar Board, who provided many leads; and a former baby sitter of my own children who is now a successful attorney. Then, as I began dialing phone numbers across the country and setting up interview appointments, nearly every woman I contacted offered, You must talk to . . . , or You have to speak with . . . Ultimately my list of prospective interviewees grew into the thousands, far exceeding the number I could actually contact. And, though that was an enormous source of frustration, certain patterns emerged in the interviews, making clear that though details vary, certain fundamentals of the sequencing option are similar among various groups of women. The consistency of these patterns across location, profession, age, and socioeconomic conditions suggests that were I to draw an additional set of names and conduct another set of interviews, the overall results would be very much the same, even though the specifics of each woman's story would remain unique.

In addition to interviews with the women themselves, I also interviewed some of their husbands, some of the employers who have hired (or rehired) sequencers, more than a dozen career strategists from across the country who specialize in advising women with both careers and families, and the leaders of New Ways to Work in San Francisco and the Association of Part-Time Professionals in McLean, Virginia. These two organizations are making major changes in the ways many Americans, including women who sequence, elect to work today. For background,

Preface

I spent many hours reading in the New Ways to Work library, which houses an exhaustive amount of material on present-day work options, and in the Catalyst library in New York. In addition, I read the work of forefront authorities in the area of corporate change such as John Naisbitt *(Reinventing the Corporation)* and Rosebeth Moss Cantor *(Changemasters)*.

This wealth of new data expands many times a framework I developed and have continually refined over the past fifteen years as an author of books for and about women and as a specialist in the area of home-based mothering: lecturer, consultant, and director of the Woman at Home Workshops, which I founded a decade ago to meet the needs of intelligent, educated women electing to raise families.

Sequencing is the result of extensive new information augmented by previous knowledge of the field and by my personal experience as both a full-time mother and a committed professional. It is my hope that the book will illuminate the challenges and opportunities available to the woman who wants to mother her own children and to enjoy stimulating, challenging, and rewarding professional activities during the same lifetime.

Acknowledgments

For a project of this magnitude, the debts are many. I am first and foremost greatly indebted to the hundreds of women I interviewed throughout the country who provided the case history material and much of the other data for the book. These women's names have been changed in the text to protect their privacy and therefore cannot be given here. Nonetheless, I express my thanks to each and every one of them.

My appreciation to the many persons who provided leads to women to interview as well as those who gave me specific information extends from coast to coast and includes Phyllis Stein, director of Radcliffe Career Services in Cambridge, Massachusetts; the entire New Ways to Work staff in San Francisco, particularly founders Suzanne Smith and Barney Olmsted and client program manager Linda Marks; Diane Rothberg, director of the Association of Part-Time Professionals, McLean, Virginia; Jane Sommer, associate director of the Smith College Career Development Office, Northampton, Massachusetts; Beth Cutting of the Parent Puzzle, a parent education program in Minneapolis; Harvard Medical School psychiatrist Dr. Katherine Poole Wolf; Jack Daley, Tymshare, Cupertino, California; Chuck Marcy, vice-president of retail sales, Kitchens of Saralee, Deerfield, Illinois; Dr. Eleanor Paradise, Cambridge, Massachusetts, psycholo-

Acknowledgments

gist; Judy Corson, partner, Custom Research Associates; Gail McClure, head of the University of Minnesota's Communications Resource Division; Carol Kanarek, founder of Kanarek and Shaw legal consulting services, New York; and Rebecca Jacobs Handler, a New York magazine editor.

My special thanks go to my agent Peter Ginsberg, president of Curtis Brown Ltd., for his tremendous enthusiasm for the initial proposal as well as for the completed project; and my friend and colleague Marge Roden for reading and commenting on the final draft. And my immense gratitude goes to Joyce Hegstrom, without whose cheerful turn-around-typing of more than a dozen manuscript drafts and frequent door-to-door service as well, this book would not have been completed ahead of its deadline.

As usual, I am most grateful to the world's best support system, my wonderful family: Dick, who was never too busy to leave the scholarly articles and book manuscript on which he is working to talk through elements of *Sequencing*'s conceptual framework and to read and comment on various drafts of the manuscript; Miriam, who willingly was interrupted from the writing of her Harvard thesis by my questions, requests for advice, and comments; Rachel, who whenever I was in a time crunch took time from her university course work to keep the kitchen running while I kept the typewriter running; and Rebecca for her extremely helpful suggestions with difficult passages as well as for transforming stacks of books and clippings into a bibliography.

Contents

Contents

PART II
THE GOLDEN YEARS

Contents

PART III
THE SEQUENCER:
A NEW PROFESSIONAL AGENDA

Contents

SEQUENCING

Introduction

The
Death of Superwoman

A twenty-eight-year-old Los Angeles advertising executive turns down a promotion to stay home with her two small daughters; a thirty-five-year-old Chicago area accountant leaves a successful career to raise her baby boy; a thirty-two-year-old New York physician cuts back her thriving medical practice to spend most of the day at home with her three-year-old son.

What's happening? Why do educated women with years of career experience leave the professional mainstream to stay at home with their children? Because Superwoman, the 120-hour-a-week dual-lifer, who worked full time at a high-powered career while trying to raise her children nights and weekends, is dead of stress, exhaustion, and the belief that her career was cheating her out of forming and enjoying the most important relationships in her life. Dead with her is the myth upon which she was founded: that every woman can have a full-time career and close, meaningful family relationships—simultaneously.

Instead, an increasing number of educated, career-experienced women are taking control of their adult lives by sequencing them into three stages: stage one, the full-time career; stage two, full-time mothering; and stage three, reincorporating a career in new ways so that family and profession complement rather than conflict.

The woman who elects to sequence enjoys both her career and her family to the fullest all in one lifetime—precisely by not trying to do it all at all times. To appreciate the reasons for a woman's sequencing choice as well as the magnitude of her decision, it is first necessary to understand the context from which emerged both the Superwoman image and the contemporary woman's decision to create a saner, healthier, and more workable alternative.

Superwoman was created and perpetuated by feminist leaders of the 1960s and 1970s as the antithesis to the "trapped housewife" of the 1950s: a woman bounded within her suburban split-level home by little education and limited or no work experience—the product of long-standing American role expectations for women that differed markedly from those for men.

Before the modern feminist movement, women were expected to marry, to have children, and to stay at home to raise them. Men were expected to get as much education as they could and then to embark upon careers, working throughout their lifetimes to support not only themselves but their wives and children. Although there were rare exceptions, by and large a serious career commitment outside of raising a family was not a role undertaken by a woman. Hers was a different social mission: bearing and raising the next generation.

Aside from the World War II years, when men were at war and women in record numbers joined the paid labor force, men and women played these clearly defined roles throughout the early decades of this century and on through the 1950s with the same degree of acceptance with which they assumed that America was great and God was good. Then the 1960s ushered in a storm of social upheaval: The Age of Discontent.

Children of the veterans who fought in the 1940s and 1950s refused to fight in Vietnam; their generation questioned America's greatness. What of the poor and the blacks? they asked as they marched for civil rights. They questioned religion, too, until some clergy moaned that we were a nation of nihilists. With state and church under intense scrutiny, and oftentimes outright attack, the institution of the family was ripe for upheaval as well. For the family was founded upon seemingly inflexible norms and values that assigned men one role in the society and women another.

There were rumblings of discontent about this role specialization throughout the years preceding the 1960s—a woman complained here, another there. Strangely, it was not the men—assigned the role of lifetime wage earners, bringing home to share with others all that they earned forevermore—who questioned the societal norms. Instead, the complaints were first heard from those women who felt social pressure to marry and to have children, as well as from those married mothers who felt imprisoned behind their picture windows in a suburban world outside the bustle of the cities in which their husbands worked. Finally, in 1963, Betty Friedan, a dissatisfied, later-divorced wife, and a mother, focused the discontent with the publication of *The Feminine Mystique*. After that, women were suddenly out of the closet, out of the suburbs, burning their bras and often their bridges.

Like the nineteenth-century women's activist Margaret Fuller and other of her feminist forebears, Friedan fervently stated that women were trapped by unrealistic, obsolete societal expectations. But she added to their arguments nearly a century of new data. Not only was it theoretically unnecessary for all women to be forced into one mode, but the expectation was pragmatically outdated as well. Women of the 1960s had families far smaller than those of their grandmothers, yet women's life expectancies had risen dramatically. The result was that a married woman could be left with no children at home by the time she hit forty with nearly half her life still ahead. Friedan officially alerted women that they could well spend the latter half of their lives in empty nests, thoroughly bored, with children grown and husbands busy with careers. For many women who already felt lonely and isolated out in suburbia while their husbands worked long hours away from them, the prospect was dim.

What a woman needed to prevent a lifetime of living exclusively through her husband, children, and the predictable empty nest, Friedan argued, was education leading to a career; fill-in jobs before her children were born or after they were raised were not enough. Rather, women needed to be stretched to the limits of their capabilities, to train for and experience "real careers" just as men did.

Through the 1960s and 1970s other vehement spokeswomen took up and amplified Friedan's cause, among them Gloria Steinem, founding mother of *Ms.* magazine. The agenda these new spokeswomen set—paid work for all women at all times in their lives—was predicated upon the doctrine of careerism: the middle- and upper-middle-class male norm which states that one's career is the central core of one's life. According to this norm, one's work determines one's level of worth, is in fact one's reason for being. Internalization of this perspective wrought changes in self-perceptions of a generation of American women who developed a different set of expectations to replace the traditional normative ones. Women affected by this changed view fell into four groups: single women; married women without children; married women whose children were grown; and married mothers of young and growing children.

A full-time career was a reasonable antidote to women's too narrow role definition *for the first three groups.* A full-scale career was beneficial to many single and married, childless women. It was tailor-made for the empty-nester. But a full-time career was never practical for all members of the fourth group of women—the married mothers of young children. Yet feminist theorists, anxious to encourage all women to pursue work outside the home, promoted full-time careers for *all* women at *all stages* of their lives. This was a critical error in a movement that has otherwise created tremendous and unprecedented opportunities for millions of women. In cases where feminism spoke to women as individuals without other priorities, the movement provided countless new choices, opened previously closed doors to a multitude of professions, and offered improved economic circumstances and new paths to personal fulfillment. But when feminism spoke to married mothers of young children, the new careerism message, which was intended to promote choice, frequently appeared to be a new dogma denigrating mothering. In addition, the print and electronic media, which continually covered the new cause, proclaimed in words and images that raising children was passé; a career outside the family was the thing for women of all ages and stages of life! Thus women with babies, toddlers, preschoolers, grade-schoolers, and high-schoolers were lumped together with single women, childless women, and women whose children were grown, and stirred into one pressure cooker. Mothers exhorted to manage careers while raising families were promised that they could have it all at once—that it could be done smoothly, happily, and simultaneously.

Who created and perpetuated this myth? Someone who had done so herself? No. Social movements are frequently characterized by gaps between the lives of the theorists who lead the movements and those of the followers who try to practice the theorists' ideas. Modern feminism is no exception. When one reviews the early media history of the feminist movement by looking at hours of tapes and reading through mounds of bound magazine volumes it becomes clear that the promises were rarely made by mothers of growing children like Friedan but, in large part, by childless women such as Gloria Steinem and Germaine Greer. Thus the very persons who redefined motherhood by fashioning new maternal-child theories for millions of women and children were not experts in developmental psychology or in early childhood development, nor were they experienced mothers or grandmothers. Rather, they were women without firsthand knowledge of the complexities of raising babies and small children.

Anxious to make careers accessible to all women, early feminists theorized that it was not necessary for children to consume their mother's time and attention throughout the day; their mothers were too intelligent and too capable to be limited to raising them. Instead, mothers should work away from their children all day just as fathers did, while they, the next generation, were in other-than-parent care. Maternal presence and participation, on a continuous, day-to-day basis, was suddenly dispensable, no longer important to the life of the mother or her child. The absentee mother became the vogue model of the day—an inexhaustible evening and weekend visitor, who brought to her role a brand new definition of raising children: she could do it with a few quick goodnight kisses and a bedtime story. That's because the role of absentee mother was predicated upon that of the absentee father; in fact, fatherhood became the very model for motherhood. Men don't stay home and raise their children. They have careers and come home to their families nights and weekends. Why shouldn't women? was the response given by feminist leaders to mothers who asked how they could possibly raise children and pursue careers simultaneously.

Emerging from this new theory was a brand new careerwoman-mother—Superwoman—who worked forty, fifty, sometimes sixty or more hours a week at a challenging career, attempting to climb a success ladder as did her husband. She smilingly got her children up and situated in the morning and returned to them after work, glowing from her fulfilling day, cheerfully prepared dinner, heard about her children's days, read them stories, then was off with her husband to a concert or play. To round out her life, she sometimes spent evening and weekend time with friends outside the family, kept up a hobby or two, and perhaps got in a weekend jog.

Such was the idealized life of the careerwoman-mother to which millions of middle- and upper-middle-class women of the early 1970s aspired, as they left their children all day for work away from them. These women, who had previously done one job—cared for their children—now began doing two. For the first time in American social history, the haves were predicating their lifestyles on those of the have-nots. Before the new feminism emerged, women who worked outside the home were those forced by economic circumstances to do so: widows with inadequate insurance, divorcees with inadequate alimony, or women whose husbands were unable to support the family. But suddenly, married women whose husbands could provide economically sought paid work but did so for reasons other than financial necessity. These women worked full time just as men did, then came home to their families evenings and weekends; but there were no wives awaiting them.

Husbands were called upon to become more active parents and, in addition, to cook, clean, do laundry, carpool, and share all that was traditionally done by their wives. Some husbands balked; some "helped their wives out"; a few wholeheartedly did their share. But even women whose husbands were highly supportive found that doing two full-time jobs—career building and family making—was a monumental task. Many women in the best of circumstances were nagged by the question, What kind of care are my children *really* getting? They realized that there weren't enough hours in the day for them to feel wholly effective both on the job and at home. Their feelings were complicated still further by concerns that their children's lives were racing by them and the added problem that "there is simply no time for me."

The discrepancy between the life of the hypothetical Superwoman and the actual careerwoman-mother occurred in large measure because Superwoman was predicated upon the lifestyle of the woman who had never nursed a child, been up all night with a sick infant, gotten a toddler into a snowsuit and to the day care center before fighting traffic to reach the office, interrupted work for a telephone conference with the teacher, left work to take her child to the pediatrician, car-pooled to a scout meeting, or spent the evening at PTA.

Yet the feminism of the early 1970s prescribed one lifestyle for all women, in spite of a fundamental error in the Superwoman design: the omission of the fact that she was female. So critical was it that early feminism inculcate *social equality* into the nation's consciousness that it bypassed the matter of *physical inequality*: that women can do some things that men can never do—become pregnant, give birth to new life, and nurse that life. Early feminism so needed to prove the woman=man, man=woman formula that it let slip the product of the difference between them and thus omitted the next generation from the original scheme.

Problems arose, however, as more and more women tried to practice feminist theories in their own everyday lives and the theorists were continually confronted with the issue they had previously let go by: the future of the human race. Their replies to questions of who will care for my children while I am gone from them all day? failed to recognize—on grounds of sexism, biological determinism, and revisionist psychology—the existence of a mother's deep desire to be physically close to her children, to establish and maintain close emotional bonds with them, to nurture and protect them. Those needs were dismissed as social conditioning that could soon be programmed out of the species. Children could be cared for by their grandmothers, by a neighbor down the block whose children were grown, by warm, loving, stimulating caretakers in excellent centers to which they could be brought in the morning and in which they would stay all day.

That these surrogate caregivers generally failed to materialize is not surprising. Who could blame grandmother and the woman down the block whose children were grown for not being available to care for the next generation? These women were perfect targets for the new message—their nests were empty—but they weren't sitting home waiting to fill them with someone else's children. They were back in the classrooms, out in the marketplaces, beneficiaries of the best of new feminist attitudes: that women who had already raised families could create meaningful places in the world beyond their homes.

And what about the center to which children could be brought to receive high-quality care from well-trained, intelligent, loving people, personalized attention, stimulation? Such excellent centers were not readily available then, nor are they in abundance now. Moreover, no one—leader or follower—anticipated the adverse reactions of the mother faced with leaving her progeny in those centers, day in and day out, year in and year out, during the child's prime developmental years.

"But what about one-to-one care by their mothers?" the speakers were asked by the children's own mothers. "They can have that, too," said the theorists, emphatically stating the creed of absentee motherhood: It's the quality, not the quantity of time that counts.

Although that argument was superficially compelling, on closer examination its implied assumption—that *more* time was somehow *less* than quality time—was one many mothers found erroneous. All agreed that five good minutes were superior to one bad hour, but none believed that five good minutes were better than one good hour. Ironically, as many a mother who tried to be Superwoman became exhausted after a hectic day at the office and a long commute, she often wondered as she hurried her toddler to bed, then tried to help her first grader with his reading, where the quality time was.

Why was it not evident from the beginning that the Superwoman paradigm would not work for *all* women? There were two very powerful reasons.

First, Superwoman had a marvelous public relations department composed of feminist organizers, writers, and speakers, who promoted careerism through the media that published their writings, publicized their statements, and covered the events they staged. The result was the establishment of a social climate that first gave permission for the new role changes and then created tremendous pressure for these changes to become normative for *all* women.

Second, within the framework of this altered social climate the new working-women-mothers had no role models apart from the mythical Superwoman. Because most of the women who initially left their children for jobs lacked advanced education and work experience, most felt tremendously insecure in the face of the new and powerful message, which was: you are inadequate unless you can succeed in the marketplace. Anybody can raise children. You must prove that you are somebody.

The undereducated, career-inexperienced women of the late 1960s and early 1970s, told by these new spokespersons that their mothering was valueless, desperately wanted to prove that they were adequate, worthwhile, successful in the newly defined terms. Since there were no previous role models, they were the guinea pigs. They could not possibly have anticipated the tremendous difficulties inherent in trying to provide their babies and young children with continuity of day-in, day-out, love, care, time, and energy while simultaneously attempting to further full-scale careers.

The prerequisite for "having it all at once" soon became clear. Women who managed to do it had to leave their children for eight-, ten-, and twelve-hour stretches in the care of others to whom they were willing to entrust their mental, physical, and emotional welfare. In addition, the women needed strong backup systems in the form of supportive husbands, and nearby relatives or close friends to help when children were ill or other emergencies arose. And they needed to get along on limited sleep year in and year out.

For many women having it all at once did not go as planned. When children were sick and there was nobody at home, when the mother became exhausted from juggling job and family responsibilities, when she felt out of touch with her children, with her husband, even herself, often she thought she had done something wrong—that it was she who had made a mistake. So she tried harder to balance the demands made upon her, to schedule differently, to reschedule, to try new surrogate child care arrangements. Yet, frequently, regardless of what she did, she felt under stress, she was tired, and perhaps worst of all, she felt cheated: where's the fulfillment? she asked. Throughout the 1970s one whispered the question quietly, and then another, and another: Is this all there is?

Meanwhile, the media barrage continued, the feminist theorists continued, and the women's support groups continued to emphasize the new norm and new values: women could and should combine full-time careers with raising families. A mother's children (referred to as "commitments," "responsibilities," and "burdens") should not be allowed to stand in her way. Correspondingly, the message of what was to constitute work escalated with each passing year. In the 1960s all women were exhorted to take jobs;

by the early 1970s they were to have meaningful careers; by the mid-1970s every woman was to become a doctor, lawyer, or executive; by the 1980s she was to become chief of staff of a major teaching hospital, senior partner of a prestigious law firm, or chief executive officer of a Fortune 500 company. When the demands of trying to combine high-powered careers with motherhood drained a woman's time and energies so that there was little or nothing left for her children, her marriage, or herself, each assumed there was something wrong with her, that she was not doing it right. Each questioned herself: What am I doing wrong?

SEQUENCING

By the late 1970s and early 1980s, articulate, intelligent, courageous members of a new generation of women began to take control of their lives by redirecting the question. Instead of blaming themselves, they placed the blame where it belongs: squarely on the social order that dogmatically and normatively assigns them dual roles, each to be performed thoroughly, well, and simultaneously.

These women have the confidence and ability to right the system that wrongs them and their children. Unlike so many of the mothers of the late 1960s and early 1970s who left their children for the marketplace, these women of the 1980s have the same degrees and career training as men do. They have succeeded through at least four and sometimes six, eight, or ten years of postsecondary education and have held responsible positions in their chosen fields. The confidence that they can handle and excel in the same professions as do males has given them the security to react against a social order that seeks to rob them of their heritage as females—the right to mother their young. They challenge a system that seeks instead to keep them in a constant state of motion from career to children on high-demand schedules with no respite year in and year out.

This new generation of clear-eyed women challenges the assumptions upon which the Superwoman system was based, as they would in the boardroom, the courtroom, or the operating room. They ask hard questions, and when they find the answers lacking, superficial, or inappropriate they supply their own, through a redefinition of the values, priorities, and perspectives with which society has inculcated them.

The first assumption they dismantle is the outmoded feminist dogma that men and women ought to function similarly in the society in all ways at all times. These women know they can fulfill their professional responsibilities as capably as their male colleagues but do not want this fact to impede them as women. They believe their education and career experience to be additional to, rather than substitutes for, their maternal birthrights. As human females they have had the right and responsibility to nurture their young since time immemorial, and they do not want a *Brave New World* social order to dictate that they must relinquish that right. Just as women were once barred from higher education and meaningful careers, they now see themselves in danger of being barred from mothering their own offspring.

The second assumption these women challenge is the belief upon which surrogate child care is based: that hired caretakers can replace the day-in, day-out love and care that they, as mothers, can give their own children. They don't stage sit-ins to make their views paradigmatic for all other mothers, but each wants her own children to receive what she considers the best care in the world. Each is confident as a human being, as a woman, and as a mother that her own care is better for her child's intellectual, perceptual, conceptual, and humanistic development than that of anyone she can hire. Each recognizes surrogate care as care different from her own, and none is willing to settle for her child being influenced and imprinted during the early formative years by a hired caretaker or a series of them.

Further, each woman feels that she can provide the ingredient she feels is most necessary of all to her child's development—consistency of love. Each believes that her own personal involvement and interaction will give her child an invaluable start in life: a sense of security, stability, and belonging, a confidence in who and whose he or she is.

In addition to each woman's belief that her decision to raise her own children is best for her children, she also feels it is best for herself. She feels that by working full time and leaving her children in surrogate care throughout their early years, she will forfeit an opportunity she can never regain.

In addition to their concern about the effect of surrogate care on their children, women now question the wisdom— for themselves—of relinquishing the opportunity to care for their young. How will I feel in twenty years knowing I let an experience I can never regain slip by? is the question asked by those mothers who feel careers can wait but children cannot.

These contemporary women have cut through the Superwoman rhetoric to the core to expose the reality that a full-time career commitment coupled with full-time motherhood can result in stress, exhaustion, conflict, guilt, resentment, and feelings of deprivation of maternal privileges far more often than it results in the feelings of freedom and fulfillment for which it was designed.

Sequencing is the solution more and more women choose of having it all—career and family—by not trying to do it all at once, at all times in their lives. Women who elect to sequence first complete their educations and gain career experience, then leave full-time work during the years they bear and mother their young children, and then—as their children grow—innovate new ways to incorporate professional activities back into their lives, so that mothering and profession don't conflict. These women—who have clearly separated the work of the house from the raising of their families—are neither "housewives" nor "jobwives" but are persons to themselves. As such, they are the most dedicated generation of mothers yet, for they are the first generation of women to be full-time mothers completely through choice. Factored out of the role—once normative for *all* women— are those women who elect to remain single, those who married but elect to be childless, and those married mothers who prefer to pursue their careers. It is therefore not surprising that this generation of full-time mothers, who have chosen above all else to raise their children, create lifestyles which they and their families thoroughly enjoy. Nor is it surprising that they solve creatively problems such as potential isolation from an adult community, which often plagued their predecessors.

In standing up for mothering as a critically important role choice, women of the 1980s who leave professional positions to mother their children have given the choice new credibility. And with this credibility has come respect for their decisions from many quarters: employers, colleagues, family, and friends.

Before leaving their jobs, many women expect their employers will be unsympathetic, but they often find instead that their decisions are applauded. A San Francisco attorney's situation is not unusual: "When I told the senior partners in my law firm two years before partnership evaluation that I was headed home to my baby instead of full-speed-ahead with them I figured they'd write me off; but to my surprise they said they understood my decision and that the door will be open when I want to come back." A Midwest executive recounts a similar experience but in a corporate setting with a female employer, who said "she regretted terribly her own decision to work during her children's early years, that if she had to do it all over again she would have done what I was doing."

Two, three, and certainly five years ago these examples would have been the clear exceptions to the rule. Although they are still not the rule today, they are not uncommon. Many women also find collegial and outside support for the sequencing decision. A thirty-eight-year-old woman who left a thriving child psychiatry practice to mother her own children says, "The fact that I am a well-trained and experienced therapist who stays home to mother conveys a powerful message. Many of my colleagues have supported my choice, and among those outside the field I often encounter curiosity mixed with admiration: they wonder what it is that I know that they don't."

The tides have definitely turned from the denigration of mothering perpetrated by feminists of the 1960s and 1970s desperate for societal support to validate their theories, to the responses these full-time mothers of the mid-1980s describe. The reason for the shift is that full-time mothering is no longer a compulsory lifestyle for the woman who is trained for "nothing else." Now it's a choice made by women who can do *everything* else of importance—who have succeeded in all of the professions our society most reveres and who believe at a certain point in their lives that raising their children is the most important choice of all.

When they are ready to reincorporate careers into their lives, these women who know what is involved both in being full-time professionals and full-time mothers are modeling creative, innovative ways to make the dream of a successful merger of family and career a reality. They are uniquely qualified to model the merger because they have taken time to learn each of the component parts completely and separately. Now they are redefining professionalism to correspond to the needs of mothers, fathers, and others in the society whose lives go beyond their careers.

Regardless of location or profession, nearly all women who elect to sequence create a means of career reemphasis that enables them to control their lives by controlling their time. Some change existing organizations so they can do it;

others become entrepreneurs. Each considers a range of options carefully to avoid getting locked in, a second time, to a situation in which her life is controlled by others.

Although different women choose to reemphasize their careers at different times and in different ways, the common denominator is that the maturity a woman develops through the experiences of raising a family and of structuring her own time and interests while doing it forever enlarges her perspectives.

Neither the decision to sequence nor its implementation is easy. The purpose of this book is to provide mothers who have begun sequencing their lives, as well as women contemplating that course of action, with a full discussion of the sequencing decision and its ramifications, a guide for making the most of their full-time mothering years, and an exploration of career reemphasis options specifically tailored to the woman who wants to reincorporate professional activities into her life without compromising her mothering priorities.

Part I, "Changing Focus," explores the conflicts involved in the decision-making process, establishment of clear priorities and realistic goals with one's mate, developing a joint financial plan to make living on one paycheck possible, the trade-offs necessary to make the option work effectively, and the potential rewards of so doing.

Part II, "The Golden Years," focuses on the full-time mothering years and solving the potential problems of the sequencing transition: creating a reinforcing community of like-minded women and an appropriate home base so that a woman can raise her children within a supportive environment; the art of participatory rather than managerial mothering; making time for personal activities, including developing avocations and a new look at the old concept of community service; and maintaining career contacts and other means of preparing for career reemphasis while mothering.

Part III, "The New Professional Agenda," details the values on which a new agenda rests. It explores implementation of the new professionalism through assessing the best time for career reemphasis, the optimal amounts of time to spend on one's career, why most sequencing mothers won't return to full-time positions, how they are instead innovating flexible professional positions within existing organizations, changing those organizations to accommodate to their needs, becoming both intrapreneurs and entrepreneurs so they can control their own time and thereby their own lives.

Part I

Changing Focus

Imagine a ladder and a spiral stair rising into the air side by side. The ladder represents the straight, vertical career path originally developed by men. The spiral stair represents the decision-making style women have evolved to accommodate the complexities of marriage, family, work, and community. In the 1970's many young women first gained access to the essentially male career ladder. In the 1980's, as some of these same women bear children, they step from that ladder to the spiral stair, often without realizing they have done so. Climbing a spiral requires constant balancing, reorienting—taking risks to round each bend. It's behavior that's confusing, even shocking, to former ladder-climbers, especially if they assumed that having children would mean simply a scheduling change on the way up the ladder, rather than a fundamental shift from linear to spiral progress.

Jane Sommer, Associate Director
Career Development Office
Smith College

Reclaiming one's birthright is not always a simple matter. Some women make the sequencing decision easily, but for others it's a complex process that frequently involves a woman's restructuring her entire value system, and looking at her present and future with an entirely new perspective. Her decision often means that her husband changes his values, priorities, and perspectives as well; and it requires of them both a strong ideological and economic commitment. For virtually all couples the decision to sequence originates with the woman and is first and foremost her personal choice, whether she arrives at it easily (Chapter 1) or with difficulty (Chapter 2). Next, sequencing becomes a joint lifestyle decision of both husband and wife, which requires the couple to develop a number of mutual expectations (Chapter 3) including a financial prospectus for its implementation (Chapter 4).

1

The
Certain Woman

WHO SEQUENCES?

Married women from all professional backgrounds, socio-economic groups, and geographical locations elect to sequence. This is not surprising when one considers that the decision to mother her preschoolers full time is the most prevalent role choice made today by *married mothers* of children under six years old. The July 1984 Bureau of Labor Statistics report states that more than two-thirds (68 percent) of *married mothers* of children under six are not engaged in full-time paid work. *Over half of them (52 percent) are full-time mothers who do no paid work while their children are under six.* (Another 16 percent work part time, some only a few hours a week from their homes.)

That the decision to mother her own children is today's most popular role choice of married mothers of preschoolers does not mean that it is an easy choice for all women who leave their careers. Women decide to sequence via two very different routes: one is relatively short and smooth; the other is longer and much more difficult.

The major determinant of who leaves her career with ease and who does so with anguish is not the woman's profession, location, whether her own mother worked, her political affiliations or—for many more than one might think—even her socioeconomic status. The primary determinant is the degree to which a woman has accepted the male career norm, which states that one's career is the focal point of one's life, and the theory of surrogate child care—that somebody else will raise the children—which underlies that norm.

The woman who accepts both the norm and its underlying surrogate child care theory often feels severe conflicts as she tries to implement that theory into the realities of her own life. The woman who never accepted the substitute child care premise is relatively free of ambivalence even if she once accepted the norm of career as central to her life.

LEAVING THE CAREER WITH COMFORT

The male career norm, which was the jumping-off place of modern feminism, rests upon the theory of surrogate child care: to do the jobs men have always done *in the ways that men have always done them*, somebody else has to raise the children.

The woman who is certain she wants to leave her career to raise her children has never accepted this premise because like most women in most cultures at most times she equates having a child with raising that child. She may initially have delayed pregnancy because of her career, to save money, or both, but the expectation that she will be a full-time mother is integral to her decision to become pregnant. Although she may have accepted the norm of career as central to her life before marriage, and even before pregnancy, she rejects the surrogate child care premise that underlies it as incompatible with her decision to become a mother.

Because having a baby and mothering that baby herself are synonymous to her, she leaves her work before the first child's birth, and she and her husband plan their finances accordingly. They almost never live on two incomes in the years before the first baby's arrival but rather use her salary for major onetime purchases or savings while living on his, so that the loss of her check is not a financial shock or economic impossibility.

This smooth, easy, almost storybook picture arises from my numerous interviews with women throughout the country who would drive the conflicted woman—who also loves her children but doesn't find it easy to leave her work—to say, "They must be professional failures; that's why it's so easy for them to leave."

It's a question I asked myself: are the women who leave their careers with such certainty in actuality the ones who couldn't make it? Clearly not, I found. Certainty about leaving a career to mother her children appears unrelated to career success; in fact, some of the most highly successful women I interviewed—as measured in present marketplace terms of salary, title, and assessment by superiors and peers

—walk away from their work the most easily. The certainty is much more related to the *value* the woman places on her career in relation to the *value* she places upon time spent with her children in a given period of her life than on the degree of success she has achieved in her field. The woman who leaves her work with certainty plainly feels no real pull between two opposing values: her children take top place in the way she chooses to spend her time at a given point in her life. Confidence in her own abilities both to mother and to work again, coupled with the feeling that a career is important but not the be-all or end-all of her life, permits her to leave easily.

Anita Crawford is a woman who unequivocally chose to be replaced on the job rather than at home. Intense, dark-eyed Crawford serves me coffee and cake at a lemon-yellow table in the paneled family room of her suburban Boston home while her three-year-old son and a playmate build a Lego ship in one corner of the room; her new baby naps in a portacrib in the opposite corner. Thirty-five-year-old Crawford speaks rapidly about the ten-year career she left as a corporate tax analyst for a multinational company: "When I first began working in 1972 I was in thrall of the idea that my career and I were going to go through life inseparable and indivisible with no interference from anybody else. I became professionally successful in terms of salary and promotions, but as years passed I began to crave what to me was personal success: a man to share my life with and children to raise. I gave a lot to my work, got a lot from it, but it simply wasn't everything. Sure it was prestigious, sure it was fun, but all that ceased to matter in the face of my new priorities.

"It was important to me to marry a man with similar goals and values about raising a family. I did not want one of those who espouses equality because he really wants to find a wife to help him support a transcontinental yuppie lifestyle. My husband feels as I do about my being home to raise our children: that I can do it better than anyone else.

"I feel that my children cannot get the kind of closeness, the love, the individualized attention, from anyone else they can get from me. Besides, if they did, I'd be as jealous as if my husband was getting closeness, love, and attention from another woman. These are my children, and it's my prerogative to care for them. I'm exercising that prerogative to the fullest."

When I asked Crawford if she missed the work she left three years ago, she responded, "Not very often. Although the other day I longed for a quiet office when my son was having a temper tantrum because I was trying to feed the baby when he wanted to go outside and she was screaming because he was screaming. At times like that I remember how I kept major executives at rapt attention during long meetings. Or, sometimes I miss the office when we're inside for days because it's raining or somebody has a bad cold; I get fleeting glimpses of my life as it used to be. I have images of myself—in a new suit, enjoying a long lunch— but I rarely feel nostalgic two days in a row. The thing is I get really involved in whatever I undertake, and now I'm immersed in mothering. I made a ten-year full-time commitment to my work; now I feel I deserve at least ten years free of it to make an equally strong commitment to my family."

But what about the money, I asked her. She surely must miss that: "I was earning a top salary when I left, more than I needed to live on when I was single and certainly more than we needed once I was married. I invested a portion of my earnings every year when I was single and nearly the entire check for the two years after I was married and was still working. While the income on my investments doesn't begin to approach my previous earnings, it provides us with an income additional to my husband's salary, and we get along well on that total."

Crawford expresses a great deal of confidence about working again in the future: "I have no idea if anything will be available at my level in my former company when I am ready. However, I have a C.P.A., an M.B.A. which I earned in the evenings while working full time, and my ten years' experience, so I will definitely find a good place. The tax laws constantly change and require that you read up on them continuously even when you work in the field every day, but the basics do not. I continue to keep up, so on any given day I could go back to work if I had to, but I hope I don't have to for a long time. I don't want work to interfere with my present plans: I adore these kids, and I want us to spend this part of our lives together."

Clearly, Crawford left her work with comfort because she very much wanted to have and to raise her children. In addition, she does not fear permanent loss of professional position, a factor that plagues many women who are conflicted about whether to take a period of years off from their work. Crawford envisions an eventual return to the same field and is confident about her chances of returning to a position similar to the one she vacated, at a different time in her life.

Confidence such as Crawford exhibits characterizes many of the women who leave their work with certainty. A woman who graduated at the top of her Columbia Law School class before she was twenty-four, landed a place in one of New York's prestigious firms, and left four years later when her first daughter was born believes, "If I want to return to a major firm, of course I'll get in again. What's the worst that can happen? Suppose I wait until I'm forty; a lot of people graduate from law school when they're forty and then start from scratch. I'll be starting with a top-of-the-class degree from a top school, plus four years' experience in a coveted firm behind me and with twenty-five or thirty years ahead of me. If I can't make something of myself in that length of time, then I doubt very much that another decade would make the difference."

A former managing editor of a publishing company is similarly confident: "I've been in publishing for nine years, have loads of contacts and an excellent reputation. With all my expertise in this field I can't believe that five or even ten years away would put me at the bottom of the heap. I'm keeping up some of my main contacts; I do some very selected consulting, and when I'm ready to return I'll watch carefully for the right opportunity and then go for it."

Almost without exception, the women who leave their positions without fear of difficulty of return are those who are basically self-confident of their proven abilities in their

fields and couple that confidence with flexibility and imagination, perceiving that they will use their career backgrounds in different ways at different times in their lives.
Thus none is fixated upon a return to a specific company
or niche, but rather envisions using her capabilities to return to the general field. The most distinctive feature regarding the career perceptions of the woman who leaves
her work with comfort is that she sees her past accomplish-
ments as collateral to take with her as evidence of her
abilities, whereas the conflicted woman often sees all that
she has done and built as being left behind her.

Although some women such as Crawford plan to return
to their previous fields, another group of women who leave
their work with certainty do so at the time they are ready
for a professional change: to a new field, to a new aspect
of a similar field, or to return to school for further training
in a specific area. Since they also want to raise children, the
readiness for a family coupled with the plan for an eventual
career change or modification means they experience little
conflict about leaving their present work, taking a break to
mother full time, then adding work or more school to their
lives later.

Petite, red-headed Jane Kranz, who left the directorship
of an in-house education program for a Milwaukee insurance company when her first baby was born, stated: "I was
psychologically ready to leave although it is difficult financially. We have to budget very carefully; there aren't any
extras, and we may not be able to buy a house for years.
But we wanted to start our family now. Later, I'll do something new professionally and be a contributor to the family

income as well. I went with my company right out of college, rose rapidly, worked there for three and one-half years, and was ready to move to something else. For me, this is really a perfect career break point. I have my past experience on my résumé and it is background for a number of fields— business, communications, or education. It should be just as good later as now. If I find it's not, I'll get a master's degree to add to it. Even if I take fifteen years totally away from work, I will have twenty-five or more career years later on." Like Crawford, Kranz thinks flexibly about a professional future, but whereas Crawford expects to return to her former work, Kranz expects to explore new options in later years.

Some women who leave careers with certainty plan an eventual return to their former fields, and others expect to change fields later. A few, however, do not plan to return to paid work, so baby and work are no contest for them. Marie Orlean is one such woman.

In contrast to Jane Kranz, who is twenty-five and who worked for fewer than four years, tall, model-thin Marie Orlean was forty when she left her fifteen-year career as a sought-after West Coast publicist to stay home with her new daughter. Now, two years later, she has a new son as well, is thoroughly involved in mothering, and looks back on her decision without regret.

"I was truly ready for this. I've had the glamour lunches, met the big-name people—the actors, the directors, the authors. There was a time when I couldn't wait to get up in the morning. It was fabulous . . . the challenge, the freshness.

PART I

"But then I got to feel what many men feel about their work, too, that once you've mastered it and gotten to the top it gets to be rote. It's when you're achieving something for the first time, when you're climbing, that it's challenging and exciting. But as time went on, and I became accomplished at what I was doing, it also became harder and harder to be enthusiastic because the newness and the challenge were simply gone.

"I sympathize with some of the younger women who have their children while they're still climbing in their careers, before they have really sunk their teeth in, gotten into responsible positions. . . . If you're not there yet, and leave, you often think you have missed something; you are constantly champing at the bit to get back in.

"I was ready for a new vista—and my children have provided it. When I was in my twenties I was too close to childhood myself to truly appreciate it, to realize the importance of what I could give to my own children. But at my age you develop a perspective on what life is all about. To me right now it's about giving my children unconditional love. I've been with them since day one, they are bonded to me. There is no way I'd give up these years with them while I put actors and authors on shows.

"When my children are in school full days, then I will need a fairly substantial interest outside of them, but I truly doubt that it will be paid work. I want to see raising them through. When I left I was asked to stay with the firm on literally any basis I wanted, but I really had no desire to do so. It's always a gamble to leave a sure thing, but I couldn't see working part time at this point. It would spoil the continuity of the present. I want this experience now much more than I am concerned about having a hold on the future."

Jane Kranz and Marie Orlean exemplify the idea that there is no one "right" or "better" age for interrupting a career and focusing on one's family. Jane Kranz is at the low age end of sequencing mothers, and Marie Orlean is near the upper end of the age spectrum.

Both Kranz and Orlean were ready for new directions when they interrupted their careers, and they consider raising their children their immediate new direction. Neither woman feels the need to meet both outside and family challenges simultaneously; each has chosen to sequence her life by placing her children in top priority at this point, deferring other new challenges.

With a very few exceptions like Marie Orlean, who plans not to return to paid work, most women who leave their careers with comfort expect their careers once again to be important in their lives when their families are substantially older. But a career is not of such major import to them that they want to spend time on it during their children's growing years. Therefore, women with no or low conflict are less likely than conflicted women to develop a way to use their career skills on a part-time basis while their children are young and are most likely to make their career interruptions a total break for a longer period of time. One reason is that they are relatively relaxed about finances. Another is that they are willing to forgo the prestige related to their work either because it's not so integral to their self-perceptions that it keeps them working, they've experienced it and don't

PART I

feel the continual need for it, or in some cases, they didn't feel much continued satisfaction from their work.

The overriding factor, however, is that women who make the decision to interrupt their careers with comfort do not weight their professions and mothering equally. They value mothering more—as a calling, a commitment, an opportunity, a gift they want to maximize.

2

The
Ambivalent Woman

In contrast to the woman who leaves her career with ease, the woman who accepts both the male career norm *and* the theory of surrogate child care upon which it rests often comes to the sequencing decision following a great deal of anguish and ambivalence. One woman is in conflict for years about whether to have a baby, fearing that career and child will conflict. Her biological clock ticks faster and faster. Finally, she decides to have the baby and then see what happens. Another woman experiences no conflict before her first child's birth because she fully expects to continue her career throughout her mothering years. Her conflict begins when she is first confronted with seven pounds of her own immortality, or when her maternity leave is about to expire and she is faced with the reality of leaving her baby every morning, or after she returns to work and misses her child in ways she never dreamed possible.

Women who interrupt their careers after much conflict typically do so when their first child is between ten and fourteen months old and is beginning to walk and to talk. Or they leave around the time of the birth of a second child, when they feel they have already missed too much with their first.

Conflicted women who interrupt their careers come to sequencing from the ranks of the nearly one-third (32 percent) of married mothers of children under six years old who work full time. Although these mothers may outwardly appear to be successfully pursuing careers while giving their children all the personalized care their jobs allow, inwardly many of them are heavily burdened by the feeling that all is far from well in their lives. On one hand, they need the benefits they derive from working, either for financial reasons or psychological rewards, or for both. On the other, they love their children dearly and feel conflicted and guilty about the time their work takes from them.

Each year more and more such women actively seek solutions to their dilemma. Many modify their work schedules once their children are born. For some that means cutting back from working ten or twelve hours a day to eight; others stop traveling or switch subspecialties to try to reduce overall work pressure; some change positions altogether; others cut down from a five- or six-day work week to three or four days; others combine work done in the office with work done at home to gain flexibility of scheduling. All those who make such changes do so in an attempt to reduce or make more flexible the time spent on their careers so as to increase time with their children.

Some women find that such modifications allow them an

effective, livable, or at least workable way to continue with their dual roles. But others feel such changes still leave them managerial rather than participatory mothers. Increasingly, women who feel this way leave their careers entirely for a period of time to become full-time participants in their children's lives. Other women find that their work schedules cannot be modified, or that employers are unwilling to accommodate their needs, and therefore leave their work entirely without first cutting back. In all of these instances, the women initially accepted the *theory* of surrogate care for their children but struggled with and ultimately rejected the *fact* of it in their own lives. This process often causes great conflict.

IDENTIFYING, ORDERING, AND EVALUATING CONFLICT FACTORS

Conflict results when a mother's desire to nurture her child on a continual basis collides head-on with the financial, psychological, and social factors calling her to continue her career. The amount of conflict she experiences about leaving her child depends upon the degree to which she wants

- To be the primary person in her child's life
- To know and grow with her child on a day-in, day-out basis
- To provide her child with continuity of love and care
- To share on a daily basis in the development of her child's personality and intellect

- To be a continual presence and a participant in the life of her child
- To avoid tight scheduling, living by deadlines, and long daily absences from her child.

If a woman feels very strongly about the above factors and less strongly about any factors pertaining to her career, she experiences little conflict about leaving it—as do Anita Crawford, Jane Kranz, and Marie Orlean. But conflict results if she feels strongly about raising her child herself on a day-to-day basis and equally strongly about one or more of the factors listed below. The extent of the conflict about leaving her career depends upon the degree to which a woman

- Needs the money she earns for financial reasons
- Needs the money she earns for the feelings of esteem she derives from earning it
- Has assimilated the male norm of careerism as her own and sees her career as *the* focal point or central aspect of her life experience
- Identifies with and feels at one with her career as giving her a place and/or power in the world
- Sees her position as a major determinant of her self-worth
- Loves her work for the personal challenge and fulfillment the work itself offers
- Identifies with her peers who continue in their careers and pressure her to do so similiarly
- Feels insecure about her ability to resume a career at a later date.

For most women, the conflict about leaving a career for her child actually centers on one or two factors or sets of factors. To a woman in the throes of it, however, it often *seems* that there is no major focus of her conflict but rather, that it is comprised of a multiplicity of relatively equal factors. Yet when a woman who is debating leaving her work actually lists and ranks in order of importance the factors that motivate her to work full time while she has small children, she nearly always finds that one or two factors are very clearly at the top of her list, with others secondary and still others mattering very little to her.

Regardless of the particulars of her story, when a woman relates how she made her sequencing decision it nearly always boils down to a fivefold process: (1) identifying factors calling her to work, (2) ranking those factors in order of importance to her, (3) dealing one by one with each of the primary factors until she has thoroughly worked each through by looking at how much, and in what ways, it matters to her, when weighing it against the time with her child(ren), (4) weighing the secondary factors against time with her child(ren), and (5) deciding after separating and evaluating the factors that time with her child(ren) takes priority over any other factor or combination of factors calling her to her work.

At the time a woman is actually going through the decision-making process, however, it is rarely so staged and analytical. Rather, the decision process is emotionally draining and is nearly always compounded by time pressure. Either it is made when a mother is working full time yet feeling that she never has enough time with her child or when she is under the deadline to return to work from maternity leave.

Thirty-two-year-old Lois Reis is currently trying to decide which path her life will take: the one marked career or the one marked full-time motherhood. Reis sits in her blue and white suburban New York living room cradling her two-month-old daughter, soothing her intermittent cries. Superficially, this blonde, blue-eyed mother looks the picture of contentment. But as soon as she begins talking it's clear that she feels highly conflicted and under the gun. "I was in doubt for years about whether to have the baby in the first place," she says. "I've been programmed ever since I can remember to have a career; I didn't see how I could give my all to both; well, I finally decided to have a baby and then see. But my conflict isn't solved at all. Right away the minute I saw the baby I was hooked . . . I loved her right off the bat. So I was immediately in worse conflict. I can't put the decision off any longer. I have to choose: what am I going to do about my job? I've got a three-month maternity leave. I've only another month to go, and then I have to decide: am I going back to my post as a health care cost analyst or am I staying here with her?"

Reis looks apologetically around her newly furnished living room. "I know it sounds funny, but if I quit, financially things will be a little tight. I suppose we can make it on my husband's salary, but without the extras. He's an M.B.A. and earning a good salary. I'm pulling down about half of what he is right now—I already left a firm where I was working seventy hours a week, earning substantially more. But when we started thinking baby, I knew I could never work under that pressure so I opted for a nine-to-five situation, but with the commute that's still ten or more hours a day I'd be gone from the baby.

"I'm really torn," Reis says pensively. "I come from a health care background, and I am strongly sensitive to our terminal time on this earth. I know I have to decide what's important to me: the baby or the money. It's not just the money for its own sake, it's the money as a symbol that I have earning power, as well as what it buys. My generation of women was not raised with the values of mothering our children. We were raised with the value of earning money even if we don't need it. My husband says, 'go ahead and quit.' That's fine with him, but I feel guilty if I don't bring in a paycheck, even if it's buying us stuff we don't really have to have. And even if I solved the money dilemma, I depend upon my job for a sense of who I am. I'm not sure I could part with that security."

Like many conflicted new mothers, Reis has just begun to sort through the issues. She talks about the need for money to support her family's lifestyle, then says she may not really need the goods the money buys but is dependent upon the symbolic aspect of the paycheck coupled with the identity she derives from her work. To resolve her conflict, Reis will be forced to separate and evaluate the major issues she has already identified: the economics, the psychological rewards she derives from earning the money apart from what it buys, and the sense of identity she gets from her job.

If Reis is like many conflicted women, clarifying the economic issues will be difficult. Some women resist exploring their finances because they suspect that they could manage without the money and don't want to admit to themselves that they work primarily to meet psychological needs. That is because many a woman today holds the view that leaving her children in surrogate care to work for money is legitimate because she is working to provide for them. But two decades of feminist philosophy still have not convinced most mothers that leaving their children in hired care to work for their own sense of self-esteem, enjoyment, or challenge is equally legitimate. If they evaluate the financial situation thoroughly and find that they are working *primarily* for psychic rewards with the money a secondary factor, they feel guilty, sometimes enormously so.

If Lois Reis and her husband now use her salary for daily living, they will have to resolve whether and how they would scale down to live without it. If she finds finances are not a major issue, she can move on to evaluate which factors are primary for her.

The psychological issue of the money is another matter. Here, Reis, like many women caught up in the careerism norm, equates her paycheck with her feeling of worth in the world. If she wants to deal directly with the genesis of her conflict, she will ask herself, as many women do, whether the positive feelings she derives from earning the money are worth more to her than the positive feelings she derives from continual contact with her baby. And since she says she depends upon her position for a "sense of who I am" she will also confront the questions, am I so dependent on my work to give me status that I will allow that dependency to prevent me from raising my own child? Can I recognize myself as a valid human being apart from the paid job I fill at the moment?

If Lois Reis works the issues through and decides that her child takes priority in her time allocations at this point in her life, in all likelihood she will stop working. If she is like the majority of women who make a similar decision, her conflicts about her career will greatly diminish or vanish within the first year of full-time motherhood as she creates a new lifestyle for herself and her family.

If Reis decides that her work is necessary to her life, she will have very clearly delineated the reasons and may then be able to continue working with less conflict than if she fails to confront the issues.

But if Lois Reis does not separate the issues and fully explore them, waiting and hoping that the conflicts will somehow resolve themselves, she may find that she remains highly conflicted for months or years to come.

Such was the case with thirty-six-year-old Meredith Martin, who was highly ambivalent for nearly two years before confronting her conflict factors and making a decision. As Martin sits crosslegged on the green and gold patterned floor of her sunny Evanston, Illinois, kitchen, cutting paper masks with her three-year-old daughter, Joni, she recalls the time when she would not have imagined herself doing so.

"Staying at home to raise a child was the last thing I ever expected of myself," Martin says. "When I was growing up in the fifties and sixties in a small Nebraska town, I looked around me at my mother and the other women—bright women, talented women, doing what? Raising kids? And I said to myself, 'You've got to be kidding. This is no way to spend a life. There's more out there.' So I looked to the men for role models—at my father, a respected attorney, at the other professional men. I knew someday I could be like them. I graduated from Antioch, then went on to Michigan Law School, where I married a classmate. We then moved to Chicago, where he went into his father's practice. I clerked for a judge for a year, then landed a job with a prestigious mainstream firm—the second woman to work there as anything other than a secretary. I really loved my law work, was enveloped by it.

"My husband and I never planned a family. Joni is an accident for which neither of us takes responsibility. Neither of us found abortion a tolerable solution, but neither of us was happy about the pregnancy. Then, in the delivery room, we both felt the magic of this little life—'My God, there is something else,' I remember thinking. But right away this magic brought with it untold pain and conflict. She was here, she was part of us, she was ours—but what to do with her?

"Disruption of either of our careers was not a consideration. My husband was back in his office that afternoon, and within a few weeks of Joni's birth, I went back to the firm in which I was by then a junior partner. First, I tried putting Joni in what was recommended by friends who use it as an excellent day care center, but I found it was cold and institutional. I told myself that it was called day care not day love for a reason—that you cannot buy your child love. But I tried to; I took her out of there and tried private care. I hired a woman who was wonderfully warm with her, so I felt my daughter was in good hands.

"But nonetheless I felt torn, resentful when I had to stay at the office into the evening—which often happened—angry because I loved my work but resented the long hours, the inflexibility of my colleagues. Most of the work I did could have been done at home. Everybody brought work home at night, but there was no allowance for doing work at home during regular daytime hours. I wanted to try cutting back. I asked to leave at five, or to work four days a week, but again they were very inflexible. So I worked all day and constantly thought about the baby; I felt guilty and that I had abandoned her. When she was a year and a half I got a call from her sitter one afternoon, 'Come quick.' I grabbed a cab and sped across town through a terrible storm to find Joni bloody and screaming, the sitter trying to comfort her. She'd grabbed a glass vase from the coffee table, tripped, fallen, broken the vase, and cut her arm on it. We rushed her to the hospital, got her stitched up, and she hasn't a scar. But I have.

"It took the accident for me to really realize how much Joni means to me. Sure, something could happen when I'm with her. Things will happen when she goes to school and throughout her life when I'm not on the spot, but after her accident I realized that for these years, I could be with her if I really wanted to be. For the first time I saw that there was a choice that was mine to make.

PART I

"I did not make it overnight; it took over three more months. First, I seriously questioned why I was working. I'd always told myself I had to work for the money. Both my husband and I earned good salaries, we saw how our friends who were all two-career professional couples lived, so we naturally thought that was how we would live, too. But then, when I had to measure that against Joni, it just didn't stack up. The truth was we could live, although not as well, on one salary. I sometimes think those of us who say, 'I have to work' for more of what we already have are hiding behind the skirts of women who really do have to work to feed their families. We need some other words in the vocabulary for distinguishing one kind of 'have' from the other.

"Once I could no longer tell myself I was working for the money, I recognized I was working because I loved it. Then I had to decide if I loved my work so much that I was willing to be away from the little person I loved, all day, in order to do it. I recognized that I could practice law in a different setting at a different time in my life, but nonetheless leaving the firm would be a major career gamble.

"If I stayed, I would not have to take any chances on my career, but I would continue to take a chance on Joni's childhood; substitute care is a chance any way you look at it. Who really knows the effect of a small child spending most of his day in the care of someone who does not really love him? What it all came down to was that I had to gamble either my career or Joni. When I saw it that way I figured I could live without being the rising star on the legal scene; that I don't have to be a man if the price is giving up my daughter's childhood. I realize that as much as my work is part of me, Joni is more a part of me. I gave notice and went home.

"I did not work for a year, then I began a limited law practice at home serving new clients who are referred by attorneys in other specialties. I limit my work and generally do it at the end of the afternoon when Joni is napping, with a sitter on hand in case she wakes up early. On the occasions when I need to meet face to face with a client I either rent by-the-hour office space or meet in their offices. Now I am free to really enjoy Joni and am also enjoying my legal work again. The difference for me is being with Joni, knowing what she is doing, feeling a sense of continuity with her throughout the day when I'm playing with her, or just having her near me."

Although she has developed a way to keep involved in her professional area, Martin says, "That kind of solution did not come easily. The conflict between career and family is something college counselors, peers, society as a whole just don't tell you about. When my friends and I used to ask our law school counselors, 'What about when we have children?' they used to say, 'Oh, you'll work it out.' Well, we're working it out, our whole generation is working it out, but it's painful and costly. If we'd been prepared for it, it would have made things much, much easier."

Meredith Martin—like many women who return to work after the first maternity leave—became more and more attached to her baby as months went by, more and more desirous of being close to her physically and emotionally on an hour-to-hour basis, and correspondingly more conflicted about her dual roles.

In analyzing the conflict factors that drew her from her child to her work, Martin's genuine love of practicing law was clearly number one. But Martin saw that the environment in which she worked was incompatible with the kind of mothering she wanted to do. To practice law, which she loved, in the prestigious firm with which she was affiliated, she was expected to center her life on the office. She willingly did so before the baby's birth. When she lived the careerism norm fully, she achieved the goal of many women of this generation: she "became" her father—the man she had long sought to emulate. It was not the financial success of her father's life that she wanted nearly so much as the fact of *doing the type of work* he and the other men did—as opposed to staying home to raise a family as her mother did.

But suddenly, when she actually became a mother, she was pulled in a different direction, away from her career as the focal point in her life, from her position in her firm, from advancement potential, from the fulfillment she derived from the work she loved doing. Eventually, she found having the traditional male experience—a full-time career—incompatible with simultaneously having the traditional female one—full-time family life. She finally opted for the latter, but with modification. Although she has abandoned the male model as an end-all in life, she has retained, along with her maternal privileges, a way to be a professional on her own terms by separating the work she enjoys from the trappings she did not enjoy, and instead she runs a solo law practice on a limited basis on a schedule and in an environment in which she is in control.

Although Martin originally believed she worked for economic reasons, when she evaluated her basic motivations she recognized that money was not a prime factor—that she didn't have an economic imperative. She became willing to alter her lifestyle aspirations because she recognized that doing so would permit her to have the years she desired to mother her daughter. Her greatest conflict was not between money and her child but between the career she loved—present and future—and her baby. Martin's comment, "If I stayed, I would not have to take any chances on my career, but I would continue to take a chance on Joni's childhood," was expressed to me in various ways by a number of women who returned to work after maternity leave expecting that all would be like before only to find that their concerns about the effect of surrogate care on their children put them into continual conflict.

As Martin and many women like her, who once embraced the theory of surrogate care, gain confidence in their own mothering abilities and standards, many of them develop the conviction that the ways in which their children spend their days during their earliest, most impressionable years will have a tremendous and irrevocable effect upon them. They hope surrogate care will have no adverse effect, but as they watch the reality of it in their children's lives they feel that it is still in the experimental stage; they fear the effects could be detrimental or at least not as positive as their own care would be, and therefore they become increasingly insecure about leaving their children all day. They are also insecure about leaving their careers. They are caught in a conflict between two unknowns: the consequences of leaving their work for a period of years versus the consequences of leaving their children in hired care. If they stay at work, they feel guilty for being unwilling to take a chance on their own careers while they let their children chart unknown territory; if they leave their work, they must later chart an unknown career course themselves.

Meredith Martin has chosen the latter route. So has Rhonda Arnold, who was drawn to her work not as much for the challenge it offered, as was Martin, but for an equally compelling psychological reward: the power and prestige she derived from the position she filled.

Rhonda Arnold's cheeks grow almost as purple as the dress she wears as she gestures furiously while describing the conflict she faced after the birth of her now three-year-old son: "I returned to my sixty-hour-a-week schedule as a television producer only a month after my son's birth. From then on I hardly ever saw him. I had to leave early in the morning. I'd rush home at night to play with him, but sometimes he would already be sleeping; I'd feel miserable and cheated. During the day, I'd call the sitter from the studio and hear him gurgling in the background. 'He's just fine,' she would assure me. But I wasn't fine; I felt hollow. Then I'd get absorbed again in shooting and be okay for a while, then the emptiness would return again.

"I flirted with the idea of leaving . . . but to leave wasn't just to leave any old job. This was a position I'd worked hard for and then in the end lucked into besides; this kind of position wouldn't just come my way again. Besides, big-time television is more than a job; it's a way of life. I was known in the world of TV—I'd walk into a restaurant and people would nod, 'There's Rhonda Arnold.' I was in a powerful spot. A lot of people wanted an in with me, a crack at my show. 'I should leave all this to be one more housewife on the block?' I asked myself.

"But the trouble was that my baby was growing up with me as an onlooker. So strangers knew me in a restaurant, but one night my son did not. When I came home, he cried. He reached out for his sitter, who was leaving, and shrieked at me. This was not manipulative behavior—this was a tired, teething ten-month-old little boy who wanted the person he knew best to comfort him. I was not that person. If I was not that person now, who would he turn to later? At five, or at ten?

"I went in tears to my best woman friend; she's also in television. She said I should count my blessings—how lucky I was that my son was happy with his sitter, that I didn't have a succession of them, three in the first year and a half, as she'd had.

"One day when my baby was about a year old I came home and the sitter beamed. 'I almost called to tell you—he walked today.' I cried that night; I missed that, too.

"Finally, when he was fourteen months old, I threw in the towel. I'd tried to have it all—but all I had was my job, which ceased to be as much fun because I was constantly tormented that I had way too little of my son. Finally it was my longing for him, my desire to be a real part of his life, that won out. Nearly two years have passed, but I am still angry that I gave up those months of my son's life; I will never get them back. I'm angry at myself that I bought the whole mess of pottage, and I'm angrier still at the liars who sold it to me.

"My fear that I would become one more housewife on the block was unfounded," Arnold says. "Actually, I'm the *only* one on the block. But I don't feel like a housewife, whatever that is—my stereotype was of a frump with nothing but babies to talk about. Actually, I talk about my son a great deal, but I've a lot of other interests, too. In the past two years since I've been home I've written two serious plays. One was produced by a local community theater. Next, I'm going to try a comedy screenplay. So, I make good use of the moments when my son is sleeping or playing quietly, of evenings, or when he and my husband spend some time just the two of them. I'd never written before, though I'd always wanted to try it. Time out from the rat race has given me this opportunity."

Rhonda Arnold's statement, "So strangers knew me in a restaurant, but one night my son did not," reflects the concern familiar to the mother who is constantly pressured by work demands and deadlines that may keep her highly visible professionally but force her children into the corners of her everyday life. For Arnold, misery that her son didn't recognize her as the person to whom he turned in need ultimately superseded the heady power given by her professional position that made strangers recognize and seek her out.

The power and prestige factors that accompanied Arnold's position clearly were the primary causes of her career-baby conflict. Money was not a major factor for her. She enjoyed the work, but that enjoyment was diminished by her often present thoughts of her child away from her, attached to someone else. That her peers were working and that a close friend advised her that she was lucky to have the child care situation she had did not keep her on the job, nor did fears about the future. Arnold did an about-face, deciding that even if she never returned to a producer's slot in major television she would rather mother her child.

Arnold's anger that "I gave up those months of my son's life; I will never get them back" characterizes the feelings of many women who come to their sequencing decisions after a great deal of conflict. It surprised me when I saw it in Arnold, and later in others, for I had hypothesized that the greater the initial conflict the more the woman would miss her work and be angry that she couldn't do both at once. But instead, I found in Arnold and in many others anger for the time they missed with their children while they were working, time they know they cannot retrieve. Contrary to my theory, rarely did those women who had been in such conflict miss their work or its benefits anywhere near as much as they or I had thought they would.

This is not to say that once at home the initially conflicted woman loses her desire to work again. To the contrary, many women find ways, as Meredith Martin did, to do some aspect of the work they enjoyed on a limited basis while making mothering their primary commitment. Others, like Rhonda Arnold, quickly take a new direction and pursue a new professional or avocational interest a limited number of hours a week. But they dramatically shift the focus. Once home-based, they tailor their other activities to their mothering priorities rather than cramming time with their children around a hectic work schedule as they previously had to do.

Arnold's serious questioning of her career commitment after her ten-month-old reached for the sitter rather than for her brings up the issue of what child care professionals call the mother's willingness to "reliquish her parental territory." This is the main differentiating characteristic between conflicted women who consider sequencing but don't and those who ultimately leave their careers. *Women who sequence ultimately refuse to give up their territory to someone else.* Usually it's because they believe nobody else can mother their children as well as they can. But Arnold alludes to another side of that coin, one Anita Crawford identifies when she says that if she did leave her child with a surrogate caregiver who was loving and involved with her child, "I'd be as jealous as if my husband was getting closeness, love, and attention from another woman."

Herein lies the catch-22 problem of surrogate care. When it's bad to mediocre, it's something nobody wants if she can avoid it. But often when it's good, or even excellent, it's something some mothers still reject. Arnold's situation illustrates that the warm, involved mother substitute may bring the full-time careerwoman-mother home as quickly as does the inadequate surrogate. There was apparently nothing wrong with Arnold's caregiver, but Arnold still found plenty wrong with the situation: her child was deeply attached to another woman on whom he relied to comfort him when he was hurt and who watched him take his first steps. Arnold asked herself, "If I was not that person now, who would he turn to later? At five, or at ten?"

A mother's rivalry with the surrogate caregiver is as yet largely unexplored by social science researchers, but will surely receive wide attention in the future. As more women enter the professions, and as many more nanny schools arise to serve their needs, we may see a great deal of discussion centering on the topic of what happens if Mary Poppins does come along: how much maternal territory will a woman who has the choice relinquish to her?

Although many women such as Meredith Martin and Rhonda Arnold chose to work primarily because of personal fulfillment, money is the primary, often the sole reason millions of women work today. Their conflict is clearly between paycheck and child, and it's not a pretty one. Many of these women want desperately to raise their own children yet feel prevented from doing so by circumstances over which they have little control.

Vivian Taylor is black, the first in her family to be college educated, and without her salary, she says she, her husband, and her young son will have to "give up our middle-class apartment in our nice neighborhood and go back to ghetto-like low-rent housing, which we thought we had gotten out of with our college educations."

Taylor, who says that "career was terribly important to me in earlier years," left her position as a research analyst with an international securities organization last year after her son was born. "There was way too much pressure and deadlining," she says. "I was exhausted all the time and missed my son terribly." Six months later, she found that they couldn't continue to keep their apartment on her husband's salary, and so she took a step which many mothers feel reluctantly forced into: "I traded down in job status and salary in order to work in a less demanding situation with regular hours." Now a secretary/receptionist with a national manufacturing organization, Taylor "works nine to five, and it's absolutely no pressure. So I can save the best of myself for my baby." But she is unhappy with this arrangement and wants to leave: "It's better than the career track at this point in my life, but working outside of my home is not what I wanted to do. I want to raise my child. But I feel trapped. I'm faced with either continuing to sacrifice my child, which I feel I am doing now by working and sending him to day care, or with leaving my job and taking us all back to the ghetto. There ought to be some other way.

"A child takes an enormous amount of energy if you are going to raise him correctly. Good parenting is a social service. The whole country benefits from a good citizen, everybody loses with a juvenile delinquent, and you can't tell me that a nation of kids raised first in day care, then with latchkeys, doesn't spell skyrocketing drugs and delinquency. I think that mothers should receive grants to stay home and do the job right."

Meanwhile, with no such grant in sight, Taylor is debating whether to sequence: "I am considering joining two other friends who already left their jobs and went to live with their husbands and children in low-cost housing. I'm afraid that raising my son in that environment isn't good for him. But I am beginning to think that doing it with me there and some of my friends around might still be better than being a part of the middle class with a nice apartment but having to sacrifice my son to being raised by strangers."

Taylor's situation is one faced by millions of today's married working mothers whose chief, often only, reason for working is money. For Taylor, quitting her job is not totally out of the realm of possibility. Her husband earns a steady income, but it's not enough to enable them to buy the lifestyle they want for the upward mobility they seek for themselves and their children. Her working means that they can have more and better materially than if she does not, but it means that her child cannot be raised by his own mother. Taylor is not at all convinced that the better apartment and neighborhood her salary allows the family compensate for its purchase price, which is her chance to mother her child on a day-in, day-out basis. Her belief that women who sincerely want to stay home and mother should get grants to "do the job right" is held by other women who deplore leaving their children but for whom the money they earn is critical to a basic, no-frills, barely lower-middle-class lifestyle.

Many of these mothers believe they and their children are missing a tremendous amount by being separated all day. These women say they need a grant, loan, scholarship, or award—money for a few years from somewhere—so they can raise their own children.

With no outside funding available, however, married mothers like Vivian Taylor who are in the lower income levels wrestle with what matters most—a basic, lower-middle-class lifestyle coupled with surrogate child care, or mothering their children themselves in an environment in which their own values may not prevail among peers to whom the child will ultimately be exposed.

Some women continue working so they can buy that lifestyle. Others gamble on themselves as the prime influence in their child's life although it means living in a less desirable environment. These mothers are most concerned with what is best for their children: some feel that to continue working to buy another lifestyle will benefit the child the most in the end. Others, like Ruby Dorman, believe that their own influence will supersede environmental considerations and will most benefit the child. Dorman, who tried it both ways, decided to leave her work and bet on herself.

Blonde hair pulled back in a bun, lines creasing her face, Dorman looks considerably older than her thirty-five years. Married at nineteen, and a single parent at twenty, she frequently breaks into tears as she describes the ten years she worked full time as a data processor while single-handedly raising her now fifteen-year-old daughter. "I got into computers early in the game in California and worked my way up. By the time I left there, when I was thirty, I was in charge of one of several data processing groups in a big corporation. But the stress was terrible—it was constantly produce, produce, one group pitted against another with raises and bonuses tied to the group's output. My daughter was raised in day care centers and was frequently ill. Many times I was caught—I had to decide whether to stay home with her when she was running a fever and to then submit to the wrath and threats of my employer, or to give her aspirin, take her to day care, pretend she was fine, and go into work—at least until the aspirin wore off and I'd be called to come and get her. Her illness took all my sick leave and more—and I was continually threatened with loss of my job if I missed more work. In spite of my absences, our group was continually on top—largely because I am an excellent manager and I worked a great deal of unpaid overtime to keep it up there. As long as we were winning, I figured they would never really fire me."

When Dorman was thirty she decided she had to make a job change and found that her computer experience was in demand. She moved to Connecticut, where she headed a data processing group in a large computer company. The next year she remarried, two years later gave birth to a son, and the following year to another daughter. At that point she decided to quit her job. "Quitting was a terrible decision to make," Dorman says. "My husband is a wonderful guy, but he doesn't earn much and he never will. My salary was higher than his. Leaving my job meant we may never own our own home; it means that our kids are not going to have a lot of the things middle-class children in this society have today. In fact, according to his salary level, we're below middle class. But there is something that our kids will have which a lot of kids with more money don't—a mother to raise them.

"I really feel that I missed a tremendous amount with my oldest daughter that I can never recapture. We're not as close as I wish we were—maybe it's just our personalities, maybe it's because I was so young, or because I was a single parent with no backup—but I can't help feel it's because we just didn't have the time together when she was small to really develop a close relationship. I have that time now with my two little ones—and I have time now for my oldest, too, so that when she wants me I can be available to listen to her, or to help with her math, or whatever it is she needs. It's a chance we didn't have in her early years, and it's an opportunity I want my two youngest children to have. Trading the money for the time is terribly expensive for us. But I firmly believe that our kids will turn out better because I'm here with them even if their house and neighborhood aren't as good as it would be with me working."

I asked Dorman about working part time at this stage in her life to supplement her husband's income, perhaps doing computer work at home. "No way," she answers, tears again in her eyes. "You have no idea how terrible it is to know your child needs you and to have a deadline to which you're committed to somebody else who's relying on you. I don't ever again want anybody to tell me I can't be with one of my children when she is sick, or to feel that I can't cook my children a meal, or take them out to play because an outsider needs something done. Freedom has its price, and for us that price is not too far from poverty level . . . but I am willing to pay it."

Dorman recognizes that at some point she will have to work again: "Once both my little ones are in school, then I will probably have to figure out some kind of part-time work—there have been tremendous changes in the computer field, but I am very well grounded in the basics. I'll be able to get back into it—but I don't want to have to do it until they are older."

.   .   .

Although money is the only reason Vivian Taylor works and that Ruby Dorman worked, for other women money is a component but not the sole determinant of their working. Prestige factors are also important, and they feel strongly committed to their work. Yet when they rank order these issues it's peer pressure rather than any of these factors that heads the list of reasons that they continue to work. Some women—even those who have long considered themselves independent thinkers—find, when they delineate the factors that keep them working, that the peer pressure of colleagues and employers is the catalyst for all the other factors.

Vivacious, olive-skinned Paula Archer discovered that she was influenced by "an immense amount of peer pressure," which was at the root of the "tremendous conflict" she felt about leaving her group medical practice. "Money mattered," Archer says, "I won't deny that. But my husband is also a physician, and so I knew we could well live on his salary alone. The prestige mattered—not only was I 'doctor' to those outside the profession but, more importantly, I was building a good reputation as a bright young comer in the medical community, and most important of all I went into medicine because of my desire to help people; my patients mattered immensely to me. But after my daughter was born I felt tremendous guilt for leaving her while I practiced medicine and equally guilty for wanting to leave medicine so I could be with her. But for over a year, I didn't recognize that peer pressure was at the root of my conflict of guilts.

"Guilt is endemic to physician mothers," Archer says.

PART I

"We've got years and years of training, we're supposed to be using it, and we feel guilty if we don't. But we've got young children who are growing up without us, and we feel guilty for letting that happen.

"Several of my female colleagues and I used to talk about this over and over—at lunch, at coffee, in the halls on the run between patients. We were truly obsessed with the conflict of not knowing what we should be doing. It got so that talking about it made it worse because sometimes I'd want to just hang it up and go home. It would be one o'clock, I'd have a full afternoon of patients, I knew I wouldn't see my daughter until after seven. But by then I was tired, frequently short-tempered, and she was often crabby, too. We really had the worst of each other.

"Slowly I came to realize that just talking with my peers about the problem was getting me nowhere . . . it wasn't that I was coming closer to a resolution of the tremendous conflict I felt, it was that talking about it continually provided an outlet for it. I came to see that my colleagues and I were constantly rationalizing our positions, providing peer support for one another. 'We have to be here seeing our cases because we are trained to do this,' we told ourselves and each other. To leave would be to capitulate to what the men always said about women—that we really couldn't do it when the heat was on. To leave would be to give up all that we'd built for ourselves, performing functions of real importance in the world, tremendous esteem in the eyes of others, excellent incomes. We kept trying to find a way to stay, to do it all.

"I slowly came to recognize that my female colleagues

really wanted to rationalize staying in full time and that was what all the talk on their parts was about, whereas I was really leaning toward leaving my practice.

"Once I saw this, I began talking my conflict over with them a lot less and with my husband a lot more. He loves our daughter as I do, but he simply has never shared my conflict. Fine that she was with her housekeeper all day— he saw her at bedtime, on weekends—that was okay with him. But he understood that I was heavily conflicted and told me he supported me fully in whatever I decided to do. Finally, our daughter began talking and began using some of the same expressions our housekeeper used. That did something. Did I really want this woman to be such a primary influence on my child? She was certainly far better than any day care worker I'd seen, the best woman I found. She was gentle, kind, and not unintelligent. The problem was not with her, I decided. The problem was with me. I was the mother, and I felt there was time I wanted to share with my daughter, were things I wanted to do with her that my professional schedule prevented. Quite simply, I was living first and foremost as a doctor, secondarily as a mother, and I was not satisfied.

"I finally just decided to hell with what anyone else thinks —there are other doctors. The patients will get along fine. But I am my child's only mother. Can it really be wrong to raise her?"

Archer worked her conflict through by isolating its major cause. Once she realized that the main reason she was practicing medicine at that point in her life was not primarily because of commitment to her profession, not for money, not for prestige, but because of peer pressure, she dealt immediately with that issue. She stopped discussing her conflict with those peers whose values were different from hers. After that she was able to deal quickly and effectively with the secondary reasons that she worked. She disposed of the money and prestige issues in short order; they were not central enough to compete with her child. The issue of her allegiance to her patients was more critical. Archer had to weigh what she could do for a given patient, or a number of patients in a day, against what she could do for and with her own child. In the end, her child won. Archer's conclusion, "There are other doctors. The patients will get along fine. But I am my child's only mother. Can it really be wrong to raise her?" is one women from a variety of professions ultimately reach. Often the woman grows to believe that she can contribute something unique and essential to her child and that contribution—herself—is one she prefers to make at a given time to her child rather than to any others whose needs she serves.

Archer's situation clearly shows that one woman's support is the next woman's pressure. For the past two decades "networking" and "support systems" have been the bywords of many a professional woman who needs peer support for her role choice and its implementation. For Archer, however, what appeared to be support was actually pressure. Superficially it seemed that she and her female colleagues shared similar values and thus similar conflicts, but in reality the emphasis of their values and conflicts was quite different from hers. Her colleagues sought support from one another for *staying* in full-time practices while trying simultaneously to raise their children. Archer, however, needed support for *leaving* her practice. She got it from her husband—a male colleague—rather than from the female physicians around her.

That was four years ago. Today, as more and more women professionals elect to leave full-time work to mother, many find peer support from other women professionals who have made a similar choice.

Sandra Conway believes the course of her life was changed because she found the support of a female peer at a crucial point. Conway was kept at her work because of the pressures of her husband and her employer (which another woman or Conway herself at another time might have perceived as support). The assistant to the marketing director of a large West Coast firm, Conway says she wanted to stop working from the time her son, Andy, was born. "But I was kept in perpetual conflict by my husband and my boss. My husband, under the guise of all sorts of egalitarian rhetoric, wanted the salary, and my boss wanted me in my job at any cost because I made his work easier. I could cut down my hours, work some from home, whatever I wanted, but he wanted me to stay. So in an attempt to please both my husband and him I stayed and cut back on hours, but it didn't work. I was still there from eight in the morning until after four, took work home, was always on the phone, couldn't relax and enjoy my baby, ever.

"I kept telling my husband I wanted to quit, but he didn't want to hear of it, and neither did my boss, who promised me a major raise as soon as the expected company merger came, which, of course, made my husband want to hear of my quitting even less. Meanwhile, my baby was growing without me and was in one after another poor day care situation. I was absolutely torn in two, constantly feeling that I was letting somebody down and without any support whatsoever from anyone for my wish to leave my work.

"Then, a real godsend appeared in the form of Marge, a woman who lived a few blocks away. I usually had no time to see any neighbors because I was only around home on weekends and then spent much of it trying to catch up on the house; but Marge stopped me when I was pushing the stroller one Saturday afternoon and we started talking. Her son and Andy are just about the same age. She had headed an advertising division in a company similar to mine, but she left it when her son was born.

"I identified with her immediately. She was living the life I wanted. I started stopping in at her house almost every Saturday. The boys would play, and we could talk. 'How is it really?' I would ask her. 'What do you and he do all day?' Finally, she suggested that I take some time off and see for myself, which I did.

"During that week, Marge introduced me to other women who had left their careers, given up good salaries, women my age who were now home with their kids. She took me on her route for the week: to the library—we spent two afternoons there with the boys, picking out books with them, reading to them. We took them swimming; we sat in the sun and played with them and watched them play. Even when Andy was over in the sandbox he'd keep coming back to me bringing me some sand or calling me over to see what he'd made. I went back to work—but just long enough to train my replacement."

Conway's situation clearly indicates that if a woman wants and needs validation of her desire to leave her career to mother full time she can benefit immensely from a role model who has already successfully done it. Further, her situation exemplifies the way a phased career deemphasis can aid the decision-making process for some conflicted women, a way that a growing number of conflicted women ultimately leave their work, particularly those afraid to separate entirely from it because of fears that they are forever risking their careers. Some women deal best with their conflicts by first deemphasizing their careers, then later leaving entirely rather than making the "clean break" initially.

THE PHASED CAREER DEEMPHASIS

The phased career deemphasis has become increasingly possible in the last several years because of employer response to a heretofore unprecedented problem. For the first time in history, employers are losing important members of their organizations to formidable competitors who can't talk, can't walk, and weigh only eight pounds. The usual inducements for retention of valued employees—higher salary, more prestigious title, greater responsibilities—fail to work against this competition. Therefore, employers are presently faced with designing a new system of retention inducements. Both employers and mothers are still experimenting to find which work best and for whom. Currently, the most prevalent plan is the optional reduced work week (usually twenty to thirty hours), which employers initiate to try to retain new mothers who are valuable to the organization.

A major study by Catalyst and several *Wall Street Journal* articles have already reported upon this rapidly increasing phenomenon. Nearly half of the women I interviewed said their employers had offered them a reduced work week, and more than a quarter of them tried it before leaving their work entirely. The optional twenty-to-thirty-hour work week seems certain to be standard procedure within the next decade for three reasons: (1) the high cost of training, (2) low birth rates and projected new job rates indicate that in the next decade the number of positions in many fields will exceed the number of persons trained for the jobs, and (3) the dollars and sense of an employer looking at a woman's past and potential contribution to an organization over a period of forty or more years rather than focusing on the few years during which she has small children. These factors combine to make many employers try to find ways to keep women throughout their mothering years.

As Sandra Conway's situation indicates, however, reduced work time doesn't address the needs of the woman who truly wants an uninterrupted period of time for mothering. Conway's employer offered the reduced time option as a means of solving his problem: to keep her on the job. This solution was incompatible with her goals: to mother full time. This difference in goals is experienced by an increasing number of employers and employees today, and it is often confusing to both.

Because it is crucial that the optional reduced work week continues to become integral to the way work is done in this country, it is critical that everyone involved recognize when the reduced work week is beneficial to mothers and when it is not. As will be fully discussed in Part III, the reduced work week is excellent for mothers of school-age children. It can also work well for mothers of preschoolers who would otherwise have no other choice but to work full time, who want to maintain career involvement until they once again resume full-time work, who would leave work altogether if they had to continue working full time but would consider working part time, or who are not sure which way to go—home or back to full-time work—and need time on a reduced schedule to decide.

The woman who ultimately decides to sequence but who suffers too much conflict to take the "clean break" approach often finds the reduced work week a way station for "phasing out" of her professional activities.

Karen Davis was a conflicted woman who "phased out" gradually and who saw that she would probably want to "phase in" at a later date. Davis realized when her son was a few months old that she could "never continue the pace of my advertising career and mother him. I was gone all the time and felt exhausted and harassed half the time on the job and much of the time at home as well. I thought about resigning for several months, and then I just went in one day and did it. That was it—I'd had it. But my boss said, 'Hey, not so fast, let's try to work something out. I think we can find ways around this to keep you here part of the time.' I was really surprised and pleased. He was willing to set a precedent for me which he knew he'd have to follow again and again for other women."

Davis is currently working three days a week in her former setting on team projects for which she doesn't bear total responsibility. "I work Monday through Wednesday, strictly nine to five," she says. "I knew if I worked every other day they'd always have something urgent on interim days, but this way I just work my three days, then leave on Wednesday for the weekend, and that's it. Period." Davis does not feel the arrangement is as ideal as it first seemed, and after nearly two years she is preparing to leave entirely.

"The truth is that I've a completely different perspective in my life now. I'm much more interested in being with my son at this point and in having another baby. Plus even working part time I still have all the child care problems I had when I worked full time—I insist on private in-home care for our son, but it's a kind of revolving door thing; I'm now on my third person and when the new one came she brought with her a new problem. My last sitter was from Trinidad as is his best friend's sitter. The kids used to play together while their sitters chatted. But my new sitter is from Jamaica, and she won't speak to my son's friend's sitter because she's from Trinidad, so the kids can't play together. This means that I now wind up spending my days off at the park with the sitter from Trinidad so my son can play with her charge—either that or my son loses contact with his friend entirely. He is already upset enough about the loss of his last sitter. He goes around saying that he is bad. Maybe she told him he was, I don't know. I don't like the loss of continuity he has with sitters or with his friend or that I am beginning to feel with him either. I'm newly pregnant again, and I've given notice that I plan to leave my work next month entirely. Before the new baby arrives I want to have some time exclusively with my son, and then the two children will keep me busy enough at home. If my firm wants me back in a few years on some kind of arrangement as we now have, say, when the new baby goes to school, I would probably like it. If not, I'll make some new arrangements when the time comes. For me this phasing out rather than going out all at once has been good because what's happened is I've developed a stronger and stronger pull to be with my son and am correspondingly less interested in having to leave him to go to work."

The transitional period of continuing to work on a reduced-time basis while becoming more involved in mothering enables a conflicted woman like Davis to reach a decision to mother full time for a period of years. As she becomes increasingly involved with her children and recognizes that her mothering benefits both herself and them, the woman becomes simultaneously less involved with her career, realizing that work will still be there later but the children's early years will not.

Although women come to the sequencing decision from two very different routes—those who leave their work with comfort and those who leave after much conflict—both groups describe very similar feelings and attitudes during their full-time mothering years. The main differences between the two groups occur at the decision-making point and at two subsequent points: the transition phase from full-time career to full-time motherhood, which is more difficult for the conflicted woman, and the point at which they reemphasize professional activities. The initially conflicted woman usually works again sooner.

The similarities among women who sequence are much greater than their differences, however, because they share a value system. For each woman who makes that decision, at a particular point in her life, nothing else is as important as mothering her children. For some women, trying to balance their professional and personal lives—the rushing, scheduling, fatigue, and dissatisfaction with surrogate child care—is a part of the picture in varying degree and kind. But in the last analysis, the heart of the matter is that each woman who chooses to sequence orders her priorities to trade a period of time from her career so she can mother her own children.

3

Joint Expectations

The decision that she wants to sequence is the woman's own. Whether and how she implements that decision depends upon the mutual expectations she and her husband develop, for her choice places him in a new role within the family unit. What are his reactions to this role? Will more mothering mean less fathering? What effect will new roles have on their marriage? Who will do the housework? How can they live on one paycheck? What financial plan can they make? Whose money is it? These are major questions which couples contemplating the wife's sequencing ask. They are answered by those couples who have already developed a set of joint expectations upon which they have implemented the sequencing decision.

HUSBANDS' ROLES AND REACTIONS

Many marriage decisions are made simultaneously by two active participants, but the decision to sequence is almost always made first by the woman, who is the primary actor, and second, with her husband, the reactor. There is an obvious reason for this order: it's her career that is directly involved because she, not he, feels pulled by their child to leave her work.

It is well known that more mothers feel the tugs and pulls to be continually with their young than do fathers. What is unknown is why. For generations behaviorists have argued biological determinism (nature) versus social conditioning (nurture) to explain a wide range of human behavior. For years it was accepted among behaviorists of a variety of disciplines that maternal instinct accounted for a woman's greater intensity of involvement with her young. But when modern feminism attempted to overthrow all role specialization on the grounds that social conditioning rather than biological determinism accounts for most differences in male/female behavior, the theory of maternal instinct became unfashionable. Feminism proclaimed that women and men could each play the other's role, that they could function interchangeably and could each do work that the other had previously done.

That hypothesis has been tested in the human laboratory of the dual-career family for the past two decades with some extraordinarily interesting findings. For in this gigantic social experiment in which feminism tried to eradicate not only gender discrimination but gender itself, we often see that men and women are capable of playing interchangeable roles. But we also frequently find that neither the man nor the woman feels the same in the role as does the member of the opposite sex. The woman who succeeds in her career and enjoys that work before she becomes a mother often changes radically toward it when she has a baby, enjoying it far less because of the time it takes from her child. Yet her husband's feelings toward his work don't usually change when he becomes a father.

In my interviews, woman after woman who continued working after her first child was born reported initial bewilderment that when she left for her office she felt she had left something precious and tremendously important to her behind although her husband rarely thought twice about leaving for work. A mother who interrupted her executive-level career when her son was ten months old says, "Before I left my job I was amazed that when my husband and I went to work together each morning he simply kissed the baby, got his hat, and walked out the door with complete ease while I left each day feeling empty and miserable." A pediatrician who is now mothering her own two children full time says she finds herself much more in sympathy with biological determinists on the issue of maternal-child attachment than she'd ever dreamed before motherhood: "My husband is gentle, sensitive, and loves our children every bit as much as I do. Yet I was shocked at the differences between us when we were both working full time after our first son was born. We both had research posts and rode to the hospital together every day. He could leave home with nary a second thought while I had a gnawing feeling in the pit of my stomach that somehow this kind of life just wasn't right for me or my baby."

There are many who will go to their graves denying that nine months of physiological oneness (coupled with months more of nursing) results in added feelings of responsibility for a child. They will say that fathers don't feel the added dimension of responsibility for their young that mothers do simply because fathers have never had to, as there was always somebody there to do it for them. But the evidence does not bear out this argument. With millions of children in substitute-for-parent care all day, millions of men are not moving heaven and earth to make more time to care for their young, but women in comparable positions to those of men in every field are doing just that.

This is not to say that fathers should not feel the same responsibilities as do mothers, but it is to say that it is evident that, *initially*, most do not. It seems perfectly plausible that the reason is that females—not males—are the biologically programmed advocates of the next generation. A man is programmed to sire hundreds of children, yet he may never be completely certain he is the father of even one of those children, whereas a baby's biological mother is never in question. Because biologically the father could be anyone and because physically a new, vulnerable, naked, and hungry creature needs an advocate, it's reasonable to assume that nature selected the child's own mother to protect and care for the child just as nature programmed the mother to nourish it. This does not mean that every woman must be the sole caregiver of her child any more than that she must be the only one to give nourishment to her baby, but clearly nature programs women to do both.

Although fathers may be far less likely than mothers to elect to be full-time caregivers to their children, husbands have a different but equally important role in the sequencing decision: that of chief moral and financial support, as well as of involved participatory parent. Many of the women I spoke with said that their husbands willingly assumed this role from the first; many received strong encouragement for their sequencing decisions from their husbands. But other men need a period of adjustment. In the beginning, a husband may be upset, threatened, even furious with his wife's desire to interrupt her career. Some men perceive the decision as a rejection of their value systems and thus of them. Others see it as an economic cop-out. Neither reaction is surprising, for a woman's reordering of her priorities flies in the face of the careerism norm, the value system in which both husband and wife were raised.

The contemporary woman's emphasis on and dedication to careerism is predicated clearly and completely upon the traditional male norm of career as the focal point around which other aspects of life revolve. In the late 1960s and 1970s, when women gained greater entry to professional schools and employment in a variety of previously male-dominated professions, women didn't question this norm. As assimilationists, they were too new at the game and thus too insecure; they had to prove that they could do it—a man's way. Now that they've proven it, women such as Maria Orlean, Meredith Martin, and Paula Archer are questioning the complete career absorption that precludes a person's other dimensions, interests, and responsibilities. They are saying, a career is an important part of me but it's not all of me; I will do my work exceedingly well but I won't give it my life. When a woman interrupts her career to raise her children, she is putting the message into action.

She is restructuring her personal priorities in opposition to the prevailing definition of professionalism. For professionalism today has come to mean not just being career-involved but career-consumed. This definition is not only prevalent among fast-trackers; it permeates the entire society. Emphasis on career begins in high school or before, as young people are pushed, and push, to achieve academically to the heights of their abilities so they will qualify for the best college they are capable of entering. They then push to excel so they will get the best positions they can or will gain admission to the best professional schools and will be tapped for the best residencies, clerkships, and appointments they can get. This is the way the men did it; this is the norm that modern feminism followed; so now this is the way women do it, too. When a husband and wife have been programmed by these norms and value systems, when both measure their worth as human beings by their appointments and promotions—and then suddenly one of them says, Guess what, I found something more important to me right now, it can't help but shake up the other one.

"You're rejecting every single thing that we've both wanted, that we've both worked for," Bob Rivers shouted at his wife, Jessica, when she told him she wanted to leave her insurance company supervisory post last year. Both middle managers, both moving upward in their respective companies, Bob and Jessica both looked toward more responsibility in their work and higher paychecks. "We spent long evenings talking about our aspirations, what we wanted to achieve in our work, what we planned to do with the money," Jessica said. "Now, all of a sudden, I wanted to do something completely different—toss the work aside, tone down our lifestyle. I found a new interest, a new focus for my energy, and Bob felt plainly left out. He felt that I'd rejected our joint values and him along with them. I had to convince him that I wasn't rejecting him but that I really felt that mothering our children was a great deal more important for all of us than my continuing my career at this point. I still want to share in his problems and joys concerning his work. Most importantly, I understand what he's talking about because I've been there. I think he is beginning to understand my new priorities, where I'm coming from, seeing that I'm not rejecting his career and the rewards it can bring. I'm simply seeing my career within the large framework of my whole life. He is beginning to see his career differently, too, I think. He sees it more as a means of supporting us all than of what he is in the world. It's something important that he does, but he no longer sees it as *the* most important thing of all."

Bob Rivers felt personally threatened by his wife's sequencing decision. Other men feel financially threatened, particularly those whose incomes fluctuate substantially from month to month and year to year and those whose wives' salaries are equal to, or higher than, their own and who therefore perceive themselves as only half or less than half responsible for the financial support of the family.

"What do you mean you're quitting? How can you expect me to pay all the bills?" thirty-two-year-old Lisa Adams recalls her husband, Paul, said when she announced that she was leaving her teaching position. "It shouldn't have come as a shock to him. We'd discussed it many, many times over the year after our son was born. But I realize now that he never thought I was serious. At first, I just thought he was being selfish, but then after he cooled down I realized that he was plain scared to death. He is a sales rep for a furniture company, and while there's always a base pay we can count on, his total income is variable.

"We agreed that I would do nothing about my leaving for three months until we could really hash the whole thing through. We talked over all the pros and cons, what changes we'd have to make in our spending habits, what kind of life we'd really be living if I left my work. This time we talked seriously—he knew I was not just theorizing about a possible decision but really meant it. We talked about how deeply I felt about being with our son, about having the chance to have another child soon and mother them both, about how impossible I found it to give what I wanted to my work and then come home and be the kind of mother I want to be. In the end, I left my job with his support for what I want to do.

"And I came to recognize how worried he is about being the only one to support us. I'm doing everything I can to keep reducing expenses to keep his anxiety level down."

Some couples aren't able to resolve the loss of the wife's check as smoothly as did the Riverses and the Adamses. It's particularly difficult when the wife earns as much as or more than her husband. "I actually considered divorce when my husband blew up over my decision to stay home with our children," Lucille Walton, a former Portland retail executive says. "I worked full time all through my two-year-old son's early days and realized that I was missing so much with him that when our daughter was born last year, I decided I just wanted to mother them for a while. Being away from them all day just didn't seem fair to them or to me when I felt I didn't have to. Jim earns a good living. We can manage on his salary, although we can't buy and maintain a bigger home in a more prestigious section of the city or can't buy the big boat he wants.

"He was just furious with me; called me lazy, unwilling to pull my share of the load. Well, damn it, where did he get the idea that our kids would magically grow up into wonderful people while getting practically no attention from either of us? To me, my share is giving them a home life, not buying my forty-year-old husband a boat.

"I extended my maternity leave from two to six months, during which time we fought continuously. Finally, I told him that if I had to go back to work full time and simultaneously raise our family, I didn't see what I needed him for. That's the lot of single mothers, it's the lot of the woman whose husband can't earn a living for the family. But I told him it shouldn't be my lot when I'm married to a man whose salary can provide for us and when I am willing to leave my work to raise our children. He said I was casting him as the meal ticket and he didn't like it a bit. I said that if I was going to live like a single parent anyway, I'd be one. I told him to decide by the time my leave extension was up because if I was going to have to go back to work, I didn't want to lose that job, but if he forced me back to it I would leave him.

"Well, a couple weeks before my deadline to return to work he came around. He said he didn't want to lose me and the children, that while he couldn't understand my feelings he would try not to argue about them. And he's kept his word pretty well, except he periodically mentions to me that there's this really great opportunity in my area. He knows though that I won't interview now, but I have assured him that this won't be forever and promised him that in a few years, when our daughter is in school, I'll work again on a part-time basis. He is more accepting of my decision as time goes on, and while I still think in his heart of hearts he'd rather have the boat and a new car and a bigger home like so many of his colleagues who have working wives, he is resigned if not content."

Bob Rivers's, Paul Adams's, and even Jim Walton's reactions to their wives' desires to interrupt their careers are not without precedent. Fortunately, however, more frequently when a woman chooses to sequence, she finds that her husband embraces her decision. In fact, for some women her choice broadens his outlook on the role of the family in his life as well.

DOES MORE MOTHER MEAN LESS FATHER?

More mother does not mean less father when the woman sequences—often it means more. Happily, there is no evidence of a return to the style of the 1950s, when father came home, read his paper, ate his dinner, kissed his children good night, and headed for his desk. To the contrary, today's father is not excluded or excused from active parental participation because his wife is mothering their children.

Women currently sequencing and their husbands say that not only does more mother not mean less father but that it frequently means the father does more fathering than he did before she left her work. The reason is that once she leaves her career and paycheck behind so as to mother, they both see their roles in their children's lives differently from the way they did when they were a dual-career couple.

"After I left my neurology practice," Paula Archer says, "my husband became more and more curious about what it was that drew me to spend so much time with our daughter. I talked about her so much, was so involved with her that he wanted more of a share in it, too. So an afternoon a week he takes off from his ophthalmology practice. He doesn't head for the golf course like his father used to, but rather after morning rounds he comes home to be with our daughter. He likes to do this more than spending the afternoon in the office or than going out for recreation. I have begun working as a consultant to an HMO on that afternoon, so he has a chance to really be with our daughter himself."

Sometimes, a wife's sequencing decision contributes to her husband's changing his own career aspirations. He may look more carefully at the way he spends his professional time and draw firm lines about how much of his day or week, month or year, he will devote exclusively to professional activities. Occasionally, he even changes directions.

When Donna Briting decided to leave her hospital post as a psychiatric social worker to raise her children, her husband, Paul, took a second look at what he wanted out of his life. "It turned out," Donna says, "that he didn't want the position he had with his mainline law firm and the hectic, pressured, unpredictable schedule that went with it. He switched to corporate counsel in a firm where he earns less and is less visible in the larger world of law, but we have a family life. Now he can nearly always plan to have dinner with the children and me and to spend weekend time with us."

My husband, Dick, left his teaching position at the Harvard Business School in 1967 shortly after being promoted so he could devote more time to our family. In so doing, he gave up an affiliation with the most prestigious school of business in the world, as well as the earning potential that went with the excellent consulting opportunities. He did it because the highly structured schedules of the more than fifteen-hour work days meant that he had to be away from home during all of Miriam's and Rachel's weekday waking hours and that he worked in his office most of the weekends as well. We had decided when I left my work with a psychobiological research foundation that I would be home full time with the children. But when we recognized, at Harvard, that we were in a situation that meant all mother and no father, all work for him and no family life, he chose to make a major lifestyle change so he could enjoy the relationships in his life as well as his profession.

The Britings and my family are but two examples of the fact that although a woman's decision to sequence leaves her husband responsible to support the family, her decision need not necessarily cause him to devote yet more total time to his work. They may opt instead to adjust their priorities. For example, Paul Briting could have worked even more hours in his firm to make up part of Donna's lost income, had the couple preferred. Dick could have remained at Harvard, and we would have had considerably more material goods. But in planning for financial implementation of the sequencing decision, a couple may well decide as the Britings did, as we did, and as countless others do to scale down their total standard of living to provide their children not only with mothering time but with plenty of fathering time as well.

WHO DOES THE HOUSEWORK?

This generation has demolished the myth that child care and housework go hand in hand. No more. No way. A couple cannot expect that the mother's sequencing will mean a clean house. For the woman who chooses to sequence to be expected—because she is "home anyway"—to do all the housework would be to repeat the mistakes of the generation of the 1960s, when many of the mothers who fled from home threw out the baby with the bathwater. These women were so inundated and bored with mundane, repetitive, purposeless household chores that when they heard the new message of "liberation" they lumped housework and children into one bag, weighed it against paid work—in a clean office—and fled the laundry, dishes, and vacuum cleaner.

In contrast, today's educated, career-experienced mothers

have left their careers for the express purpose of caring for their children. They did not leave their positions as attorneys, physicians, editors, nurses, educators, secretaries, computer programmers, therapists, or executives to clean house!

At the time of the initial sequencing decision, most of today's couples set all housework into a category *completely separate* from caring for the children. They then seek ways to solve the problem of the household tasks. For more and more couples one solution is to list all housework, then drop half the items from the list immediately. (Nowadays people don't do prophylactic dusting, scrubbing, or vacuuming. They ignore at least 50 percent of what their grandmothers once did, even grandmothers with fully machined homes.) Once the couple decides what *really* is necessary, each member of the pair decides what he/she is willing to do, then they either ignore the rest, divide it, or in some cases hire someone to do it. Other couples agree to do as little as possible, each pitching in and doing what absolutely needs to be done; still others hire regular or occasional help for general cleaning, splitting the marketing, cooking, and meal cleanup themselves. Most women elect to do the weekday cooking and often do it as a joint activity with their children. In some families she routinely cooks, he routinely cleans up from the meal, and they market as a family. In other families the woman does the marketing because, as one mother says, "At first we all went together on the weekend, but I thought 'this is ridiculous.' I can do this with the kids during the week as an activity, then we can all go on a picnic or do a thousand other things we'd rather do together on Saturday instead of wasting half a day in the supermarket in prime-time crowds."

When *Woman at Home* was published in 1976, I was sure that my views on the boon it is for the home-based mother to hire help with housework would place me at best as an elitist, at worst as exploitive. (At that time, any woman who hired another woman to clean her house was called "exploitive," although it was perfectly fine for a man or woman to hire another man or woman to clean his or her office.) To my surprise, reviewers lauded the idea of hiring household help as if it had been newly invented, the book's housework section was excerpted in a number of newspapers around the country, and, most important, I received letters from many mothers who identified themselves as having modest incomes and who thanked me for giving them permission to concentrate on their children, forget the house, and consider hiring some modicum of household help.

A decade later, I don't have to validate the issue. Now, many couples at least consider hiring help, and it's not unusual for a number of them to do so. Sometimes parents give the couple a gift certificate for a certain number of months of cleaning help, particularly right after the birth of a child.

In days past, when household help was prevalent and relatively cheap, many households whose income corresponded in today's dollar to "middle class" retained a full-time housekeeper, who concentrated on the house while the full-time mother focused her time and energies on her children. Now, with the advent of technology and, as important,

PART I

the changed values as to what constitutes a clean house, full-time cleaning help is not necessary. But many couples still find they can use some outside help, particularly when children are too young to pitch in and clean but old enough to create a mess.

WHAT EFFECT DOES SEQUENCING HAVE ON THE MARRIAGE?

In nearly every case when the woman worked after the birth of one or more of the children and then left her full-time job, couples agree that more time for the marriage is a major benefit of her decision. Yet, interestingly, time for the marriage is rarely mentioned by women discussing their conflicts before leaving their full-time work. Then, the real pull is between children and profession, with strain on the marriage recognized as a price exacted by two people trying both to maintain their careers and raise their children. "Husband comes last is the way it was," says a woman who left her public administrative post two years ago. "It had to be—I felt so guilty for leaving the baby as much as I did that I wanted to spend every minute I was home with her. But once I left my work to be home full time, I no longer felt torn. . . . I am with her all day, so when we put her to bed in the evening I have no remorse and can relax with my husband. This is a delightful benefit that I didn't count on but that he and I both love."

Husbands concur. A man whose wife left an executive track last year says, "Life is far less hectic with my wife at home, yet what's interesting is that very little has changed with regard to what we actually do around here in the evenings. It's the *way* we do it that's so much better. Before, I'd pick the kids up from the family care home, she made dinner. Then we'd all eat frantically—it was four people converging on each other after ten hours away. One of us fed the youngest, our three-year-old tried to talk to us both, and we sometimes tried to talk to each other but without much luck. One of us would clean up, while the other read stories. Then we'd each take one, bathe him, and get him to bed. The whole thing used to take about three hours from the time we left work until the kids were in bed. By then, we'd be tired, tense, fixed on getting things lined up for the next morning. There was no time for us.

"Now we eat in a much more relaxed manner when I get home. I am the only one who has been gone all day, so it's only one person to reincorporate into the family instead of that major convergence of us all on each other. I clean up from dinner. Then we take turns bathing and reading to the boys. It's flexible, it's relaxed, and in fact it's so calmed down around here as opposed to before that it's like night and day. The best part is that my wife and I actually have time to curl up with each other in the evening after the kids are in bed. Neither of us is too pooped or tense to relax together."

Less stress on the marriage is a definite joint gain of sequencing, and thus more time for each other is a plus which couples contemplating sequencing can well expect. As part of this joint gain, many couples report a feeling of cohesion, both in their marriage and as a family, a feeling that there is time for them to share activities together, knowledge that their children are growing within a secure family unit, certainty they are able to be the primary contributors to their children's development, and knowledge that their children will receive individualized parental attention, love, and care.

4

The
Economics of Sequencing

Sequencing is the premium-cost child care option. There-fore, how can we afford to live on one paycheck? is the first question couples seriously considering the option ask. On closer analysis, however, the question is not so much, how can we afford it? as it is, how badly do we want to do it? for the loss of thousands of dollars a year requires most couples to revamp their spending patterns and, more important, to rethink the values that underpin them.

In the two-parent family the decision of whether both partners will work full time is almost always a values decision. I do not make this statement lightly. When I first began researching *Sequencing*, I assumed that the woman's decision to leave her career would be positively correlated with her husband's income—that the more he earned the more she would be likely, if she wanted to leave her work, to do so. And I assumed that, correspondingly, the less he earned, the less inclined she would be to leave. But this is not always the case. Husband's income and wife's sequencing do not necessarily go hand in hand. Some lower-income couples, for whom the husband's pay is under median income, feel that at all cost the woman should be able to mother their children. They go to great lengths and sacrifice to make it possible. In contrast, other couples, for whom the husband's salary is in the high five, even six figures, maintain a standard of living that requires the wife also to work full time.

Couples at each income level have to grapple with what it is that they value most, and it always boils down to the same question: what money can buy versus their child spending his or her days with his or her own mother. For many, losing the wife's paycheck means a giant step backward in living conditions and correspondingly in socioeconomic status. For Vivian Taylor and her husband, her sequencing would force them to give up their "middle-class apartment with all of its nice furnishings and go back to low-cost ghettolike housing." The trade for them is her mothering their child versus living in a far less desirable environment near the bottom of the socioeconomic scale. For others, like Ruby Dorman, her sequencing means the couple will rent in a lower socioeconomic area and will never own a home, or at least not for many years. For others, her sequencing means their owning a smaller home in a less prestigious neighborhood than they would on two incomes. For yet others it means giving up a second home or a lake cottage. It's all relative, and it all depends upon what a couple most values at a certain point in life.

As previously indicated, the women who leave careers with certainty differ markedly on the issue of money from those who leave after much ambivalence. Because most of the certain women decided some time before the birth of their first children that they wanted to mother full time—some knew it for years—they are much more psychologically and actually prepared for one-paycheck living than are women who suffer conflict. In many cases, once married, low-conflict women rarely use both salaries for daily living. They and their husbands almost always divide the incomes. His is used for all daily living expenses—rent or payments, taxes, food, and the like. Hers goes for major one-time purchases, savings, or both. Therefore, one-paycheck living is a de facto way of life before she leaves her career.

A former interior designer "in the sixth year of maternity leave" says she "hoarded nearly everything I earned for the four years before our first child was born. That savings account now produces an income that, when added to my husband's present earnings, gets us through." Others may have a house partially paid for, or at least predicated upon one income, as do Anita Crawford and her husband. "When we were house hunting before our first daughter was born," Crawford said, "it was extraordinarily tempting to buy a home we could have afforded on our joint incomes. But we were sure that I wasn't going to continue working, and we knew that the house would be a terrible stretch for my husband alone. We didn't do it; we bought one that his salary covers, and we've never regretted it."

In contrast, most of the women who suffered initial conflicts have no expectation before the birth of their first children that they will want to take time from careers for full-time mothering and as a result live on two salaries. For them, when she decides that she wants to leave her company, her students, her clients, or her patients—and not incidentally her paycheck—to nurture her child, or children, it is a matter of major concern.

It is therefore essential, even if both partners are ideologically committed to the premise of sequencing, that a couple who has lived on both paychecks detail a thorough economic plan to prevent misunderstanding, conflict, guilt, and recrimination along the way. She cannot pursue the goal of raising their children for a period of time unencumbered by career responsibilities unless she is correspondingly unencumbered by economic responsibilities. If the checkbook fails to balance month in and month out and she begins to view each day with her children in terms of number of dollars foregone, or as a luxury rather than a necessity, or if she thinks he does, there is bound to be trouble.

Barbara Morris, a Seattle woman who interrupted her law practice three years ago to raise her two sons but had no strong economic plan, found just that: "We simply never cut down our expenses in the way that we should have—we got used to living very well when I was working full time, and I must admit that we felt resentful at having to cut. So we really didn't. As a result, we are heavily in debt. I will probably have to resume practicing law on a full-time or close to full-time basis within the next six months, and it saddens me immensely to have to do so. If we had simply cut down in the first place instead of thinking, 'Oh, well, we'll figure it out,' I would be able to continue at home for several more years. I feel embarrassed, too, because with our backgrounds the whole thing was inexcusable. Certainly I'd never run my law practice the way we've run the family finances, nor would my husband function that way in his business dealings. Now he is really up against a wall because of our debts, so he keeps saying to me, 'I think you're bored at home. You were happier in your practice.' Actually, I'm not at all bored, and I'd be delighted to be home another few years, but that's his way of saying he can't handle the financial scene."

There are many variations on this theme. A woman decides to take time from her career to raise her children, her husband agrees, and they figure they'll play it by ear. They like the concept but don't plan its implementation. This lack of planning then results in a clash between partners when their expenses continually exceed their income. The only way for a couple to ensure against conflict is to prevent it in the beginning through a thorough exploration of personal and joint values and a strong financial plan—subject to frequent updating—for implementing those values.

DEVELOPING A FINANCIAL PLAN

To effect a strong, workable financial plan husband and wife need to take all their financial documents and schedule a series of uninterrupted conferences with each other to evaluate the financial needs to implement the new lifestyle decision and the necessary trade-offs to effect it. Or they may elect to consult a third party—a banker or a personal investment counselor—to help them assess their long-range financial picture as well as to help them look at the trade-offs from all angles.

This financial evaluation is their written values statement, the answer to how badly do we really want to forgo what the money will buy us so that our child can be raised by his or her mother on a day-to-day basis? Some couples opt to trade down to well under $20,000 a year to provide the woman with a period for mothering, but others do not elect to cut from many times that. *Performing the financial evaluation enables couples to see for themselves just what trades they are and are not willing to make for the sequencing decision to work.*

The financial evaluation involves three steps: (1) current financial analysis of income and outflow on two salaries, (2) analysis of projected income and expenditure with one salary, and (3) evaluation of trade-offs to determine which goods and services will be cut.

The first step is self-evident. It entails a careful look at how current income is presently being spent. The second step involves evaluating how the projected one paycheck would be spent. Certain items will be dropped from the first list to the second. They are reduced or eliminated because they directly relate to the woman's full-time career and include major child care expenses (although some baby sitting and perhaps household help will still be retained as an expense), work wardrobe, transportation, and non-expense-account lunches.

In addition, the total tax bite is reduced so that the take-home pay from one check is considerably higher than the take-home pay from that same check when both spouses were earning. Even accounting for the tax break, the reduction in child care costs, and the omission of her work-related expenses, the projected expenditures will often exceed the single paycheck.

Step three, then, is the point at which the heavy evaluation and real decision making begins. Couples must look carefully at what they believe they can forgo from the projected expenditures column—what items they are willing to trade to achieve their goal.

The fixed expenses are the most problematical, with the residence almost always topping the list. The couple may have to reconsider where they live. Sometimes this analysis shows that the rest of the budget must be tailored to accommodate monthly rent or house payments; other times it may mean moving to a less expensive place.

A Denver woman who left her post as a buyer for a women's ready-to-wear chain says, "In retrospect it was unrealistic of us to have bought such an expensive house without giving any thought at all to the possibility of my not working. I just never expected to want to be home with the baby, but once I knew, it was a very clear choice— either work to pay the mortgage and taxes for a house which would be empty all day or buy a smaller house in a different section of town, where I could be home with the baby. I opted for moving; I just didn't want to live there badly enough to give up my mothering years."

Not everyone has such a radical choice to make. A woman who left a management post in a St. Louis pharmaceutical company to raise her two sons says, "When I first announced to my husband that I really had to leave my job, he alternated between anger and panic. We'd just bought a new house. How could I possibly leave work? How could he alone give us the kind of life we'd been leading? But the other side of the coin was, how could I possibly stay at work because things were absolutely miserable around home. In fact, it was no kind of home atmosphere, just rushing and tension. We sat down and figured that we could manage without selling the house as long as we didn't do anything more to it—we never put in the carpeting, never furnished as we'd planned to."

For some couples the change of lifestyle means they abandon or defer plans to buy a different home. One woman who left her banking post says: "The dream house in the suburbs never became a reality. Instead, we kept our falling-apart house in the city."

In addition to the house and neighborhood, other trades which couples deciding on a sequencing option frequently consider include furnishings, number and makes of cars, leisure activities, and traveling.

In discussing trading money for time, most couples find that their entire system of values is called into question. Both partners need to clarify, perhaps for the first time, just what it is they want out of life—what each hopes to give to and get from his/her relationship with the other and with their children, what each hopes to contribute to society as a whole. Often such discussions take not one but many evenings, sometimes days and weeks.

Very frequently, such searing lifestyle exploration intensifies a couple's joint resolution to make whatever changes are necessary for a woman to interrupt her career to give time to the children. Often couples who make drastic lifestyle changes report that they are happier than they formerly were, in spite of the dramatic alterations in their standard of living. A woman who left her work as a medical secretary in a Los Angeles area hospital says, "My husband is a teacher. My income loss means we have had to cut out all the extras; I shop much more carefully for food now, as well as for the kids' clothes. We used to take weekend trips with the family, and now we don't travel anymore. But we don't have to go away to relax; the pressure is way down on our marriage with me away from the hospital. We're not living as we formerly did, but we are much happier in spite of it. Eventually, when the children are in school, I can go back to work. My husband can be home after school, and his vacations will correspond to theirs. So we won't always be living on such a close budget."

A Connecticut mother who interrupted her career as a Manhattan corporate cost analyst says, "Our financial change meant we look at ourselves in a new light; before we were a pair of yuppies who happened to be raising a son. Now we are a middle-class family—it's barbecue in the backyard instead of a three-wine restaurant dinner, but somehow at this stage we find this way of life much more rewarding."

Sometimes, however, couples who thought they were ideologically committed to sequencing find that in making a substantial lifestyle change, the price tag on maternal care is too high; when measured in dollars the cost of her staying with their children while he supports them all is not one they are willing, or feel able, to pay. Some couples, when faced with the realization that leaving *her* career for a period means a major lifestyle change complete with changing *their* spending habits, perhaps changing *their* place of residence, or *their* moving to a less desirable area, decide *her* time with their children is not as important as it seemed. They then opt to provide themselves and their children with more material comforts and opportunities and correspondingly less maternal time.

There is no judge and jury to arbitrate material versus maternal values or to hand down a decision of "right" and "wrong." What is right is that if a woman feels she wants to interrupt her career, a couple takes the time to thoroughly discuss joint priorities and the economic issues involved. They are then in full position to evaluate just how much the woman's taking time from her career to raise their children means to them.

Often it is only after a woman decides she would like to interrupt her career—or is seriously considering it—only after she and her husband discuss it at length, only after they play out the financial aspect of the question that they can determine whether she will, in fact, leave her work or whether she will merely fantasize about it. Here are two contrasting situations.

Lois Reis in Westchester fears cutting down from their joint six-figure income to high five figures if she interrupts her career. Mary Wagner in Somerville, Massachusetts, feels differently: "I left my position as supervisor of twenty visiting nurses to take care of our first baby. Because I'm thirty-six and we wanted more children, I got pregnant again almost immediately. It was at this point that my husband decided on a mid-career switch and left his steady job to start his own business. It didn't go as well as he expected, his annual income doesn't exceed $20,000 a year. In fact, last year it was only $18,000. Sometimes, when things get really desperate, I work weekend shifts as a staff nurse for a few weeks to help pull us out. Then Bob is with our daughters. But I absolutely do not want to go back to regular work, and Bob is in complete agreement with me. With the pressure he is under, coupled with the pressures I'd encounter if I take a full-time administrative job, the kids wouldn't have a chance at the kind of childhood we want them to have. And if I tried to work staff nurse shifts around Bob's hectic and unpredictable schedule, I know full well there would be constant trouble. I would be frustrated all the time at the hospital from being at the bottom of the heap instead of administering, I'd be tired and cross when I'm home with the kids, and I'd never see Bob. So we're budgeting tightly, and I'm going to stay with the children; I think that, in the long run, will prove to be the best decision we can make all around. Sure, we can use the money in the worst way now, but we're eating. I feel if I go to work I lose their childhood. I've waited too long for this experience to let it get away from me."

The Wagners' solution is the bottom-line answer to almost every couple who are philosophically committed to a woman's interrupting her career to mother their children and who ask, how can we afford it? In nearly every case, the old adage about will and way prevails, so that the couple for whom sequencing is truly a top priority, who have established that they value maternal care for their children above all else, manage to adjust their standards and live in a way in which they can implement that value.

EMOTIONAL ACCEPTANCE OF ONE PAYCHECK

Some couples who seriously want the mother to be home with their children and who believe that they can manage to pay the bills on one paycheck still worry and ask, what will it really be like? Will a reduced standard of living change our images of ourselves? How will we look to our friends? Will we be dropped socially by those with whom we can no longer keep up? How will it feel to stretch the beef for stew rather than put a roast in the oven? What if we can't give our children the lessons we want them to have? The list is endless. The question is the same: how will we feel in a new and unfamiliar financial situation?

When Ruth Anders left her executive position with a Chicago area fashion chain and an excellent salary, both she and her husband were "quite scared. He earned a good salary, but still, all of a sudden, our income was effectively cut in half. We knew that we could maintain our home and continue to eat, but still we would be radically trimming everything else. Our savings program for one thing—there would be no more cushioning—traveling, just the freedom to buy what we wanted or felt we needed without having to think very much about it. We wondered if my being home would be worth it, or if we'd start to be resentful of my not earning and resentful of each other. We wondered if we'd have the same friends if we couldn't dine out with them. We were full of fears."

Anders says that their fears turned out for the most part "to be unfounded" because they both discovered that her being home meant that they were getting new rewards: "However, we definitely lost some of our friends . . . funny thing, though, it turned out that we recognized they weren't so much friends as they were social acquaintances with whom we enjoyed an evening dining and dancing, but they weren't people with whom we had any real deep rapport. Once we couldn't afford to add sitter costs to fifty-dollar dinner tabs and started inviting them over for an evening of conversation instead, we found we really had not much to say to each other. I would say a definite side benefit of leaving my paycheck was that we lost the resources to keep superficial social arrangements going and instead developed some more meaningful friendships over potluck suppers and the bridge table in each other's homes."

Andrea Barnett has been away from the practice of law for four years and says that while she was deciding whether or not to leave she was "terrified at the prospect of the income loss. But we established a budget, and we stuck to it so that after a few months I began to relax and see that we really could do it. However, I like going to a good sale as much as the next person, and I thoroughly miss getting the "steals" on the clothes I don't really need anyway; and I would love to take some of those great package deals to

Europe I read about in the travel section, and I'd adore to go to a good restaurant without thinking about how many meals I could make for one I'm eating. But I am no longer frightened about whether or not I can live on less as I initially was. I simply miss the things that more money can buy, but I don't miss them enough to leave my kids and go to work for more money right now. Someday I'll be back at the salesracks, and I'll jet abroad again, and I'll eat out after a long day at the office; I can wait. Right now I'm happy out in the sandbox. It's a trade, and I figure I'm ahead."

The key to a woman's dealing with the emotional aspects of her paycheck loss is to maintain a feeling of control, knowing that if she finds she cannot live on less or that she is truly unhappy without earning she can work again. Rather than feeling that she is without recourse, she is constantly aware that she has made a trade and that her decision is not irreversible.

Clearly, nobody can give a woman contemplating sequencing a crystal ball complete with promises that she'll love living on less money. But those women who have done it agree that the prerequisites for making it work are a philosophical commitment to being at home with one's children, making and sticking to a budget, and feeling in control, knowing that the choice is theirs and believing that the freedom from having to leave their children to go out to earn money outweighs the loss of what the money can buy at a particular time.

WHOSE MONEY IS IT?

Clarity about the psychological aspects of one-paycheck living is as fundamental to the sequencing decision for many women as is analysis and projection of spending patterns. Some women have no trouble accepting the one-paycheck premise: that she will forgo hers to mother their children while he foots the bill; others are fearful of the implications of his becoming her enabler. A woman's decision to interrupt her career effectively returns her mate to the race of the sole breadwinnner from which feminism liberated males two decades ago. Does his acceptance of that responsibility fulfill the feminist nightmare that it will imbue him with ultimate power in the marriage relationship? Does it mean that the woman will now be one man away from poverty?

These fears that some women have about losing their incomes are based on the belief that economics determines the power distribution in the marriage. Women who have actually left their careers, however, rarely report that these fears become realities. One reason appears to be that before they left their work many discussed their insecurities with their husbands and arrived at a way to try to deal with the psychological effects of the income loss. "It all boils down to your philosophy of who is earning what and for whom," says a former travel company executive: "My husband suggested when I left my job that he turn his paychecks over to me. He always hated to pay bills anyway, but we used to each pay half. He said it was fine with him if he never saw another bill, and what's more he didn't care how I allocated the money just so we stayed in the black. This helped immensely as I am totally responsible for the allocation of all of our money. Of course, I talk major matters over with him, but I don't feel that it's his money—it seems clearly to be our money."

A physician who left her medical practice drew up an agreement that in case of divorce her husband (also a physician) owed her a certain amount of money for every year she was away from her work. (The figure was based on what she had been earning at the time, corrected for inflation and for projected increase in her practice.) "This was my way of ensuring," she says, "that if we were ever to divorce he couldn't claim the major portion of our assets on the basis that he had earned for a period of more years."

Although so far this kind of pre-career-interruption contract is a rarity, it could be used more frequently, like the prenuptial agreement, which is almost always drawn up in advance of the marriage by partners who have been previously married to protect inheritance intended for the children of each spouse, as well as to ensure their own economic protection. Any couple in which the woman is leaving her career to raise their children could draw up a similar agreement, which would protect whatever they want to protect—that in event of a divorce, she has appropriate assets, that she is not penalized for the years she was not earning, that she will get a certain percentage of his income as child support, that she will be paid by him for a certain length of time while she retrains and reestablishes herself professionally.

The Economics of Sequencing

Whether the couple chooses to deal with the psychological aspects of her income loss by having her control the spending while he manages the earning, whether they draw up a pre-career-interruption contract, or both, or neither, certain facts remain. The educated, career-experienced woman of today is simply not in the same position as was the trapped housewife of yesteryear, who had little education and no career experience and was dependent on her husband not only for her current needs but for all of her future income. If he died and was not well insured, or if he divorced her without sufficient alimony, the best she could hope for was a low-level job and generally a great reduction in the standard of living to which she had become accustomed.

Today, a woman who chooses to sequence has as insurance her education and her professional experience. She has proved that she can earn a good living independently or that she can be a prime contributor to the joint family income. Both partners know that she has done it before and can do it again. If they decide that she will take career time out to mother their children, that does not mean that she needs to defer to him in any way. It means that they concur that her primary contribution to their family lives can be best made at a particular time through attending to the needs of their children rather than to the needs of clients, customers, or patients. They both perceive his pursuing his career and her caring for their children as equally important, worthwhile, and necessary to their individual and joint well-being, as well to the total family lifestyle.

PART I

The one-paycheck family is predicated upon both partners' realization that it is a given that the money earned is *their* money, even though it may all be earned by one partner at the moment. The checkbook and savings account are joint, and all spending and budgeting decisions are mutual. She is caring for *their* children, not only hers; he is earning *their* living, not only his. The name of the game is not power but interdependence, which enables the family to function as an independent unit. The husband depends on his wife to take charge of the minute-to-minute, day-to-day care of their children; she depends on him to finance that joint priority. This *interdependence* means that the parents are free to raise their own children *without depending* upon third-party caretakers; children can depend on a parent for their day-to-day needs and concerns rather than having to depend on an outsider to the unit.

To many couples economic interdependence is not unusual. They see income sequencing as part of a total career sequencing decision because they may already have sequenced their incomes. At some point she may already have been the sole provider while he finished school.

An urban affairs specialist says, "I worked full time for five years while my husband was in a joint medical school, Ph.D. program. Now it's his turn. I didn't lord it over him when I was doing all the earning. I never said, 'It's *my* money, so I'll decide how to spend it.' I never felt that way. It was ours when I was earning it all; and it's ours now that he's earning it all."

Some couples feel that at another point in their marriage the woman might well be the sole full-time financial provider. An architect married to a newspaper editor has been away from her work for the past four years while at home with her children. "I have no feelings of inferiority or of dependency here," she says. "True, he's taking on the whole financial burden for the lot of us now. But his dream is to leave the paper someday to be free to concentrate on his own writing. That will mean I'll be the primary, or maybe the only, wage earner in the family."

Clearly, today's sequencing woman and her husband recognize interdependence—emotional, physical, and financial—as the best way for them to operate their family unit. They see interdependence as a means of maintaining their independence from harried schedules, allowing them more time with each other, and ensuring that their children will be cared for by their own parents.

Part II

The Golden Years

I highly recommend taking some years out to people; it was a wonderful experience for me and for my children. If you don't you miss some golden opportunities that you can never regain.

Dr. Katharine Poole Wolf,
Psychiatrist,
Harvard Medical School

5

From Career to Home-Based Mothering

The "trapped housewife" syndrome—the vicious circle of housework, boredom, and loneliness that plagued millions of full-time mothers in previous generations—is virtually nonexistent among today's sequencing women. The obvious reason women today don't feel trapped at home as did some of their predecessors is that these women freely chose to be there. Further, they aren't "housewives" repeating the mistakes of women of the 1950s and 1960s, who confused polishing floors with nurturing children.

The full analysis goes far beyond this explanation, however, and reaches into the deepest values of our society. I have carefully observed women's changing lifestyles since 1963, the year *The Feminine Mystique* was published and my first child, Miriam, was born. I felt from the early years of the modern feminist movement, from sheer observation of the other mothers around me during the mid-1960s in mobile Cambridge, Massachusetts, then in the later 1960s in the settled suburb of Belmont, Massachusetts, then in Minneapolis, Minnesota, the heart of the American Midwest, in the early 1970s, that the feminist cure for the trapped housewife—a job away from the family—was based upon a misdiagnosis of the problem. The problem as feminism saw it was that the trapped housewife lacked feelings of self-esteem and fulfillment because she was missing out on what the men had: job titles and paychecks through which men defined themselves and through which the society defined them.

But I am convinced this was not the real problem. The core problem was that the trapped housewife had not defined her own role, values, and goals. She lacked a clearly defined sense of purpose about what she was doing; she lacked the vision to perceive herself as responsible for raising the next generation. Instead, she continually confused the baby with the bathwater and was bored by the mundane "wife" to "house" chores and by her lack of validation of her own needs for stimulation outside the family. Because her values and goals were not self-defined, she was ripe for external forces to define them for her. And they did. True, the trapped housewife lacked feelings of self-esteem and fulfillment, but the feminist solution—"the trapped jobwife" otherwise known as Superwoman—was not the answer either for mothers of young and growing children.

My own hypothesis was, and is, that the answer lies within the woman herself. I became convinced of this during the 1960s as I witnessed firsthand that there were as many—if not more, though they were quieter about it— happy, satisfied, fulfilled women raising families during that stormy decade as there were unhappy ones. I was sure that there were certain factors which differentiated the trapped housewife from the woman who is successful in her home-based mothering role. But what were these factors?

I began searching for the answers to my question in 1972 through a cross-country investigation of women raising families. This research resulted in the establishment of my Woman at Home Workshops in 1974 and the publication of *Woman at Home* in 1976. My findings were clear: certain factors do, in fact, differentiate women who are happy at home from those who are not. The factors that contribute to a full-time mother's sense of happiness, satisfaction, feelings of self-esteem, and fulfillment are: (1) a very clear sense of who she is and why she is at home raising her family; (2) a supportive husband who values what she is doing; (3) a community that reinforces her own values; (4) the woman's making a very clear distinction between the children and the work of the house with a minimum of her time spent on the house and maximum on the family; and (5) her recognition that she must have time to develop and maintain interests apart from the family.

In contrast, the trapped housewife, who was miserable at home, did not have a clear idea of who she was or what she was doing—her role and goals were not at all clear to her. Because she did not herself value what she was doing, she was in no position to enlist the help of her husband or of an outside community. She constantly confused the baby with the bathwater, and she failed to realize that she required time outside the sphere of the family for personal development.

PART II

What is distinctive about today's sequencing mothers is that they very closely parallel in attitudes, values, and actions those women of a decade and more ago who were happy and satisfied in their roles, and they in no way resemble those who were not.

Today's sequencing mothers are clearly on top of their roles: they are very definite about why they are home: to raise their children. They are usually supported morally as well as financially by their husbands and have constructed supporting communities of like-minded women who reinforce their values. In addition, they recognize their needs for meaningful activities outside, as well as within, the family.

The reason these women are making a success of home-based motherhood goes beyond the fact that it's now a choice. It's also because women have found the male career norm robs them of time and energy for interpersonal relationships. They now want close relationships badly, and they have recognized that each loving, trusting relationship has to be slowly built, nurtured, and developed over time. Therefore, these women have left their professions with very clear-cut goals: to put the best of their time and energies into building enduring relationships with their children. They come to their new roles as full-time mothers with excellent tools for doing so: the positive lessons they have learned from feminist philosophy on housework, networking, and self-development which ensure that they establish optimal conditions in which to develop close relationships with their children.

These women don't get trapped by the syndrome of the 1950s—housework, boredom, or isolation—because they are accustomed to negotiating, dividing, and delegating housework and recognize that the upkeep of the family living quarters is not the woman's sole responsibility, whether she is away all day or at home. They know about the advantages of networking and support systems from their professional lives and transfer this information to their lives as home-based mothers. And feminist philosophy has made them recognize continued self-development as their birthright. Therefore, they expect and seek stimulating, meaningful activities outside the family as well as within it.

This is not to say that because the trapped housewife is gone, today's home-based mother is free of problems in her new role. To the contrary, precisely because she is a career-experienced professional who has spent years immersed in the careerism norm, she often brings home from the office a set of problems new to this generation of home-based mothers. These are feelings of loss of identity, feelings of loss of a set of expectations and rewards, and loss of a collegial community.

This set of problems is almost always limited to the transition phase—the first few months to year that a woman is full-time mothering—because the women themselves limit them. For along with the problems, they bring home from the marketplace problem recognition and solving skills gained from their work, positive open attitudes, and the firm resolve to make a success, in their own terms, of their home-based mothering years.

COPING WITH FEELINGS OF LOSS OF IDENTITY

Feelings of identity loss affect a woman who leaves her job in direct proportion to the degree to which she has accepted the male careerism norm. Therefore, women who felt a high degree of conflict in the first place are the hardest hit. When a woman's entire being is tied up with her occupation and then she leaves her job, she cannot help but suffer feelings of loss, anxiety, and even grief. These are the same feelings experienced by the man who, at retirement, finds himself bereft because he has *been* his occupation and now feels that without his job he's without a self. Like him, she must look at herself in the mirror as a human being rather than as an occupational identity whose job defined her personhood. Unlike him, she has the chance—relatively early in her life—to separate herself from the occupation for which she was trained and to move on to form a definite sense of self, independent from the work she does at a particular point in her life.

This separation is often difficult. The entrapment of a woman's identity in her occupation is an integral part of her thinking. To change her perception she has first to understand how she has come to equate herself with her work.

When feminists bought the male career package, they accepted with it the entire system of derived identity fundamental to careerism: that one's identity is synonymous with one's paid work.

Their only complaint about derived identity was that women were deriving it secondarily—as wives of the men who *were* their work. Thus feminists insisted that women transfer their derived identities from their husbands' occupations to their own paid occupations. Paradoxically, just when feminist philosophy espoused that women needed greatly to expand their self-perceptions to develop the sense of who they really were, it dramatically restricted self-development by maintaining that the one way to develop was to derive identity from careers, in imitation of men.

They did not critique the fact that many men live one-dimensional lives for and through their work, often collapsing into grave depressions at retirement, if not into the grave itself. They did not analyze the lives of "career-successful" men, who all too often fail to build close interpersonal relationships, whose marriages crumble, who barely know their children, who lack interests outside their work. Instead, women rushed out to emulate them.

In so doing, women joined full force as participants in the perpetuation of the socioeconomic stratification system wherein persons are classified by occupational categories, then placed on a hierarchical value scale. (Each profession has its own complex internal stratification system as well.)

They then came to see themselves as their occupations, to believe that their professional reputations defined them. In the last several years, however, more and more men as well as women have come to rethink the entire career norm because it is incompatible with their other agendas.

They find that acceptance of their occupations as all-encompassing self-definitions is too restrictive, even though they may be highly successful at what they do for a living. These people view their professions as a part of a much larger story. For instance, a forty-two-year-old man who heads one of the country's prestigious law schools sings every summer with an Italian opera company. "What I love most about my summer work," he says, "is that in Italy I'm known as an American tenor—nobody calls me 'the law school dean.' It's great to be known within an entirely different group for what I can do within that sphere; it's my range of voice, not my occupation, that identifies me to them. Singing there makes me realize I'm a many-faceted person, that I don't have to live by one dimension alone."

A recent medical school graduate says, "I'm really ashamed for people to find out I'm a doctor before they know me as a person. Doctor used to connote healer . . . but now to a lot of people it connotes insensitivity and moneygrubbing. When pressured to give my occupation in a group of strangers I feel I have to qualify it . . . 'I'm a doctor *but*. . . .' "

These people are simply saying that there is a lot more to them than their work, that they identify themselves in far broader terms and want to be identified accordingly.

REDEFINING ONESELF

For the woman who feels a loss of self in the sequencing transition, redefining it entails unraveling the wrappings and trappings of the profession to which she was bound. It means recognizing that the occupation in which she was enveloped was an aspect of herself, perhaps an integral part of herself. But even if she was programmed from high school or earlier for that occupation, even if she trained for it for years postbaccalaureate, even if she has won coveted honors through it, the real self is far broader and deeper than the occupation to which she applied it.

Erica Sellers recognized this after she left an executive position in a Fortune 100 company, along with a high salary and a staff of fifteen, to stay home with her infant son. "I went through a complete metamorphosis," she says. "I'd been with the company for ten years, worked terribly hard to get where I did, and really enjoyed my work tremendously. My whole life was bound up in my work, in the company, with my colleagues there, with the problems one or another of my staff would encounter.

"I went through a lot of soul-searching before I decided to leave, but once I made the decision I was comfortable about it—that is, when I was home with the baby. But when I went out—to parties or even to open a new charge account—and someone asked me, 'What do you do?' I was stymied. 'I'm the director of . . .' I'd start to say and then catch myself. 'I *was* the director . . .' then I'd wonder, 'My God, what am I now?'

"After several miserable months of this I began to question myself . . . was director of sales to have been my total self-definition until I became vice-president of sales . . . would I always *be* whatever my job title was; or not *be* at all if I lacked one? My baby inadvertently helped me to find an answer. As I watched him play in his crib one day, I asked myself what I wanted him to grow up to become. Would this wonderful little creature someday be vice-president of sales—or president of the company . . . was *that* to be his sum total?

"Then I began to really take stock. I wanted him to become a whole, wonderful, happy, healthy, compassionate, creative, competent human being. What he might do for a living didn't even figure in. I mean, he could do any number of things . . . it wouldn't matter . . . what matters is his values, his sensitivities, what kind of *person* he becomes. Well, then I started doing a lot of thinking about my own values and attitudes. I came to recognize that my occupation might change several times in my life but that I won't ever again fall into the trap of letting it be my sum total, of letting the job define me."

Erica Sellers's new understanding typifies the self-perceptions of many women, who once away from their ocupations perceive their identities as much more complex than simply the work they did at a particular time. They come to recognize their identities as the sum total of all of their qualities, thoughts, and actions, not merely their occupational activities at a given period. For a truly secure sense of self comes from within, is developed through recognizing what is unique in one's own right, in reveling in it, and in transmitting it to others in a myriad of ways, not simply through doing a particular job.

The process of separating one's identity from one's previous occupation appears to take women from a few months to a year. After that, many women say they become much more secure of themselves than they have previously been. For they can recognize themselves as individuals over and apart from the work they are trained to perform or the particular place they held in their fields.

For instance, one woman says, "The first months I was home I told people who asked what I did, 'I am an accountant . . .' because I kept thinking, 'Damn it, I am an accountant even though I'm not doing that work right now.' Then I started saying 'I *was* an accountant,' but now after a year I realize that I am a person, trained as an accountant, who has a lot of other abilities and interests besides. Even when I'm working again, I can't imagine ever narrowing myself into the 'I am an accountant' slot."

Many of today's home-based mothers describe their present activities to themselves and others by using an action word rather than a noun. So the answer to what do you do? is almost always, I'm mothering."

When I first began interviewing for *Sequencing* I was intrigued that women from coast to coast would say, "I'm mothering," because I had not heard "mother" used as a verb before. First, I thought it was just a catchy byword, then I began to see that the change of terminology from "I am a mother" to "I'm mothering" has profound social implications. No longer do women consider that their biological relationship to their children determines their place in the social structure as in "I am a mother." Rather, they see "mothering" as something they are doing for a period of time in their lives; correspondingly, these women who have parted from their careers for a period no longer view what they *did* as what they *were* any more than they see what they *do* as what they *are*.

Once a woman comes to terms with her initial feelings of identity loss by the internal realization that her identity is much larger, deeper, and greater than the activity she performs at any moment and that her self cannot be compressed into, and classified by, a one-word descriptor, she feels much more comfortable in her new situation. Although some women raising families experience identity problems in the transition stage, within a year most see the concept of occupation as identity in a new and broader perspective. There are no easy "how-tos" for developing this broadened perspective; interviews with women who have radically changed their ways of looking at themselves once away from their work made it clear that this change is a product of experience. It is analogous to living in a new culture in which suddenly one sees what mattered in one's former society in a new light and reevaluates it according to new values. What is so interesting about this broadened perspective is that it not only affects women's thinking about themselves during their full-time mothering years but frequently has a major impact on their thinking when they reincorporate their careers into their lives at a later date.

RECOGNIZING LOSS OF SET OF
EXPECTATIONS AND REWARDS

When first away from their professions, some women experience a loss of a pre-defined set of expectations and rewards—a feeling of total loss of accountability. That's because most professional positions carry with them a job description; even top-ranking executives, physicians, and attorneys work within a system of expectations. They know what is expected of them by superiors, peers, and constituents. In addition to the external standards of their profession, they have internal standards; they know what to do, and they know when the job is well done. They are accountable both to others—colleagues, clients, patients, students, customers—and to themselves for the quality of their work, and they are accustomed to receiving acknowledgment for what they do.

Like their male counterparts, most achieving women were raised within such a system of expectations and reinforcements and thrive on it. These women are accustomed to besting a series of clearly defined hurdles: taking a test and getting an "A"; doing what is expected and receiving commendation in their professions; doing more than is expected and receiving extra commendations, reinforcements, and promotion. They know well how to succeed within a system of clearly defined expectations and rewards.

Mothering, however, is not systematized—there are few "how-to's" beyond providing food and warmth for one's child and no readily observable system of reinforcement.

Marge Hermon, who left her post in a Chicago advertising agency to raise her son, expresses the insecurity and frustrations of the woman who is accustomed to high career performance within a clearly defined system, then finds herself at home with a small child and without a set of standards and reinforcements. "You never know exactly what you should be doing—you just feel your way and hope for the best. . . . What's worse, there's no review. You never know how you're doing. In my work there were raises; there were promotions. You had a continual peer review and a review from superiors as well— plus, of course, client satisfaction or dissatisfaction in and of itself, as part of the general review. You knew what was expected. You were told if you weren't meeting those expectations, and you were praised when you were. You got continual feedback at meetings and on a one-to-one basis.

"Now, at home, who are you going to ask? The baby? If it were even as it was when I was a young child in the fifties —when women were all home—a mother got a peer review from the neighbors whether she wanted it or not . . . 'your kid's face is dirty,' or 'haven't you taught her any manners?' . . . but now you're really isolated. You may be doing really well, but you don't know it . . . you don't know for sure."

SETTING ONE'S OWN STANDARDS

Although at first a woman may perceive as a negative that today society provides few external expectations and no system of accountability for mothering, many come to recognize it as a positive. For one of the prime advantages of home-based mothering is that a woman is free to develop her own expectations, to find her own rewards in what she does, and to do so without accountability to anyone else.

Blair Coming, a forty-year-old Seattle woman who left a corporate position in which she held the top spot on the executive ladder, says, "At first it was truly baffling to find myself in a new situation without role models and with nobody else telling me what it was that I was supposed to accomplish. Although I left my position in order to concentrate on motherhood, I found that I hadn't defined very clearly what my objectives for myself and for my children were. So, I had to spend some time figuring them out. I decided that the long-range plans of industry weren't applicable to raising my young daughters, beyond the usual parental concerns that they be decent, ethical human beings. So I established a goal which I felt was appropriate: that my children should see in each day something special, that we do some special things together—it doesn't take much to please a child, you know—picking apples from a neighbor's tree, making cookies, making up dance steps to a new record, going skating, a trip to the library. In a way, doing special things seems to be a really short-term goal. But if each day has something special, and it's a happy experience, all the days should add up to a pretty special childhood for each of them . . . and that's essentially what I want them to have and what I want to help provide.

"With that as my set of expectations, my reward is being part of making it happen—being a part of each special day with them. It's a very personal, private reinforcement, but to me it's better right now than any promotion. What I found really rather unsettling in the early months was that this is the first time in my entire life that I have been accountable to absolutely nobody. Now I find it exhilarating. In the long run, I'm accountable to my daughters, of course. But in the short run, I'm accountable to no one else, and I must say I am enjoying it immensely."

Blair Coming is one of many women I interviewed who found that by thinking through her own objectives and creating her own standards, expectations, goals, and reward systems, she turned the lack of a structured system of rewards and accountability from a negative to a very positive factor.

Learning to develop one's own structure, one's own system of expectations and rewards, does not come overnight. But teaching oneself to do so can be one of the greatest unexpected benefits of sequencing. It means that the woman herself *(1) must decide what she wants to accomplish in a day, a week, and a month and (2) set the objectives, goals, and standards. (3) She must evaluate herself and decide whether or not she has met her expectations. (4) If so, she has a method for proceeding on further self-determined challenges. (5) If not, she can evaluate the reasons for the problem and then try new ways of meeting future goals.* Strange as it seems, a woman may be highly successful in her career role and yet not have developed these skills, for many organization men and women report to someone else, or to a team, and lack ultimate responsibility for defining the actions they take.

Many women find that becoming their own bosses is one of the most maturing aspects of the home-based mothering experience. No longer reliant on somebody else to reward them with promotions or money, they pride themselves on deciding when something is well done. The high rate of sequencing women who become entrepreneurs when they reincorporate professional activities into their lives is no accident. It occurs because many of them find structuring their own environment and developing their own reward systems so appealing that once having tasted freedom they don't want to be in somebody else's employ again.

LOSS OF REINFORCING COMMUNITY

The almost universal problem faced by mothers newly at home is feeling lonely and isolated. For some women in the 1950s and 1960s feelings of loneliness were a perpetual part of the trapped housewife syndrome, whereas for women of the 1980s it's almost always a temporary problem caused because the woman is in transition beween two lifestyles. She has clearly left the former one but has not yet created a new one. Two major factors contribute to her loneliness during this transitional period. First, a new baby generally sleeps a lot, doesn't talk, and therefore isn't much of a companion from minute to minute. Second, her former colleagues and peers are at the office, which seems a million miles away, in another lifetime, even though she may have left it only a few months previously. Although her professional peers may have been a wonderfully collegial group, they are of absolutely no help at the moment because there is no shared daily activity.

Most women who choose to sequence agree that being at home with a new baby is like being new to anything: it takes a while to feel comfortable and successful in new activity patterns, to grow to know one's child, and to create a reinforcing community.

"The first year at home was pure hell," says blonde, blue-eyed Peggy Erickson as she helps look-alike seven-year-old daughter Jill take a sheet of chocolate chip cookies out of the oven. Three-year-old Tommy and a playmate dash into the room, swoop up as many as their hands will carry, and, in a flash, are gone again.

PART II

"It's a busy scene around here now, and I love every minute of it," Peggy says, sitting down and passing me a plate of cookies, "but I had to grow into my mothering role just as I grew into my career responsibilities. I worked for the telephone company for eight years after college, the last four as a supervisor with ten people reporting to me, a lot of responsibility and a really good salary. I grew into that job gradually—it didn't just happen. I gave notice that I wasn't coming back before Jill was born, but nobody really believed it. They'd call me nearly every week. 'Have you changed your mind?' 'Aren't you ready to come back yet?' Meanwhile, I was terribly lonesome at home. I had absolutely nobody to talk to, Jill slept a lot, I didn't know another at-home mother, and I was really missing the collegiality of my job. But I'd sworn up and down that I'd be home to raise my children. I decided I had to give this a real try.

"The worst part was that somebody at work always seemed to know just when I was the most down and they'd call, telling me how much they missed me, needed me, really wanted me back. 'Why can't you just stop this and let a person live with their decision?' I wanted to shout. Finally, as the first year went on, things gradually got better. By the time Jill talked and walked, I really started having fun with her. We walked the entire neighborhood. We met other mothers and children, made friends among them. It all worked out wonderfully, and I'm forever grateful that I had the tenacity to stick that first year out—but, I wouldn't want to go through that year again."

Peggy Erickson's comments that she had to grow into her full-time mothering role just as she grew into her career with the telephone company pertain to all mothers, I think. I realized as she and I talked that it wasn't until Rachel, our second daughter, was over a year old that I began to feel confident, not until she was three or four that I was very confident and felt that we had such a wonderful family life that we had to have another baby so we could share it with more people. By that time, I'd been mothering for seven years. I realized as I listened to Peggy Erickson talk about her growth in the role that in deciding to have Rebecca I had, in effect, awarded myself tenure.

As I talked with these sequencing mothers and thought back on my own mothering, I realized that as with any other responsibility of major importance it's perfectly normal for it to take several years to feel totally confident and on top of what you're doing. It's toughing out the transition year that is pivotal in a woman's coming to achieve a feeling of mastery of her mothering role, a real sense of communication with her child, and a loss of feelings of isolation.

Different women deal with the isolation problems of the transitional year in different ways. Peggy Erickson sought out other women in similar circumstances for networking, companionship, and stimulation—an excellent method used by women throughout the country (detailed in Chapter 6).

Alexandra Sandry talked herself through the transition period. Sandry, who left her post as personnel director for a large manufacturing company to raise her infant son, expresses it well when she says the sequencing transition takes "time, patience, and a strong ego. At first, it wasn't easy. My baby slept a lot, and after all even when he was awake he couldn't talk to me. I felt isolated, and I felt lonely. I had to keep talking myself through to keep from going back to work. I kept asking myself, 'suppose you would have quit after four months of college, remember how hard it was to get adjusted then?' Freshman year was no picnic. As a matter of fact, neither was the first year of marriage—'suppose you would have quit after six months of marriage?' I asked myself, 'look at all you would have missed.' I kept talking that way to myself until gradually things got better—I got to know my little boy, and he really knew me—he began to do more; he started crawling, then talking and walking. Now every day is challenging; every day is interesting. I want to have another baby soon, and I know that it will be much easier the second time. First of all, there will be more going on, and secondly, I'm accustomed to what I'm doing and feel much more confident about it now."

My own experience as a new mother was that, like Sandry, my feelings of isolation and loneliness faded quickly when my first baby learned to talk. After years of schooling and work when I was constantly involved with other people, I was suddenly home, alone all day with one infant and a black labrador, who, for the first few months of Miriam's life, was substantially more communicative than she. I was miserable much of the time. When I analyze how I came to love full-time mothering, I realize it all began when Miriam started talking. That changed everything.

From then on, being home with her became better and
better as I realized I was growing a real, live person. (Once
I practiced on Miriam, I knew immediately when Rachel
was born three years after her, and Rebecca five years
after that, that I was raising real people.)

Not only did I develop wonderful friendships with each
of our girls, over and above our mother-daughter relationships, but I also developed a host of new peers and new
interests as well during my home-based years. But it did not
happen overnight. I developed each relationship gradually
and each interest in its own time. In retrospect, I realize I
developed close relationships with my girls because I needed
their friendship and companionship; and I built a community of friends, neighbors and colleagues because I needed
them, too. Had I stayed in an office all day, I could not
have developed the relationship with each of my girls that
I did. Of necessity, I'd have done a lot more managing and
a lot less participatory mothering. I'd have seen them only
at the end of the day when they and I were tired, when
we'd each have had the worst rather than the best of one
another. And I know that I'd never have had the time for
the new colleagues, peers, and community that I structured
for myself and for our entire family unit. In addition to
investing my time heavily in relating to my husband and
daughters, I spent a great deal of time building personal
friendships for two main reasons. First, I needed friends so
that I had a feeling of camaraderie and community while
raising my children. Second, I recognized that in this mobile society our family unit needed to be augmented by
others at times—such as Sunday afternoons, birthdays, and

holidays—to simulate the extended family security of the pre-nuclear-family days. Building the relationships within my own family unit, investing myself, in addition, in building other close personal relationships to provide emotional backup for me and for the whole family meant that I structured a new lifestyle.

Although I found mothering to be so immeasurably worthwhile that there is no comparable life experience, the transition from career to mothering can take time, and structuring a new lifestyle is a process that requires not only time but work, thought, and care.

The following three chapters detail how today's sequencing mothers structure their new lifestyles and in so doing trade in potential feelings of loneliness and isolation for feelings of community (Chapter 6), close personal relationships with their children (Chapter 7), and time for their own personal and intellectual development apart from that which they derive within the family unit (Chapter 8).

6

Seeking and Creating a
Reinforcing Community

HISTORICAL BASIS

The friendship of another mother or of several mothers who share similar values during the period in a woman's life when she is home raising babies and small children is essential. My current interviews confirm my findings over the past fifteen years that regardless of her age, occupational background, or geographical location, when a woman has a strong, positive, reinforcing peer group she is far happier in her full-time mothering role than when she does not. This has nothing to do with her children or with her relationship with them. It is because raising children in isolation can be terribly lonely.

It is therefore critical that the mother who elects to sequence create a reinforcing community to counteract loneliness and isolation. She must have available the collegiality and companionship of other mothers who have made a similar choice. She will not necessarily spend time with them every day or even every week. What's important is that she knows that a sustained, reinforcing community is available to her.

There is ample historical and anthropological basis for this need. In most cultures and in most generations, a woman spent her days raising her children within an extended family of women who were also raising, or had raised, families. But today, she's on her own. The extended family is largely fragmented. One set of grandparents may live on one coast, another grandparent on the other; aunts, uncles, siblings, and cousins are distributed throughout the country, each hundreds and thousands of miles away from the others. The woman who once would have lived within a group of other adults who also cared deeply about her and her children today finds her connections with close kin limited largely to long distance telephone calls, videotapes, and occasional visits. It is essential to her happiness and well-being that she simulate an extended family by creating a reinforcing community.

In the post–World War II years, when job mobility first began seriously to fracture families, the neighborhood served as the extended family substitute. Full-time mothers of the 1950s and early 1960s had only to open their front doors to find other mothers engaged in similar activities. But today a mother can no longer assume that a reinforcing community will be on her doorstep; she must actively seek it out or construct it herself, thereby recreating—albeit in different form—an extended family structure, historically a necessary part of raising a family. *Seeking it* means finding and moving into a neighborhood where home-based mothers raise their children; *creating it* means finding mothers from geographically disparate areas and making the effort to meet with them and their children at regular times. In the latter instance, the issue is making friends. In the former, it's finding neighbors.

SELECTING THE RIGHT NEIGHBORHOOD

Aside from a loving, supportive husband and children with whom she is closely involved, the greatest reinforcement a sequencing mother can have is a neighbor to whom she feels close. Such a person is a combination of a relative, colleague, and friend, often meeting the needs of all rolled into one: the feeling of responsibility of a relative, the physical proximity of a work colleague, and the ear and heart of a friend. Such a neighbor is a person one probably would never have known had she not lived nearby and might well never have become close to had they met casually at a party. Yet often a neighbor becomes one's best friend in life.

Finding a neighborhood of like-minded women—intelligent, articulate, and sharing my mothering values—has been a chief priority for me since we made the mistake of leaving a tiny apartment in such a neighborhood in Cambridge, Massachusetts, early in my mothering years and moving to a more spacious suburban house where I was the only home-based mother around. In retrospect, I learned that we had traded community for space, an error I would never again repeat.

PART II

In subsequent moves we selected homes and apartments around the country and the world wholly on the basis of location and community. This does not mean that I wanted to socialize with my neighbors all day; I most certainly did not. I wanted primarily to be with my girls, and in the time when they were otherwise occupied to pursue a myriad of personal activities. But I also wanted to walk outside my door as I'd have walked outside my office and find a collegial group of educated, intelligent women to talk with from among whom to make friends. In addition, there is "parellel play" involved in full-time mothering—when one's own children play with other children for brief and then for longer periods; when children run back and forth to mothers; and in between when the mothers talk with one another. When my children were younger, it was during those times that I wanted intelligent conversation with like-minded women, as well as the give and take of friendships with those with whom I shared a common bond.

Even with all the fun I had with my girls I would never have enjoyed my home-based years as much without the wonderful reinforcing community of my neighbors, who made it all even better: one whose children were enough older than mine so that she could tell me what stage to expect next in their lives and in my own; another, who with her three children, my three and I would go sliding or stage a joint play; yet another, a full-time mother and award-winning writer, who translated my "someday I'll write a book" into "you can start with twenty minutes today."

Neighborhoods where there are full-time mothers and

small children exist in most areas of the country today, whether it's Brookline, Massachusetts; Minnetonka, Minnesota; Winnetka, Illinois; Austin, Texas; Westchester County; or parts of Manhattan. The difference between the 1950s, when almost all married mothers of preschoolers mothered full time, and now is simply that there aren't as many neighborhoods where women are home during the days.

There are, however, cluster areas of home-based mothers in most locales, but now one has to search for them rather than just assume they will be there. Sometimes it takes nothing more than a walk to a library story hour; other times it requires considerably more sleuthing. A former suburban Seattle public relations director who felt "enormously isolated at home with my toddler with no neighbors around" took matters into her own hands and ran an ad in a community paper asking for calls from mothers interested in forming a play group for their one-year-olds. She got so many inquiries that she split the group on the basis of location. She kept on her own list the several mothers who lived within a few blocks of her, and gave the other list to another mother a mile away.

Some locations, however, are motherless and childless during the day. If couples find that they are living in one of those sections they may want to consider a move. On the surface this may sound radical, but in actuality it is well worth it.

Today, many couples rent an apartment or own a home for years before having children, and whatever their criteria for selection, a community of home-based mothers and children was probably not on the list. For even when couples buy a home anticipating children, they often expect that husband and wife will be working away from home, that the children will be in surrogate care, and that the home will be a bedroom and weekend retreat rather than a center of daily activity for most of the people in the family.

When a woman sequences, however, home takes on an entirely different meaning. It becomes the locus and focus of activities for most family members for the majority of their time, usually at least during the preschool period, which could be six to ten or more years. Therefore, it seems reasonable that couples who may have purchased a home with one time allocation for its usage in mind take another look at their living quarters within the context of the new usage patterns.

It stands to reason that when the majority of the family members shift the locus of their activity to home, when both the mother and her children need—in addition to one another—a reinforcing community with age peers for each, whenever possible home ought to be located within such a community.

This in no way a polemic in favor of moves from city to suburbs. The liberation movement of women in the 1960s from their homes began in suburbia, where women who preferred metropolitan areas felt stultified. If a woman prefers city life, loves the proximity to galleries and museums, thrives on being part of the hustle, and wants to expose her children to all its advantages, it behooves her to do all in her power to locate her home in the city even if it means an apartment with markedly less space than is available elsewhere. There are areas of many cities throughout the country where families can live without tremendous cost, providing they are willing to live in older apartments or homes or in reconstructed areas or are willing to sacrifice a great deal of internal and external space for location.

Whether she prefers a city, suburb, or town, if a woman decides she'd like to relocate so as to live in the midst of a community of peers, finding such a community requires effort. A Realtor is not always the best way. Since most of their clients focus their searches upon internal space, Realtors often concentrate on selling an extra bedroom or den rather than knowing who is home during the day in the neighborhood.

When a woman wants to live among other full-time mothers and their children and feels she can't count on a Realtor for counsel, she has to identify the neighborhoods of choice herself, then investigate whether other home-based mothers live there. Some mothers try out the area by taking their children on walks in those sections on weekdays and to play in parks there. In addition, they ask about other home-based mothers at libraries, community centers, public schools, nursery schools, or churches within those areas. Once one meets another mother or gets names of one or two other women it's usually easy to get further information about the neighborhood from them. Prior investigation is essential, however. No one should make the error a suburban Kansas City woman did when she and her husband decided to move because there were no mothers and children around their area. They house-hunted on Sundays, bought a home in a neighborhood with scores of young children, and then found out, after they moved in, that those children spent their days in day care centers while their mothers worked away from home.

CREATING A NETWORK OF
LIKE-MINDED WOMEN

Finding a reinforcing community of women with similar interests within one's own neighborhood, or moving to a neighborhood where such a community exists, may be an ideal solution to a mother's need for collegiality, but sometimes it isn't possible. Yet a woman may badly feel the need for such a community. She may find that although she enjoys being with her child or children, she is otherwise completely alone all day without other adults with whom to talk.

She then has to solve the problem in other ways. Unlike women of the late 1960s and early 1970s, who fled home in part because of feelings of loneliness and isolation, sequencing mothers of the 1980s almost immediately recognize loneliness as a potentially serious problem and, rather than succumbing to it, seek to solve it by forming extended family and neighborhood substitutes. They form groups of mothers from geographically disparate locations, they sometimes find mentors among these women, and they make individual friendships within the group. They initially do so through their own efforts, or by participating in community programs, taking courses, or having their children take classes as a means to meet other mothers.

Seven or eight years ago I first noticed what I now realize was the beginning of a trend for women to create solutions to the isolation problem when I was asked to address an evening meeting of a group that called itself simply Mothers. The group consisted of about twenty women, most in their early thirties, all of whom had left careers in which they had invested a number of years to raise their children.

They met once a month both to socialize and to attend a program on a specific parenting issue. When I asked how and why they formed their group, they explained that not one of them had a neighbor at home raising children and that each of them was hungry for the interchange of ideas with other women who shared their basic philosophies. They had formed their group, largely through the efforts of one of the members who knew, or knew of, several of the others and had called an organizational meeting the previous year. Then, as each met other interested women, new members joined.

Almost every woman said she had formed at least one close enough friendship with someone in the group so that they saw each other with their children between meetings. Many of the women credited the group with having a great deal of meaning in their lives. As one woman said, "I have always considered myself a highly independent person, and still do, but I live in a neighborhood of two-career couples, where I am the only mother at home with my children. I absolutely need to know other women who share my values and need to make friendships among them."

Like these women, many of today's home-based mothers, who lack the ready-made support system of the extended family or neighborhood group, instead build reinforcing communities through their own efforts, energies, and creativity. One way they do so is through networking, as did the Mothers. One woman takes the initiative, calls a friend or two, they set goals for the composition and purpose of a group they'd like, and each friend calls another friend until they get six or eight women for a starter session. Then they meet to see whether they have enough commonality of interest and background to continue.

PLAY GROUPS

Many mothers around the country form play groups. Several mothers and children meet together at regularly scheduled times. These are not the rotating-location play groups of the 1950s and 1960s, which were a form of neighborhood baby-sitting arrangement (although some of those play groups are popular today, too). Today, when mothers refer to going to the play group, they usually mean they have revived the old kaffeeklatsch tradition of mothers, who for generations past met to talk with one another while their children played together alongside them.

Some of these play groups meet transitory needs and thus come and go out of existence fairly quickly. Some serve as a meeting place for women who then form one-to-one friendships through them but who don't feel a need for the whole group. Other groups last.

A suburban New York play group, formed more than five years ago by two mothers who happened to meet at a party, has lasted from the days of the women's first toddlers through the births of subsequent children, until now, when some of them no longer have preschoolers. "We still meet," says one of the mothers, "but now instead of a morning a week, it's one late afternoon every two weeks. Our needs and schedules have changed. For two of us, our children are now in school and we're working again part time, one of the original members has moved, and two others have come into the group. I expect that we'll keep on in some way even after our children are older and we all return to work because we've formed some real lasting friendships here. I remember laughing at my grandmother, who used to talk about going out with the 'girls'—the 'girls' were sixty years old. But now I can just hear myself at sixty saying 'I'm going to play group.' "

Many women who have found these informal networks enjoyable cite diversity of occupational backgrounds as a reason. As one woman says, "From the time I entered law school until the time I left my firm to care for my first child more than ten years later, all my personal friends were in some way connected with the legal profession. Through our play group I've found friends from other areas of life— medicine, writing, airline hostessing—and it's really refreshing. Making friends among women whose backgrounds are so different from mine has been an educational experience of its own."

PROGRAMS AND CLASSES

Other ways in which home-based mothers network with one another are through local community centers, Y's, churches, and synagogues. Some women take parenting courses separately from their children, some participate in gym or craft courses with their children, others enroll the children in courses and meet other mothers while they watch.

Many women say they take a parenting course, not primarily for the information—though often they find that very helpful—but to meet other mothers. A Brookline, Massachusetts, mother says, "The classes entail a lot of discussion so you get to know one another pretty well; then you make arrangements outside the group to get together with someone who particularly impresses you. I've formed two very close friendships in this way."

An increasing number of community centers, Y's, and exercise and dance studios throughout the country offer Mothers and Tots programs so that mother and child can participate together in a joint activity such as gymnastics, swimming, arts and crafts, and yet each can also meet age peers. A Santa Barbara mother speaks enthusiastically about the programs she and her nearly three-year-old son attend twice weekly together, one a gymnastic class and one in art: "It gives us a mutual out-of-home experience and gives us something to practice together when we are at home. Further, it enables us each to meet other pairs of at-home mothers and children. We have one set—another mother and her son—from a class we took last semester who we now see an afternoon every week. She and I have lots of similar interests, and her son and mine play well together."

Sometimes mothers enroll their children in courses ostensibly so that their children, who lack both the dozens of

cousins of yesteryear and the neighborhood groups of yester-
day, can play with other children. But usually beneath the
surface is the equally compelling reason that the mothers
want to meet one another. A former Manhattan stock-
broker laughingly told me that she "bypassed the one-to-
six-month-old gym course—you know, 'stretching'—for my
son at a nearly Y, but later I placed him in a series for
nine-month-olds. I did it mainly for me, so that I could
meet other women. It worked wonderfully, too, because it
turns out all the other mothers were there for the same
reason. Six of us found we had all sorts of things in common—four of us had strong business backgrounds, two
were attorneys. We'd each worked for anywhere from six
to ten years in our fields, now we were all at-home mothers.
When the course was over, we decided to continue meeting
on our own. So we started our own play group once a
week, rotating apartments. Of course, nobody has space
like the Y, and sometimes things get kind of hectic, but we
have a good time."

INSTITUTIONAL SUPPORT

In the last few years, mothers have been aided in their
initiatives by new enterprises which are springing up in an
increasing number of locations throughout the country in
recognition of the need of full-time mothers to network with
one another: the Parent Connection in Bethesda, Mary-
land; the Family Resource Center in San Antonio, Texas;
Family Focus in Evanston, Illinois; the Family Center in
Miami, Florida; Birth to Three in Eugene, Oregon; and

thirty-three Mothers' Centers (the original in Hicksville, New York) around the country try a variety of ways to meet mothers' needs. In 1987, Joanne Brundage, founder of FEMALE, a Chicago area network of formerly employed mothers, wrote a letter published in *Ms.* magazine. That launched national publicity which resulted in a nationwide organization with a newsletter and chapters in many cities.

FINDING A MENTOR

In addition to making friends among women whose children are of like ages, many woman feel that finding a mentor for mothering is every bit as important as having a mentor on the job. Finding a mentor is, in a sense, like replacing a mother who may live too far away or be too career-involved to be much help. A mentor is another mother who has more children, or whose children are older—although not necessarily very much older—than one's own; she is someone who has been through it, who knows the ropes, who can encourage one over the rough spots, and who serves as a positive role model for mothering.

Sometimes having a child just a couple of years older than one's own, or having one more child, enables a woman to be a senior adviser or role model. Such an advisor is often crucial to a new mother, who, although she may have excelled in business, law, or preschool education (which presumably would give her expertise on small children), finds mothering is different from anything she's done previously.

As one woman who taught kindergarten for eight years said, "Now I realize how much I thought I knew and didn't. I think every teacher should be required to do field work, spending at least a year living in a family setting that has young children. Until you've been part of the continuous day-in, day-out living situation with children you just don't know what it's all about. When I go back to teaching I will know what I'm doing in a way that I simply did not know before."

Because participatory mothering is so different from any other life experience, every full-time mother can benefit from the advice of a mentor who has participated actively in the growth and development of her own children (as long as that advice is solicited, rather than freely dispensed).

One mother, formerly in a responsible industrial position, says she felt very insecure when she was first home with her small son: "I don't think I could have enjoyed him half as much as I have if it hadn't been for a friend who became a very positive role model. Her second child and mine are the same age, but her first one is three years older, so she has been through everything once before. She calms a lot of my worries but most of all, just watching her with her children makes me more relaxed with mine."

In Cambridge, when Miriam was a toddler, my next-door neighbor, who had three young daughters, was, as far as I and most of the other women on the street were concerned, the resident expert. Because she had more children than any of the rest of us and because her oldest was older than anybody else's and because she spoke so sensibly and authoritatively, we all looked to her for advice. After we moved to Minnesota, I lost touch with her for well over fifteen years, but when we lived again for a year in Cambridge a couple of years ago, she and I picked up as if no time had passed. I told her then how much her advice, support, and help had meant to me and to all of us whose children were fewer and younger than hers. She was floored. She had viewed her relationships with us as completely reciprocal and had never realized that we counted so heavily upon her. From her standpoint, the mentoring she now realizes she was doing was purely natural, and the relationships she enjoyed with the rest of us seemed to her to be a two-way street. So, it seems in this case, at least, the mentor may not even realize she has been elected for such important work.

Whether a full-time mother establishes friendships by moving into a neighborhood that serves as a reinforcing community, creating a substitute community, finding a mentor, or all these means, many women feel these relationships come to have a larger, more lasting value in their lives than the immediate needs they serve. A former investment banker, now raising her children full time, says of the friendships she's made through a play group, "As I now have time to enjoy and build these friendships, I recognize that my work-related relationships were somewhat different . . . not as deep or as varied. I shared business problems and even personal problems, but I rarely had the leisure to talk about real feelings or to talk on a great many issues."

Many home-based mothers say that they feel the friendships they make among one another are more like their college friendships—made when going through a specific life phase together—than like work relationships, which are often less leisurely and less oriented toward feelings.

Mothers of older children who have resumed careers express sadness again and again that they have so little time for their friends. Looking back on their home-based years, many of these women say that the friendships they formed with other women during that period remain among the most meaningful in their lives.

EXTENDING THE FAMILY

In addition to serving the primary need of providing the mother with collegiality and companionship, the reinforcing community she creates may also play another important role for her, her children, and her husband. The family units of the neighbors and friends a woman makes during her sequencing years are often the persons with whom she and her family come to celebrate holidays and birthdays or have Sunday afternoon picnics. They often come to know well and to care about each other's children, providing them with a continuity of "almost like family" relationships as the children grow. Conversely, the children sometimes become like nieces and nephews.

One of the bonuses I would never have dreamed of in my early mothering years is that the now grown children of some of my friends and neighbors have become friends of mine in their own right, apart from my relationships with their mothers or theirs with my daughters. One once small blonde neighbor is now a tall, striking resident who for the past several years has kept me abreast of how she and other of her women classmates view their roles as emerging physicians; one once little dark-haired boy with whom I've pitched softballs since he was four is now a bearded English major with whom I exchange short stories for critique and comment.

7

Quality Care
in
Quantity Time

What do you do with your children all day that you couldn't hire done? is a question women contemplating sequencing frequently ask former colleagues who are now full-time mothers. The question cannot be answered in a word, but it can be responded to through a look at several separate but interrelated dimensions of the mother-child relationship: the responsibilities assumed by the mother coupled with the freedom of the mothering choice, the lovegiving and memory-building with her child which are a part of the mother's everyday life with him or her, the fun they have through sharing each other's lives, and their shared bank accounts of joint memories.

There is no one thing the full-time mother does that she couldn't do if she were working all day and thus with her child only two or three of his waking hours instead of ten or twelve; but she would do only a fraction of the things she does, and she would do them without continuity. Her continued presence, allowing mother and child to share intimately in each other's lives for years, distinguishes the relationship of full-time mother and child both quantitatively and qualitatively from any other relationship in life. There is no other relationship of this intensity. A husband and wife typically spend all day every day together only on a honeymoon, on vacations, and perhaps after retirement. Colleagues may work long hours together but leave one another nights and weekends. In contrast, a full-time mother and her child are together nearly twenty-four hours a day for years with only short breaks.

The relationship they develop is dependent on the *quality* of the time they spend together during this tremendous chunk of both of their lives. Nearly every woman who left her career for full-time mothering told me she believes that she can provide her child with higher-quality care than anyone else can, and each wants a large quantity of time in which to do it. Each does it in a different way, for each mother gives love differently, builds memories with her child differently, communicates differently, and shares different activities. Each realizes that she has taken on an enormous responsibility.

RESPONSIBILITIES

By being the person who is continually there with and for her child, by being the one to whom he turns for love, attention, guidance, assurance, and reassurance, the mother becomes the most important person in her child's life. At this level of responsibility, power is at stake—not the power of managing somebody else's dollar, but the power of influencing somebody else's character, personality, and use of intellect. At stake is the transmission of all one is and of all one believes, of imprinting it upon the open mind and heart of the next link in one's own chain of being. At stake is the formation of the security, confidence, and sense of mission which one's descendants carry forward; at stake in what one transmits to one's child is a microcosm of what one hopes the world will become.

This realization is frightening enough to send a woman back to managing forty employees whose lives still remain pretty much the same whether she or someone else is in charge. For modeling a belief and value system day in and day out that will live after you, that will be transmitted by your children to their children, is existentially terrifying.

No less terrifying is grappling with the constant stream of one's child's unanswerable questions—How do you *know* when something is bad? Who makes babies? Why do good people die? Where do the stars come from?—when they are first tendered. Those responses, coupled with the modeling of one's own behavior day in and day out, determine to an extraordinary degree what the child believes and values.

When a woman decides to leave her career to mother her child, she chooses *not* to leave the transmission of beliefs and values, the perspectives on life's more elemental and crucial questions, to anyone else, but rather elects to take the ultimate responsibility herself.

PART II

LOVEGIVING AND MEMORY-MAKING

A woman's role as full-time mother is not merely that of caregiver; it is that of lovegiver. Lovegiving is the consistent communication and activity with one's child through which one builds the reservoir of memories that makes up the fabric of early and basic life experience. Stella articulates this concept while her hands expertly massage mine, as she snips cuticle, chastises me for chipping nails at the typewriter, and asks what I'm now writing. "Ahhh, mothering," she says, her eyes growing misty, "I'm glad that I had that. I can still remember my mother sitting in her lattice-backed chair sewing. I was right down at her feet. She had her sewing box and I had mine; I used to just sit there—we'd talk and talk about everything—all the while I was waiting for scraps to fall. She made clothes for all five of us girls. I was the baby. A good day's work for me was one where I gathered lots of different scraps—bright red print calico, glowing green muslin . . . I'm so glad I had that. She died when I was five, but I still collected pretty scraps of material wherever I could; and when I played with the smaller neighbor kids I'd sit on the porch with them at my knees, playing mother and child. Later, when I had my own daughters, I used to buy remnants of fabric and make doll dresses with them. So I guess a bit of my mother lived on and got passed down to her grandchildren." Although she died when Stella was only five, her mother did a lot of lovegiving in those early years. In fact, if richness is to be measured by the memories of what one transmits through the generations, Stella's mother died a rich woman.

Quality Care in Quantity Time

Stella's recollection illustrates that lovegiving and the memory-making which is part and parcel of it aren't just special occasion phenomena. I am repeatedly struck by the importance that full-time participatory mothers and full-time careerwomen-mothers alike attach to such infrequent events as their children's birthday parties or class plays. Mothers who work away from their children, regardless of how crowded their schedules or demanding their careers, almost all circle those special dates in red and arrange to be there. These special events are unquestionably important to our children; witness the child whose mother can't come. But special events are only a tiny fragment of the whole.

I asked two of my own daughters, individually and out of earshot of each other, to name for me off the top of their heads three of their happiest early memories. Topping Rebecca's list (she's now fourteen) was "having tuna sandwiches and carrot sticks across the street by the river with you," and topping Rachel's (she's now nineteen) was "you and I having lunch at the small round table in the living room of our old house." I was astounded. Rebecca and I had picnic lunches nearly every day, fall and spring, from the time she was two until she was in first grade. We had a minimum of five hundred tuna sandwich and carrot stick lunches by the river. Similarly, Rachel and I lunched to-together from the time Miriam began first grade, when Rachel was three, until Rebecca was born two years later. Rachel is remembering perhaps three or four hundred lunches together, not one birthday party (of which she always had two per birthday) or school play (in which she appeared at least twice a year).

After asking my girls that question, I became curious enough to ask other teen and college-age people to talk about what they most happily remember from their childhoods. Again and again it was not the major life events but the seeming nonevents, the repetition of the ordinary moments, which, when repeated time and again, became the framework and fabric of their childhoods. This is especially revealing to me because throughout my twenty-two mothering years I have been very conscious at birthday and holiday time that today's occasion is not simply the festivity at hand but tomorrow's memory. In making each party and holiday special, I was consciously involved in memory-making. Recognizing this, I'd try very hard to make the party or holiday wonderful so that it would be happily remembered by my children. But I hardly thought at all about the tuna sandwiches at the river or lunch at the small table. That was just what we did every day. Apparently, however, it was the repetition of the occasion that each child and I had to talk privately, leisurely, and uninterruptedly for a lengthy time in a place different from where we ate our family meals that made it wonderfully special. What they remember best and most happily is what we did frequently and routinely together. It was the everyday things, not the occasional special events, that counted—the everyday things that add up to a childhood.

A JOINT BANK ACCOUNT OF STORED MEMORIES

The greatest reward of participatory mothering is the chance for some of the most pleasurable memories in life to be associated with one another. For just as a magnificent sunset on a Venetian beach is most memorable when shared with a loved one, so are the simplest pleasures of daily life more memorable for mother and child when shared.

Rarely do I see a flower today that I don't associate with my mother. She took me on daily walks from the time I can remember (and according to photographs and her recollections, from my preconscious memory days as well). On every walk she exclaimed over each new chrysanthemum, rose, or iris that we saw. She'd stop, stand almost reverently near each bud, branch, or bush, smell it and lift me to smell it, tell me its name, and talk to me about it.

We planted flowers in our own garden together each spring and fall, watered and cared for them, nourished and watched them grow. Peonies, iris, lilies, my mother, and knowing she was always there or near are all wrapped up in my memories of an idyllic and immensely secure childhood. In talking with Mother today there is little that I remember of my childhood that she doesn't remember as well. We share these banked memories in a very private account; nobody else has the number.

It's this concept of sharing a bank account of stored memories that sets full-time mothering apart—for mother and child—from any other experience. The mother who leaves her career to be with her child through his preschool years spends at least ten thousand more hours with that child during the first five years than if she were at the office. This means that he spends ten thousand more hours in the care and company of one who loves him dearly, for whom he is central, than he would if his mother were at work. Both make hourly deposits in their joint memory bank. At the end of five years the mother and child who have had ten thousand more hours in which to make those deposits are richer in shared memories than the mother and child who have lacked those hours together. It is not that the mother who is absent for those hours loves her child any less; it's that she has less time to show it.

Because each mother provides that time and love differently, each mother and child has a memory bank completely different from that of every other mother and child. This is because every mother brings what is unique to herself to participatory motherhood: her imagination, beliefs, attitudes, and preferences in everything from food to people. She becomes an enormous influence on her child. As one mother said to me, "It's serious to think how much effect I have on my little girls. I see it in the way they walk and talk, their expressions, their ways of dealing with other people. But the only thing more serious is having them influenced to this degree by anyone else."

FUN

It's often necessary to put the realization of the seriousness of one's responsibilities as a participatory mother on hold so as to have fun with one's children. The most important requisite of enjoying one's mothering years is a sense of humor. Next come imagination and creativity. No person is devoid of these characteristics, but sometimes they are nearly programmed out by work environments in which one restrains her sense of humor so as to appear professional, or she has worked in a situation in which imagination and creativity are somebody's else's department.

One mother who rose up the corporate ladder to a middle management post, then left to raise her young son, says she had to "unlearn my focus on the output of getting a job done in order to enjoy the process of raising him. I was accustomed to managing a series of relatively short-term projects. The emphasis was on productivity, on the process of getting the job done quickly and efficiently. So that didn't translate very well to making a pie with my little boy or even to helping him build a tinker toy structure. I wanted everything done perfectly, efficiently, smoothly—but he just wanted to have fun. Finally I learned from him if we got flour on the floor, so what? If the building we designed fell flat, it didn't matter—the pie and the sand castle aren't for posterity—but our relationship is. So I started having fun for the moment. Once I began really letting loose and having fun with him, he and I have both had a great time."

To my mind, the very best thing of all about participatory mothering is the sheer fun of it, especially because fun has been in short supply for many women for a long time. We haven't heard much about fun during the past couple of decades, at least not for women. We've heard about fulfillment and enhancing one's self-esteem, about power, and about presenting an authoritative image. We've heard about being professional, we've heard about staying on top—in the boardroom and the bedroom—but we haven't heard much about fun. Yet participatory mothers have the opportunities to share lots of fun with their children. This is important, for not only is the laughter and gaiety of shared good times wonderful for the spirit and the soul of the mother, it's the lifeblood of children.

Participatory mothers have the chance to foster a fun-filled atmosphere for their children. They have not only the opportunity but the responsibility because if they don't, who will? We don't hear much about fun for children anymore either; we hear about fostering a "sense of responsibility," about making the child independent, and about maximizing his cognitive skills from an early age, but we don't hear much about his having fun anymore. Fun is not the focus of the institutional settings in which most children spend the greater part of their days after age six; nor is fun really the focus of kindergarten and preschool programs or day care settings—institutions wherein large numbers of children must be managed in ratios anywhere from one adult to several children to one adult to twenty-five or more children. Institutions do not specialize in fun. Their purpose is to provide the child with "creative play options" and a "stimulating environment"—as defined by the particular institution—and preparation for future institutions. A child may have fun in an institutional setting as a by-product of a particular activity, but if you ask any institutional principal or manager what the goals of the program are, fun is not usually on the list.

Fun, however, is a major part of participatory motherhood. From the mother's point of view, part of the fun is the return to the imaginative play of one's own childhood —from a different perspective, to be sure, for as an adult, reality has established itself; unlike the child, who has not yet made the distinction, the adult is presumably grounded in reality and escapes it to play happily. Part of my daughters' and my shared memory bank are the sandbox days, our tea party days, our dollhouse days, and our writing and performing plays in the attic days.

It's true that it was I who had to use my experience in reality to caution, "don't spill lemonade on the baby's head" or "hey, Cinderella off the stepladder," but except for the health and welfare responsibilities I was free to have as much fun as they, and maybe more because absorbed as I'd become, I still appreciated that it was play as somehow distinguished from real life, whereas children don't yet have to make that distinction.

INTEGRATIVE ACTIVITIES

Playing games with one's children is a delightful part of mothering, but it's only a small part of the fun, only one chapter in the total story. The rest of what full-time motherhood is all about is what I call integrative activity; it's everything else.

It's the part of mothering that is ignored in studies constructed to reassure full-time working mothers that they really aren't missing much time with their children. In her book *A Mother's Choice,* Deborah Fallows, former associate dean at Georgetown University, who left an academic career to mother her two sons, systematically analyzes press reports based on studies that "prove" that full-time mothers and absentee mothers spend nearly the same amounts of time with their children. She compares the press reports to the actual studies, carefully analyzes the methodology of those studies, and provides her own penetrating analysis of where the studies fail miserably. "The only time that counted as time spent with a child was all-out, undisturbed, down-on-the-floor-playing-with-the-blocks time," she says.

What studies don't measure is hugs and kisses while getting a baby or toddler dressed, a mother and three-year-old splashing in the swimming pool together, a trip to the supermarket, a visit to a friend's, a stop at the library, a walk around the block. What they don't measure is the consistent camaraderie of a mother and her junior colleagues. What they don't measure is the hours and hours of conversation during all those shared activities.

It is the constant physical communication, plus the steady stream of verbal communication, that characterizes the intensity of the relationship of mother and child who spend several years of their lives together. It is the quality and quantity of this communication which is threaded through the particulars of the activities mother and child share that the tests don't measure. And it's precisely that large quantity of high-quality time that tests don't measure —how many hugs and kisses did you have today? How much did you talk to each other today?—in the car when you were riding, in the kitchen while you were cooking, by the lake when you were walking, during lunch together—

that is the *quality mothering that requires quantity time.*
This is the integrative shared activity that full-time mothering is most about.

Sharing one's favorite activities with one's children is
another part of participatory mothering. For one mother
it's getting her child a pair of ice skates and looking forward
to the winter as the season to share a favorite sport; for
another mother it's including her child on a daily jog—
at first he may lag, but within a few years he'll go faster—
for another mother it's raising her own tennis opponent as
I did with Rebecca. I geared my game down to hers from
the time she was a preschooler until she was about eight,
when our games were equal for two or three years. Then she
so far surpassed me that I now present her no challenge.
The same thing happened with Scrabble.

Sharing activities is not limited to sports and games but
has no limit. Mothers across the land have fun sharing their
interests in everything from watercolors and photography
to cooking or computer programming with their children.
And their children benefit tremendously from this shared
involvement and love it.

I've been able to do a wide variety of things during my
past two mothering decades because I've always made my
children a part of the activities I most enjoy, and I've learned
and shared in new activities with them. For instance, I've
integrated exercise, which is essential to my physical and
mental well-being, into my life with my children throughout
the years. When Miriam and Rachel were small we took
long walks, which not only accomplished my exercise goal

but gave us a mutually enjoyable activity, shared conversation, communication with one another, socialization with friends and neighbors we'd meet along the way, and sometimes unexpected pleasures: a blazing red tree, a purple tulip, a first robin.

Rebecca and I walked, too, but walking was never our major activity. By the 1970s, the nation was in an exercise craze, and Rebecca and I joined it. We cross-country skiied —she was on skis the year after she learned to walk—we played tennis, we swam together. As if this weren't enough, we took a joint mothers and preschoolers creative dance class.

Today, I still take walks with one or another of the older girls. We use walks for the nonstop discussions we've been having throughout the years. Miriam and I sometimes meet at a campus pool to swim. So exercise, which has been a part of my life, is a shared activity that I enjoy with members of my family. I can similarly trace avocations and community participation throughout the stages of my family's growth so that I was able consistently to engage in activities I enjoyed and considered important, sharing them with my daughters. The same goes for everyday family meal preparation, as well as holidays and birthdays. I've never done it alone. I learned early that any hand that can form a ball of clay can make a meatball. Contrary to popular belief, two-year-olds can clear tables without either hurting themselves or breaking anything. What's more, at that age they love it!

LIBERATION

One reason that today's participatory mothers are enjoying the fun and freedom of their roles—perhaps more than any generation before them—is that they and their children don't stay home all day.

Although today's sequencing mothers are home-based in that they are not office-based, it's pretty hard to find one at home unless it's during naptime, somebody's sick, or there is a snowstorm. Otherwise they are out doing things with their children—taking advantage of community center programs, parks, zoos, museums, sports activities, on picnics, or participating with their children in a host of other activities. Sometimes it's just mother and one child, or mother and children; other times it's two or more mothers and their children out enjoying the exploration of their environment together.

April through October, and any sunny days above 60 degrees the rest of the year, my preschoolers and I used to go "park-hopping," a favorite activity of Miriam, Rachel, and me. We'd go to several parks in one day. One had a better slide, at another we could count on finding a friend Miriam liked, at a third, Rachel liked the sandbox crowd, and at a fourth the horsey swings were better. We'd stop and do errands as necessary, in between, generally picking up groceries on the way home. Rebecca and I used to follow a similar procedure in nice weather, sometimes stopping by "big school" to take Rachel and a few of her friends complete with their brown bags or hot lunch trays out of the lunchroom to the park across the street from the school. (I'd get advance permission from each girl's teacher each year to do this so that the outing did not have to be negotiated at the time. Rebecca and I showed up in the lunchroom, and sometimes half the class would come running to join us.) Rebecca was always too busy to eat because of the excitement of playing with her sisters and their friends, so afterwards we'd go by the river and have the tuna sandwiches and carrot sticks she so fondly remembers.

Many of today's sequencing mothers find as I did that sharing everyday life with their children is immensely free and liberating. Marcia Lenger, a former Washington, D.C., government litigator who is now raising her two children full time, says, "After over three years I still can't get over the freedom of being able to spend every day outdoors. I'm in the park with the kids most days, unless it's heavy rain. We go morning and afternoon for a total of perhaps four hours. It's glorious . . . I never realized how much I hated the confinement of all that concrete." This sense of freedom which Lenger articulates is one sequencing women have mentioned to me so frequently that I can only laugh. I was on the playground in the 1960s, when mothers flocked away from the swing sets deciding that liberation meant being able to spend one's days in an office. Now it's delightful to be back on the playground talking with career-experienced mothers and hearing them say that liberation means being free to swing with their children in the park. Clearly, freedom is being able to choose and to do each in its own time.

When I look back on my twenty-two years of mothering I

am grateful that I stayed on the playground because of the large quantity of high-quality time our girls and I have had together. All of my daughters are generous lovegivers. The best part of my lovegiving has been the love receiving —the loyalty, affection, and friendship I have from each of them coupled with my bank account of joint memories with each and with all of them, which is overflowing with warmth, happiness, and the fun we've had together.

8

Time for Me

Every full-time mother needs to recognize her right to and need for continued self-development outside the sphere of the family by taking some time just for herself each week. In the vernacular of women's issues it's called "time for me."

The fundamental lesson of modern feminism—that each woman should continue self-development throughout her lifetime—applies as much to the full-time mother as it does to the full-time careerwoman. What differs is the definition of self-development. For the latter, self-development takes place primarily and often exclusively through her job, whereas for the former, self-development is twofold. It takes place within the context of her family through the woman taking the tremendous responsibility of raising other human beings. It takes place outside the realm of the family as well and is expressed through participation in a variety of activities at different periods in her mothering years: it can be reading a book or writing one, exercise, avocations, community activity, and part-time paid work. Self-development is limited only by a woman's own interests and imagination.

The mother of preschoolers needs to make it a point to keep a few hours a week aside for her own personal activities. When children are all in school full days a mother has a significant amount of time for personal activity. She can allocate that time in one or several ways so that she can still remain a full-time mother yet do a great deal else besides.

The form a woman's personal activities take varies with each woman and among women. In my own case "time for me" for the first three or four months after the birth of each new baby was simply a break in the routine: a nap, a quiet cup of tea, or reading a magazine. When Miriam and Rachel were preschoolers at home all day, it meant limited avocational or community work, taking an evening course, organizing a community project, or attending a lecture. At still another point, when Rebecca was a preschooler, it meant writing a book in small bits and pieces of time, which totaled six or eight hours a week. Later, when all three girls were in school full days, "time for me" expanded three- and fourfold to twenty-five hours a week, three-fourths of the year, in predictable chunks (except when one of the girls was sick). For the past near decade I have divided that time between writing, teaching, returning to school first to complete an M.A., then to a doctoral program, swimming every morning, and some limited community work mostly in my daughters' schools.

MAKING THE PERSONAL "TIME FOR ME"

Mothers with all their children in school have built-in "time for me" during their children's school hours, but mothers of preschoolers need to create that time because there is no way that it just happens. No one needs periodic breaks for refreshment and regeneration more than full-time mothers of small children, yet no coffee breaks come with the position. In fact, as mothers of toddlers will testify, one can scarcely arrange unaccompanied bathroom breaks. So each mother needs to watch the rhythms at each stage of the family's development, carve some time out for herself, then jealously guard that time so it doesn't get eaten away by errands or phone calls.

With additional help, women make personal time through trading time with a friend or neighbor, hiring a baby sitter, or leaving the children and her husband together one or two evenings a week or on a weekend afternoon. Even without additional help, many mothers make small amounts of time for themselves by using the nooks and crannies of daytime when children are playing quietly, larger amounts of time during their naptimes (if and when they nap), and in the evening when children are sleeping. Whichever ways a woman chooses of making and taking time for herself, she has to recognize and validate it as a necessity to be put ahead of routine household chores.

It is especially important to validate time when the mother does not leave the house because it's easy to fall into the trap of filling children's naptimes or few minutes of quiet play with a succession of small tasks. In the long run, it's far more valuable to both mother and child for the mother to look upon her children's nap and quiet times as a period for her either to rest herself or to do something else of personal interest. Because this "nook and cranny time" is highly unpredictable, it is not a substitute for an afternoon or evening of leaving the children with a husband or sitter. It is time, however, in which the mother can put her feet up and read for a few minutes or, if she has a focused project, to chip away at it. Paintings are done with individual brush strokes, and many projects are effected through a long succession of phone calls and correspondence, so if one has materials out and knows exactly what comes next, amazingly large inroads can be made on major tasks in one or two separate ten- or twenty-minute periods a day. But this approach works only if a woman is relaxed about what she's doing. It isn't worth attempting to work on a project during short, disparate bits of time if it causes pressures on her.

Some couples use time when the children are in bed for the night, after stories and "one more glass of water," partly as individual "time for me" for each of them and partly as time together. In addition, if a woman takes "time for me" an evening or two a week, or a Saturday afternoon, it not only gives her time for her own pursuits, it gives her husband time as the sole adult with their children.

Some women whose children play well together trade an afternoon a week caring for each other's children. This means that one's child is with another mother and child he knows very well, and it avoids sitter costs, but it may also mean that one, in turn, has four or five children for a length of time. A baby-sitting cooperative in which a group of mothers exchange hours rather than dollars is an extension of this concept and can work well if one knows the other mothers in the group and agrees in principle with their standards of care.

A healthy trend among today's generation of full-time mothers is for a woman to hire a few hours a week of day-time sitter help (in addition to hiring a sitter when she and her husband go out together). In the 1970s women in my workshops would argue that they couldn't justify to themselves the cost of a sitter to take time out for personal interests although they knew they needed to do so. They viewed sitters as replacements for working-outside-the-home mothers; because they had opted to be full-time mothers they felt guilty about hiring help. Today, however, most full-time mothers recognize "time for me" as their right and therefore juggle budgets accordingly to ensure time for themselves.

The uses to which she puts her "time for me" vary from woman to woman and from time to time in each woman's life. For some women at some times it's simply unstructured breaks in the routine; at other times it may be a community activity or avocational pursuits.

BREAKS IN THE ROUTINE

Sometimes a woman simply uses personal time for a break in the routine rather than earmarking it for some specific outside activity. One home-based mother of two small children says, "I have six hours of sitter help a week, when I am basically home, catching up on reading or phoning or writing friends."

When Miriam and Rachel were small, I hired a neighborhood teenager to come in for a couple of hours at the end of the afternoon once or twice a week. I rarely scheduled regular commitments during that time. Sometimes I spontaneously went out to a campus event or used the time to relax and read. This was discretionary time, which I used in any way I chose, providing me with some flexibility at the end of a day for a change in our usual routine. As it happened, I sometimes chose to take one of the children out with me as a special date for us both, as I would do with any other friend. But when I wanted that time all to myself I knew I could expect it.

EXERCISE

The woman accustomed to exercising each day usually plans to continue doing so once she's home-based. The mother who previously had no opportunity to exercise when rushing from office to home can make the opportunity for regular exercise when home-based if she desires. Some mothers do aerobics during their children's naptimes, others incorporate their children into their bending and stretching routines from an early age. Babies love to watch; toddlers love to participate. Other mothers take daily walks with their children in carriages, in strollers, by the hand, on their backs, or in combination. Some mothers prefer to exercise during their personal time. For some it's a jog either before their husbands leave or when they come home; for others it's an early morning or late evening swim; for others still it's an exercise class. Whatever the means, "time for me" and exercise go hand in hand for many of today's mothers of small children. As their children grow, exercise frequently becomes an integrative activity as the mother shares it with her child and uses her personal time for other pursuits.

COMMUNITY CONCERNS

Community participation is something many women do as a shared activity with their children when it involves schools, churches, or community centers. At other times it may be personal activity, apart from the family.

Community work has taken on an entirely new complexion in recent years so that now one is frequently asked, what do you do in the community? meaning "what do you do that's *not* for pay? That is because "not for pay" has taken on new status as professionals of both sexes find things they want to accomplish apart from their paid work. It's also newly valued by women who have found out what men long knew: that community participation is a means of making valuable contacts or gaining useful experience that leads to future professional activities.

Today, sequencing women are taking a new look at ways nonpaid work can meet particular needs for a host of motivations, including socialization, effecting social action on an issue of passionate concern, influencing the reinforcing institutions of their children's lives outside of home, and extending, augmenting, or contributing to their own professional development through civic leadership. In other words, this work is done for its own rewards. Different women have different motivations: the same woman may elect different volunteer activities at different periods during her sequencing years.

Mothers who elect a community activity for reasons of socialization usually do so when first home-based and in search of adult companionship, or when they move to a new location, or through the desire to meet people in fields other than their own. In many cases, once the socialization goal is accomplished, the woman may discontinue the volunteer activity. In other cases, she may like what she is doing and continue it even though her initial need is met. A physician who began League of Women Voters work, attending "a meeting a week in order to get to know women with other than medical interests" when her children were small, continued her community work long after she resumed medical practice. "I enjoy the women I've met and don't want to lose contact with them," she says, "plus I feel the importance of the work the League does."

Often a sequencing mother assumes a position of community leadership because of an issue of passionate concern to her; it may be a longtime interest that her career coupled with marriage and family precluded, or it may be an interest she develops as a direct result of mothering. One former executive spends her "time for me" speaking on the necessity for nuclear freeze, an issue she says "went right by me until with motherhood I suddenly realized that the world doesn't stop with me. Now I want a planet to leave my children."

The desire to extend one's parental commitment into the

reinforcing institutions of her children's lives almost universally leads sequencing mothers, regardless of their profession or location, into their children's schools. Most women begin involvement when their first children begin school and continue those involvements for years.

Some mothers prefer to be involved in policy discussion and decisions on committees or boards. Other mothers like to have an occasional or a regular classroom experience. A child psychologist who was home full time for several years with her children, then practiced part time for the next decade, says she has never been too busy to be part of her children's Parent-Teacher Association. "I believe parents really must be in there," she says. "Most teachers are good, but occasionally you get someone who is extremely naive about children, about teenage rebellion and that kind of thing, and you have to be involved in a capacity where you have input and leverage."

Some women escalate their volunteer involvements into major commitments. A Los Angeles area woman says, "I began to get involved in the schools when my oldest son began kindergarten. By the time all the children were in school I brought my local PTA efforts to bear in my successful campaign for school board—I figured that would keep me in a top decision-making post in citywide educational problems and programs during my children's early school years and net me some political experience and visibility which later I plan to use on a state political level."

Many other women opt for "hands-on" classroom involvement. A former executive says, "Because I left an excellent job to be with my children that time is extremely precious to me. I only do volunteer work on a highly selected basis when it's directly related to my children's needs and highly visible to them such as teaching Sunday school or helping one of their classroom teachers. In this way, I am a part of my child's classroom experience, I see firsthand what is going on, I meet all his classmates and assess the dynamics of his day."

Some of my own community work was directed toward my children's schools when our section of Minneapolis was part of a huge federally funded educational alternatives experiment in which a tremendous amount of time, effort, and funding was spent on art, music, and drama to the near exclusion of reading, writing, math, and science. I vigorously opposed the system at the state and city levels and helped organize other parents to donate professional and personal time to the cause of educating our children.

With three-year-old Rececca as my assistant I gave a weekly interpretive literature course, with much reading assigned in the interim, to a group in Miriam's fifth grade and a similar but less intense course, coupled with creative writing, to Rachel's second/third grade class. To this day, some of the children from both classes come back from high school and college and thank me for introducing them to techniques that helped them throughout their school years. Friends who taught science and math classes have had similar experiences. As parents we managed to turn a situation that could have had detrimental educational consequences for our children into one that benefited them and us tremendously through the experience we gained and the rewards we derived from filling a serious gap in their educations.

Some women deliberately choose to keep their professions separate from community work. Others just as deliberately perform civic leadership in their professional spheres, for sound reasons. Women who expect to work again within large organizations stay visible and make valuable contacts in this way. Entrepreneurs in every field develop client and customer bases through their civic contacts. An attorney, away from the practice of law for eight years, opened a solo practice last year and brought with her what she calls "a small but economically viable client base" developed from personal contacts she made while on the board of directors of her children's school. She continues to be active on that board and attracts clients impressed with her clear, quick thinking and negotiating strategies.

Community work can strongly enhance a résumé. For some sequencing women even a small amount of community work over a period of years adds up to a significant show of continued involvement in their fields. For instance, Louise Kevins before home-based mothering taught in an excellent dramatic arts academy. Because Kevins wanted her own and other youngsters to learn to love theater, she arranged to hold rehearsals and performances in the social hall of a local church and every spring announced through a note in her community newspaper that she would direct a children's play for which neighborhood grade-schoolers could try out. Kevins was clever with the casting and crowd scenes so that all the aspirants got a part, and they also served on crew, costumes, and lighting.

Although she did it with the intent of sharing her love of her work with the children, the productions looked terrific on her résumé. When she went to reapply to teach again at her former academy, she took with her scores of letters sent her by grateful parents lauding her coaching abilities and management skills. She now teaches there again and gives a wider range of courses than before. Although she had previously taught only acting, through the neighborhood productions which she single-handedly produced, directed, cast, and stage-managed, Kevins gave herself the equivalent of several in-depth courses in other areas pertinent to theater. She says that although her original motives were strictly for her own enjoyment and to share what she loves both with her own and other children, she later was delighted that her volunteer work proved professionally useful to her.

Kevins's case illustrates that regardless of a woman's motivations in doing community work at the time she does it, that work belongs on her résumé. When on a functional résumé community work is described according to responsibilities and services performed, the job descriptions are often every bit as or more impressive than those previously performed for salary.

Many women who perform community service during their sequencing years find that work later leads to a career decision or opens new options. For example, a woman who left her newspaper position to raise her children donated a few hours a month one year to a community program in which she helped senior citizens with autobiographical writing. She became so interested in issues relating to the growing numbers of seniors in this society that, when her children were in junior high school, she enrolled in a doctoral program in gerontology and is now teaching at a major university where she also researches problems of the elderly.

Clearly, community participation constitutes "time for me" for various women at various stages in their mothering for various reasons. Although community activities are almost never "time for me" for a woman to spend individually, such participation constitutes "time for me" as a member of a larger group. It's time in which a woman can express herself as part of that group according to her own needs and the needs of others.

AVOCATIONS

Time to develop a new interest or pursue an existing one is the frosting on the cake of the sequencing mother. Some women take advantage of the opportunity with delight. Patty Front, who left her position as an insurance claims adjustor six years ago, says, "Even when I was single I was so career-bound that I had no chance to enjoy any of the hobbies I so loved as a child; once I married and the children were born there was never a minute for anything but work and family until I left my job two years ago. But now I'm enjoying art work again through taking a course in watercoloring a night a week. I spend many more hours painting, mostly with the children; some afternoons we put on smocks and set easels up in the basement; in nice weather we take our supplies outside."

Front's avocation was a return to a former interest; other women explore new areas. For an attorney home full time with her two young sons it's a music appreciation course at a nearby college, "something I never had time for before but want to learn about"; for an art historian it's a course in computers: "It's the wave of the future; I may as well learn." Whatever the particular background of the woman or the particular interest, full-time mothering gives her the opportunity to explore new dimensions. Some mothers are so delighted with the opportunities to take courses in new areas and to learn new skills or pursue existing ones that they find it hard to choose what to do first.

I was interested to find that it's the women who are *not* planning to return to their former fields, but who plan to make a career change in later years, who participate the most and the most diversely in avocations while raising their families. For them the avocation is an opportunity to explore new dimensions of themselves, to test new areas unrelated to their former vocations. Since they do not perceive themselves as having a permanent vocation, they view the totality of their mothering years as a time for self-exploration and each avocation as part of that exploration. For some women the avocation is simply an opportunity to enjoy a new activity; for others the avocation influences a change of fields and becomes a new vocational direction. A nurse turned professional photographer; a high school teacher started her own costume jewelry line.

In contrast, some women who expect to return to their former fields feel guilty about using avocations as "time for me." Not that the woman feels guilty for leaving her chil-

PART II

dren long enough to take a class when her husband may be with them anyway, or for leaving them with a trusted sitter two hours a week. Rather, she feels guilty because she knows that she has earning potential and feels that the time spent on a hobby is "wasted" or "luxury" time as opposed to time spent at a job.

A former information analyst says, "I do some volunteer work at my son's nursery school which I see as a part of his everyday life. But every time I think of taking a course for self-development, even though the dollar cost of the course is negligible, I think that if I have time to do *that*, then why am I not working."

A dental hygienist, now full-time mothering, says, "I feel my husband would think, if she has time for needlepoint why isn't she working at least a little? Even if he didn't *say* it, I feel he would think it." A former travel agent says, "I feel terribly guilty whenever I take up some hobby while my husband works to pay the bills for all of us. I mean, he doesn't have time for his hobbies, why should I? If I could make and sell some art or craft kind of thing then that would be a different story. But I don't have those kinds of talents."

Actually it is erroneous to perceive avocational time as "wasted" or "luxury" unless it produces income, for then it is not an avocation at all. One answer to a wife's guilt because a husband hasn't the time to pursue avocations, too, is for her to help him make the time—to encourage him to take a course, to buy him a book on subjects of interest to him, or to use evening or weekend sitter time jointly to pursue a mutual interest whether it's square dancing, tennis, bowling, or an ancient history or French course, combining "time for me" with "time for we."

Some women put their avocations in the "time for all of us" categories and enjoy avocations with their children by participating in sports from swimming to gymnastics, or a variety of arts and crafts. They don't feel guilty because it's part and parcel of joint interactive time. In this way the woman gains exposure to a new activity or participates in a familiar one and also provides mother and child with stimulating and creative joint experiences. (Community centers, Y's, and the like across the nation have "Dads and Tots" or "Dads and Kids" weekend courses and athletic programs so that fathers have their chance to pursue avocational interests with their children as well.)

Clearly, avocations serve various sequencing women differently. For the mother in the process of self-exploration, avocations give her definite "time for me" to try various activities, some of which may be brand new to her. Although making a vocation of it may not be her prime motivation—at least at a conscious level—an avocation may ultimately become, or dovetail with, a new vocation. These avocational activities may well be shared with the family, as Patty Front does with her watercoloring, but the primary purpose the avocation serves is "time for me" to expand interests.

PROFESSIONAL DEVELOPMENT

The woman with a vocation firmly in hand and mind frequently has another agenda for her "time for me," using some or all of that time for professional development, either keeping up contacts, reading literature in her field, effecting a very limited career reemphasis while she still has pre-schoolers at home, or engaging in professional activities during their school hours once they are older. This use of such time is the subject of the next several chapters.

9

Preparation for Career Reemphasis

The great majority of women who leave careers to mother their children plan to resume working again. Well over 90 percent of the women I interviewed plan to resume (or have resumed) some career activity; nearly two-thirds return, or plan to return, to the same field; another third take, or plan to take, new career directions. *In nearly every case the woman wants to work part time long before she wants to work again full time. It's not surprising, for resuming a career on a part-time basis is doubly advantageous to the woman.* It enables her to preserve her mothering priorities, working around her children's schedules, and it means that a career reemphasis is never a critical life change. Women who resume working part time gradually integrate their work back into their lives so that their career commitments grow as their children grow. When the children are older, those women who wish to make a more substantial career commitment already have years of continued work experience behind them and current contacts as well. This means that they are not concerned with the problems of reentry that were central two decades ago to women returning full time to the work force after fifteen or twenty or more years completely away from either classroom or office. Also, a great many sequencing women today elect to become entrepreneurs, beginning when they wish and working part-time hours of their own choosing.

This chapter is a bridge between Part II, which has focused exclusively on a woman's years at home with her children, and Part III, which will discuss major aspects of career reemphasis: the new professional agenda sequencing women seek; the optimal time to resume career activities; the desire of the overwhelming number of women for flexible schedules; the preference of the vast majority for part-time professional positions and their means of creating and negotiating them; a range of entrepreneurial options; and the return to full-time work for those who want it with discussion of the levels at which they return.

Preparation for career reemphasis as a connecting link between the full-time motherhood years and the woman's career reintegration focuses on three main topics: (1) maintaining professional contacts during the full-time mothering years to promote ease of reemphasis; (2) keeping up on the literature during those years away from active professional participation; and (3) discussion of who needs to return to school and of the best time for those who need to do it to do so. This chapter is geared to both the woman who plans to *reemphasize in a former field* and the woman *planning to change careers*. These two groups of women have different objectives, and therefore preparation is different in each group.

For the woman planning to resume in her former field, keeping up contacts and keeping abreast of the literature of her field can be of tremendous value, and she may not need more formal schooling. Career switchers have less need to keep up contacts and read the literature—sometimes no need—but frequently additional schooling is a prerequisite for the new career, and preparation includes evaluating what additional education they'll need, deciding when to get it, and getting it!

MAINTAINING PROFESSIONAL CONTACTS

Career strategist Marilyn Moats Kennedy, the author of *Office Politics*, says in her June 1985 *Glamour* magazine column, "If you keep up your contacts you can take time out and move back in with relative ease . . . when asked why you took time off you have an acceptable and plausible explanation . . . I wanted to get my child off to a good start and she is." My findings are compatible with Kennedy's. Keeping up professional contacts is a critical factor in career reemphasis. Keeping up contacts means both keeping up with former colleagues and employers and keeping up certifications and professional association memberships as well.

Women who plan to become entrepreneurs need to preserve their contacts as much as do those who expect to be employees, for the independent relies heavily upon personal contacts for the development of customers and clients. The only women who, as a group, don't find it necessary to make a conscious effort to maintain contacts are those who are married to men in the same professions. For them professional contacts are built into their personal and social lives.

There are two main ways women maintain their contacts: on a one-to-one basis and through their professional associations. On a one-to-one basis, women keep up with two categories of former colleagues: those with whom in addition to a professional relationship they developed a personal relationship and those who were primarily business associates. The question facing the sequencing woman is how to keep the relationships mutually advantageous once she no longer has a day-to-day involvement in the field. This generally poses little problem when the relationship was closer than simply collegial. Sequencing women find that many of their former female colleagues are very curious about full-time motherhood. A former public relations specialist who has a standing first-of-the-month lunch date with a former colleague says, "Besides the fact that we like one another there's something in it for each of us; for me it's keeping up a contact in the field while I'm out of it, for her it's learning from me what's involved in mothering. She's starting to think 'baby' so she is really interested in what I'm doing and how I feel about being out of the field, all the things I wondered about myself a few years ago."

A medical technologist who keeps up with a group from her former clinic by bringing her baby to join them for an occasional lunch finds similar interest among her former coworkers: "They are all married, one is pregnant, and the others are thinking about it. I'm one of the few mothers any of them knows well, and I'm the only one they know who has taken off. So they are very interested in hearing what I do, in watching the baby develop, and, I think, in watching how effortlessly the baby and I interact."

Of course, interest in how full-time mothering works is not the only reason personal friends remain friends. Usually whatever it was in the two personalities and backgrounds that meshed in the first place still holds even though their daily activities are no longer parallel. "One of my colleagues and I used to talk about literature," says a woman two years away from her work in a genetics laboratory. "We both had vacillated between careers in the arts versus the sciences, both opted for the sciences, and each held a very great longing for what we gave up. Since we both read avidly we'd have lunch every week and never talk shop, always books. None of that has changed except that I have more time to read now than she does. When we get together we still talk books, books, and books."

A Wall Street broker in her third year of mothering sabbatical says, "My friendships all transcend time, place, and activity. I pick up with old high school friends in five minutes, see college friends after years and don't miss a beat. It's the same way with my former work colleagues. I used to go for a drink with my teammates—except for me it was an all-boys' club—every Friday afternoon, and I still do meet them some Fridays, same place, same time. I was accepted from the first because I'm a lot of fun, and we still have fun together. If I don't show up for a few Fridays in a row, one of them calls to say they missed me and to ask if everything is okay. I love seeing them and talking trade—it's fun and it underscores to me how much I am not missing. I always go home happy to have seen them but delighted with the choice I made."

Often women find that making the time to keep these contacts is not easy; their own lives move quickly, as do those of their former colleagues, each in a different orbit, with different priorities and interests. "There's a strong temptation on my part to let my relationships drift," a former advertising account executive says. "But I force myself to resist that temptation, to be sure to see people in my field even if our daily activities are vastly different right now. I am usually the one who takes the initiative. They have people right there to go out to lunch with; I have to plan in advance, get a sitter, and make a half-day project of it."

Whereas keeping up with professional contacts who were also friends usually works very well for the women who make the effort, keeping up with those who were primarily business associates without real friendship is more of a challenge. After all, if you lunched together only to discuss business and if now you are not actively involved in that business, you will be of less interest to a former associate. When one wants to maintain a particular contact, however, there are ways other than lunch or cocktails —sending a pertinent clipping with a note attached when you see something in a publication about her, or that you know will interest him; dropping in for a quick "hello"; writing a memo if you get an idea that you feel would be of high interest to a former employer or colleague. Whatever the means, the point is that it is up to the woman who is presently inactive to let the other person know she is still interested. That way, when she is ready to reemphasize, she doesn't have to preface any inquiries with "remember me?" For example, a former merchandise manager says, "I make it a point to drop in to see my ex-boss once or twice a year, even if it's only a two-minute visit between his appointments. We were never friends, but it was always a pleasant working relationship, and I want to be sure to keep up the contact. Then I won't be a stranger knocking on his door looking for work someday down the pike or somebody he hardly remembers asking for a letter of recommendation. As for what's in it for him to want to see me, he was always impressed with my fashion sense and ability to predict trends. So when I stop I always leave him with something which may be helpful to him—a comment, suggestion, prediction, or question, something to make it worthwhile for him to talk with me."

One of the easiest ways to keep in contact with former colleagues, employers, and other associates—beyond the one-to-one—is through professional associations. It's important that the woman who plans to return to her profession keep up one or two of the most important of the professional association memberships, chalking the cost up to the insurance budget. (She should obviously keep up all certifications as well if her profession requires it.) Some women find that attending meetings from time to time is sufficient. Others work actively within their professional associations at some point during their home-based years as a way of keeping visible, maintaining contacts, and doing work they consider valuable but wouldn't have time for while working full time. "For two years I'd been asked to accept a board position in my professional businesswomen's group," a former corporate sales director says, "but I was working full time, had a child and no time. When I left my job to stay home, I said I would accept the board position. It was precedent-setting for somebody who was unaffiliated with a corporation or board post. I'm now in my third year at home and was just elected the organization secretary. Because of my visibility and continued networking I have had several job feelers and have already turned down a good offer because I'm not yet ready to go back."

Active participation in a professional association and attending a local conference or two every year and perhaps a regional or national conference, especially in the year before one wants to reemphasize, is important. There is no easier way to maintain contact with those who were purely professional associates than through these memberships and meetings. If one is still seeing others from the field, reading in it, and interested in it as well as in a variety of other issues, one finds that the gap between being currently active in a field and being inactive is not terribly great. For the commonality with former colleagues is *interest in, knowledge of*, and *new ideas about* aspects of the field as well as present participation. This is especially borne out by women who keep up well in the literature of their fields and often find themselves in demand by former colleagues.

KEEPING UP WITH THE LITERATURE

Regardless of her particular profession, it's important that a woman away from active work in her field keep up with the literature through the professional or trade journals and through reading articles in general publications pertinent to her field.

A pharmacist who hasn't filled a prescription in three years says, "While my speed is down a little and will take a few weeks to get back up, in terms of information, I am so much farther ahead of most of the men and women out in the pharmacies today that it's hard to believe. I read all of our publications, I know literally every new drug, its uses, contraindications, and interactions. My former colleagues in town know that I keep up, in fact, that by keeping up I am keeping ahead of them. I often get a call from another pharmacist asking me about a particular new drug or drug interaction."

An internist speaks of similar experiences: "When you're carrying a full patient load you haven't the time to keep up on the *New England Journal of Medicine*, the *Lancet*, or the subspecialty publications," she says. "Since I've been at home for the past two years with my young sons, I have had the time to really read. I'm in close touch with my former associates, who pick my brain for the new material."

Sometimes, regardless of how well a woman has kept up on her field in general, once she has a particular position in mind, or has secured it, she'll still find she wants or needs to cram. In her autobiography, *Ferraro*, the 1984 Democratic vice-presidential candidate discusses her overnight jump in 1974 from years of full-time mothering to working full time in the district attorney's office. "A whole new criminal code had been written in the interim," she says, and asks, "what was I going to do?" Then she answers her own question, "Take the new statute . . . and plunge in, studying all the new laws and legal terms—that's what." Geraldine Ferraro's solution is the same one scores of other women in various fields implement when confronted with the need to get new information for a new job: they find out what they have to know, then give themselves a crash course in it.

USING PROFESSIONAL SKILLS DURING THE YEARS AT HOME WITH PRESCHOOLERS

Some women use their professional abilities in a limited time frame while they are home with preschoolers, through a community activity, as discussed in the previous chapter, or through a few hours a week of paid work, as will be discussed in subsequent chapters.

Other women write to keep visible. A literature professor who left her university tenure-track position to mother her two children spent an evening a week in the library of her home and Saturday afternoons at a nearby university library for the eight years she was full-time mothering. The result was several publications in prestigious journals, which led directly to a tenured position at another college in her area when she decided she again wanted a teaching position.

An attorney who's been away from the practice of law for three years while mothering her two children writes articles for her state bar association publications: "As a direct result, I've gotten feelers from a couple of firms asking if I'm ready to come back. I'm not yet, but this visibility keeps me confident that when I am I won't have much trouble finding something to suit my needs."

ADDITIONAL COURSE WORK OR DEGREES AS REFRESHERS

When I began the research for this book, I assumed that most women, in most fields, would find it advantageous if not downright necessary to take additional course work or degrees before resuming their professional activities after years away. This, it turns out, is not the case. Most women who have already reemphasized their careers find that they don't need formalized course work as refreshers because they say they don't forget the basics and that they quickly integrate new materials into the existing frameworks, which they remember well. For instance, none of the M.B.A.'s I interviewed who have thus far resumed working felt that a return to school for more course work is necessary, nor apparently do the employers who have hired them. As one executive who recently rehired a woman who was away for several years explained, "The substance of the course work doesn't really matter: what matters is the problem-solving abilities which she already has. The on-the-job experience is better than any classroom."

Attorneys who have resumed working told me they did not need to take any new courses, but for the first few months back they needed to do more research than they did

at the time they left. The time spent on the research, however, was far less than the time they spent when first out of
school and on their first jobs, when much of the first two
or three years was devoted to checking precedents and
protocols.

To my question, "What did you do to regain skills and
information in preparation for returning to work?" women
who have resumed professional activities in a variety of
fields repeatedly answered, "Nothing." Many use the expression, "It's like riding a bike." That particular expression
was used by Gretchen Nyman, who returned to an executive-
level position with a Fortune 500 company nearly a decade
after leaving, by teachers, by computer programmers, by
attorneys, and even by physicians such as Dr. Katharine
Poole Wolf, now a Harvard Medical School psychiatrist,
who fifteen years ago left her practice of medicine entirely
for nearly five years when the first of her sons was born.

Dr. Wolf explains the "bike riding" phenomenon this
way: "Once you understand the flow of the blood into the
system, for instance, forever afterward when you listen to
someone giving a paper you know if they are talking theory,
nonsense, or if it's real . . . you can detect an authenticity.
If there is new work you may not know every fact, but you
can get those; it's the methodology which once you have,
you always have." What if you are listening to a heartbeat
instead of a paper? Dr. Wolf, formerly a pediatric car-
diologist, switched subspecialties when she returned to
medicine because she did not want to face the day-to-day
conflict of leaving her own children to practice emergency
medicine. Had she not switched, she says she may have

"spruced up for an additional fellowship year just to be doubly sure," although she doubts it would have been necessary. When she began her new residency she found she had not forgotten any of her clinical training. (Some physicians after the first year or two away from medical practice arrange to practice one or two half-days a week to maintain their skills. Some women in some of the high-tech fields do similarly. But that seems to be where practice for skill retention ends. Some women from all fields return to professional activity on a limited basis after only a year or two away, but most do not, and those who do almost always do so for reasons other than fear of forgetting valuable skills or information.)

In many fields, keeping up with the literature constitutes a refresher course because processing the new material requires one to use the old. Attorneys, cost accountants, and security analysts, for example, feel that reading while they are out keeps them current, sometimes ahead, in vital matters—that many laws change so frequently that even when working full time in the field one must continually keep up. Scientists, as previously discussed, often find that by keeping up with the literature they are ahead rather than behind in the field.

Some fields have yearly certification requirements. Those fields—such as education and nursing—require a certain number of hours of course work each year to ensure that one remains fresh and current. Because these were traditionally "women's professions," and because women traditionally left them to have families—and a percentage always returned—it's possible that as more women leave and return to more professions other fields will institute similar guidelines. If so, women who have already sequenced should take the initiative in instituting the regulations so that requirements are few enough in number of hours or flexible enough so that no woman is precluded from them because of her mothering priorities and that requirements are pertinent, that they really address the information, issues, and areas that will be beneficial to the woman reemphasizing her field.

The major key to successful career reemphasis regardless of the profession will continue to be a woman's understanding her field very well in the first place, so she can continually fit new information into that framework.

CAREER SWITCHING

In contrast to women returning to former fields, many women who plan to take new career directions desire or require more formal training, in some cases new degree programs, as a route to new careers. These women fall into two main groups: 1) those who switch areas *within* the same field, such as those who want to leave hands-on practice and become administrators, to switch subspecialties, or to stack a new specialty onto an existing one; and 2) those who switch fields completely.

Switching Career Directions within the Same Field

The largest segment of women who make career switches within the same field formerly did "hands-on" work in businesses, schools, or hospitals and now want to switch to administration. They have their basic four-year degrees and want master's degrees as tickets to higher levels of position, pay, and responsibility. In many corporations, schools, and hospitals there is little chance that a person with a B.A. or B.S. can proceed past a certain level regardless of on-the-job expertise, even if he or she has been working without a break in the field for years. Thousands of persons in business, health, and educational fields work full time by day, then go to school at night to get admission tickets to higher administrative levels in their professions. Therefore, the woman who left the field as a practitioner and wants to return as an administrator will similarly need an additional degree. It stands to reason that she should seriously consider getting the degree before she returns to the field because it will enable her to return with greater flexibility and negotiating strength. (Obviously, this does not mean that every manager, nurse, or teacher will want an advanced degree before working again; it simply means that those who want to make a switch to administration in their fields will probably need another degree to do it. And, if so, it helps to get the degree before returning to work because mothering, working, and attending school is a no-win trio.)

A second group of women who switch within a field and benefit from more training before they reincorporate professional activities into their lives are generalists who want to become specialists. Many of these women acquire a new specialty to make them unique in the field rather than returning to a field in which even the persons already working full time are having difficulty finding growth and challenge.

Even in fields in which positions are plentiful, a new skill can give a new twist to an existing profession to make one highly desirable. For instance, a new skill area of the present and foreseeable future that facilitates many new options is computer application to almost everything. A physician who took a series of computer courses elected not to return to private practice but set up and ran a new diagnostic system for a health maintenance organization (HMO). Because she has unique credentials she wrote the job description and named the hours. A pharmacist who acquired computer expertise draws upon it for her work in drug interactions for the consulting practice she established; an art teacher learned computer graphics and returned not to teaching in elementary school as she had been but on a college level. The list is as endless as the possibilities, but the point is that when one has an additional special skill to add to one's profession, it can catapult her into a far higher-level bargaining position than the one she was previously in.

Some women switch within a field because the thrust of their profession doesn't mesh with the way they want to continue mothering. They find that the work is incompatible with family because it can be done only under great deadline pressure or it keeps them constantly on call. Dr. Wolf encountered both problems when she decided to switch subspecialties and leave pediatric cardiology, in which she had built an excellent reputation in the Boston medical community, because pediatric cardiology meant leaving her children on a moment's notice to rush to care for someone else's child. She chose psychiatry within an academic setting because it is far less emergency-oriented. Hers is the kind of a subspecialty change which she believes women now entering professions can avoid by asking themselves at the start: If I have children, will this field enable me to mother as I want to?

Complete Career Change

Some women decide at the time they leave their careers that they will make a complete career change before working again in the future. Others decide once away from their work that they didn't like it enough to go back to it; still others feel a real calling to do something else; others acquire new interests and perspectives while mothering which ultimately take them in new professional directions.

Whatever their reason, many women in this group need more schooling before they proceed. Examples include one woman who switched from public relations to law and one who switched from dental hygiene to teaching art history. For them more schooling was not optional; it was a necessary prerequisite to do the work they found they wanted to do. These women, as well as those who make switches within fields, return to school with one of two time goals in mind: to get the further education as "time for me" while they are raising preschoolers so that when their children are in school they are set to work again, or because they plan to go back to school when all their children are in school.

PART II

When and How to Return to School

The crucial factor in deciding *when* to return to school is recognizing *how much time* one can comfortably spend on it. For if a woman wants to continue to meet the mothering goals she established in leaving her work in the first place, she will need to regulate the hours she spends in school and on her schoolwork carefully. Otherwise too much school can create the same pressure and interference with a woman's mothering priorities as can too much professional activity.

A mother taking courses in a degree program must, besides factoring in the time she spends in class and the time she spends preparing assignments, be aware of Murphy's Law: one of the children will always run a 103-degree fever the night before an important exam. Therefore, the mother may arrive to take the exam after a sleepless night in which she got absolutely no studying done. Cramming, which may have served her in earlier years, does not serve her now—she has to learn an entirely new style: being prepared for all assignments and exams well in advance of the deadline.

Anita Roberts found that she had to change both her studying habits and her timing plans when she returned to an evening M.B.A. program shortly after the birth of her second child two years ago: "At first, I thought I'd zip through, take two courses a semester, study during my baby's naps when my son is at nursery school; but it was totally unrealistic. She didn't always nap when he was gone, and besides all I was doing every spare minute was schoolwork, it was always *there*, always on my mind, always more to be done. I could do it, but the cost was way too high. I was tense, always rushing the children so I could fit in more study time. This was totally antithetical to the kind of student or the kind of mother I'd been. I was always a sure A in the classroom; all of a sudden I was killing myself for the A or even a B; and besides that, my mothering slid from the A I'd always awarded myself to a C, maybe C+. After a year of this, I cut back to one course a term and that is what I now plan to do throughout the program. Now I'm an A mother again, and my A's in school are coming pretty easily again, too. It will take four years to finish this way, but I would not be looking even at a part-time job before that time anyway.

Roberts's experience, that a course a quarter or semester can work well whereas more is too many, is a theme I heard often in talking with women who pursue degrees while raising families. But even a limited amount of course work can be too much for the mother of preschoolers if the woman does not enjoy the course subject matter or if it entails a great deal of time pressure. If she is in a program that appeals to her and the course work is interesting, stimulating, and challenging, her schooling may well add a positive dimension to her time with her family; if, however, schoolwork creates pressure, school is merely a means to an end, or there are many tedious requirements, she may well seriously consider waiting to enroll in a formal program until her children are all in school themselves, when she will have large blocks of time to zero in and get it all over with. That is surely preferable to letting school be a constant intrusion during the years she has with her small children and thus interfering with her mothering choice.

Choosing between a day or evening program can sometimes be a major determinant in deciding when to return to school. Day school programs are often incompatible with the schedules of mothers of preschoolers, and tuitions are often high. In contrast, many universities throughout the country offer evening school M.B.A., M.P.H., M.E.D., and a host of other programs that facilitate both the full-time careerperson and the full-time mother through the scheduling and spacing of courses, the flexibility of the number of years required to complete the program, and the lower tuitions.

Molly Welter found that an evening school approach, once her children were in school full days, worked well because she could do all her studying while they were in school and take her courses twice a week while they were with her husband in the evening. Welter was a charge nurse for eight years before the birth of the first of her two sons and was away from nursing entirely for seven years before she began an evening M.P.H. program. "I had looked into the daytime program at one nearby university, but the courses were given in short time slots every day. I would have had to be away from the boys too much. So, when they were in school I enrolled in an evening program designed for professionals, all of whom were working full time, or a few like myself who were home with children. The program was staffed by people who knew we were all busy adults, and we were treated accordingly. Courses were concentrated into seminars meeting once or twice a week for three years. While I cannot pretend that I loved much of my course work, at least it was concentrated, moved quickly, and there seemed to be a reasonable justification for most of the courses given within the perimeters of the goals I wanted to achieve. My husband was with the boys the evenings I had to be in class, never over two nights a week. I did almost all my studying when the boys were in school, so I rarely was pressed by it when they were home with me, and best of all, I went on school vacation when they were."

Alberta Carter, a fifty-two-year-old mother of four grown children, took a Ph.D. in business when she was over forty, and now runs her own human resources consulting firm, a major switch from teaching second grade, her profession nearly thirty years ago. Carter says, "I am glad that I waited until the children were all in junior high and high school because then I was able to become totally immersed in my own course work. I took classes during their school hours, then came home in the afternoons, was with them and my husband through the dinner hour, and then when the kids hit the books at night, so did I."

Clearly, to enjoy a return to school and to get the most from it, returning at the right time is crucial. And the time that's most right for one woman can be wrong for the next. Each woman can best find for herself her optimal time by (1) assessing realistically her present schedule and determining exactly when class time and study time would fit into that schedule; (2) starting out gradually with a single course for the first quarter or semester; (3) when adding more, trying the course times and load that look as if they will best fit; and (4) not hesitating to cut back if the course demands interfere with family priorities.

It is very difficult to assess just how school will fit into one's life without first trying, cutting, trimming, and adjusting. Each woman should realize that it may take more than one attempt to get the right fit so that she will not get discouraged if she finds on the first try that she wants to reduce her course load or even postpone entirely completing a program.

What's important is that a woman keep her initial priorities in mind—that she left her career to have time with her children—and recognize that if course work robs her of that time, she may want seriously to consider alternative schedules, or a postponement, until she finds the balance that best suits her all-around needs.

Part III

The Sequencer:
A New Professional Agenda

Your work should fit your life. It's terribly important to make lifestyle the principal objective . . . if you subordinate your career to your personal predilections invariably the career will fall into place. If you do the reverse you may never achieve the personal life you want.

Professor Joseph Auerbach
Harvard Business School Bulletin
April 1985

The following section of the book discusses at length the major question which nearly every woman who leaves her career to raise a family faces at some point: how will I reintegrate my career into my life? This part is divided into four chapters. Chapter 10, "Going Forth on New Terms," in an overview to the rest of the book, explores the search for a new professional value system prevalent among many men and women today and discusses the leadership of sequencing women in that quest. The chapter shows that in their career reemphasis choices most sequencing women want control over their own time and that, although a return to full-time positions is usually much easier to effect, most of those who return to work in organizations want part-time professional positions with growth opportunities; many others select entrepreneurial options.

Chapters 11, 12, and 13 illustrate in detail what Chapter 10 sets forth: that women in literally every profession and location are creating the opportunities they desire. Chapter 11, "Controlling One's Own Time," shows the ways in which women can control their time by detailing the optimal times various women resume working, how much time women find they can comfortably spend on careers while still preserving their family priorities, and the differences in time allocation between mothers of preschoolers and those with school-age children. Chapter 12, "Changing the System," focuses on ways women in a variety of fields are designing part-time professional positions to work for them. Chapter 13, "Beyond the System," details how women in a host of different professions are creating entrepreneurial opportunities for themselves.

10

Going Forth on New Terms

NEW VALUES FOR A NEW MILLENNIUM

On the eve of a new millennium, sequencers are striving to make the contemporary woman's dream of a truly successful integration of family life and professional activity come true. In the third stage of sequencing, they are attempting to reincorporate work into their lives in new ways by developing a new agenda of professionalism. The new agenda they are designing supplants the rigid, hierarchical norm developed by males of another generation, who had no other focus to their lives beyond their work. In contrast, women from one coast to the other, in reemphasizing their work in scores of different professions, are saying: I want my work to be a component of my life, not the entirety.

Although this is a story I'm delighted to relate, it's not the story I had expected to hear. Before I began the book I assumed that women who were leaving the marketplace for families were expecting to spend a relatively few years mothering before returning to full-time careers. The issue I planned to address in this final section of the book was total reentry: How do you return to a full-time job, to a comparable place with your former employer or to another comparable place in your field? These are the questions I asked women in my initial interviews. The first woman I asked, an attorney with a Ph.D. in political science, told me I was asking the wrong question. "I'd never return to that kind of situation again," she said of the prestigious law firm in which she'd worked for five years. "I'd have to be crazy. Ask me what I want out of my life; how law fits into it, but don't ask me how I plan to go back to give my life away."

I thought at first that I'd drawn the exception to the rule. After all, she did have both a Ph.D. and a law degree; even among my well-credentialed sample she was unusual. So I continued to ask the same questions of women already working again as well as of those contemplating doing so. The response of a forty-two-year-old psychologist and mother of two was typical: "Why not ask what role I fore-see for my profession in my future?" she said. "To ask how I plan to return to what I left doesn't address my needs. What I need is balance in my life. Returning to the organiza-tion in which I headed the testing service would mean a completely one-dimensional life again. My family would get relegated to the corners. I didn't want that when I left the first time. Why would I want it now?"

After scores of such responses, I finally realized that, indeed, I was asking the wrong questions. For I came to recognize that women are not concerned with going back but with going forth. The model I had envisioned—full-time career to family to full-time career—was built on the woman of the 1960s and early 1970s, who was just getting into a profession after many years of mothering and who had no prior experience with the Superwoman routine. Then, the big as yet unanswered question for millions of women was, Can a woman who has never been in the labor force get into it at age thirty, forty, fifty, and more? For a smaller group of women of the late 1960s and 1970s the question was, Can a career-experienced woman get back into her field after years away without permanent professional loss? The answer both groups of women found was yes—if they were willing to work full time. And they were.

RETURN TO FULL-TIME WORK

Most women today believe that the question of whether a career-experienced woman can return full time to her field at a comparable level was settled by their predecessors. Because of the women who have already led the way, precedents are now established for women to return to partnership law tracks with full credit for number of years already served; federal law protects tenured government employees with three or more years of service so that they can return to the same or higher-level positions after years away without penalty. Public school systems typically give five or more years of leave to tenured faculty with level of reentry protected.

A Philadelphia attorney was four years into a partnership track when she left six years ago. She has now returned to a different firm that gave her full credit for the four years she had worked. A reading specialist who had seniority in Ohio when she left her position eight years ago began teaching again last year in Wisconsin at a level comparable to that which she left; a classical vocalist returned to an academic music appointment three years ago after twenty-five years away. At the national level, Geraldine Ferraro spent nearly a dozen years as a home-based mother, and Sandra Day O'Connor spent five. Both went back to their careers full tilt, and each made history.

Therefore, today's sequencing mothers know that the model of a return to a full-time career in an existing organization is possible. Many women today report being offered good full-time positions in their fields when they are ready to reemphasize their careers. (Specifics of search procedures are detailed at the beginning of Chapter 12.) Returning to a full-time job, however, is not the choice most of the women I interviewed made or intend to make.

Fewer than 10 percent of the women elected to go from full-time mothering directly to a full-time position in an existing organization. Those few women who decided to take a full-time job included elementary school teachers, morning shift nurses, and a college professor, all of whom can schedule their work around their children's school hours. Others were an attorney who had to return to full-time work to support the family while her husband returned to school, a widowed advertising executive, an ophthalmologist, and an editor of an airline's inflight magazine. The latter two went back full time with the express plan of cutting down to part time once they become reestablished. The ophthalmologist, who had been away from practice for three years, retrained for several months by her own choice ("I wanted to be *sure* I remembered everything"), then joined an HMO; the editor went back to senior editor status at a competing magazine.

As the experiences of these women evidence, mothers who want to work full time again find that full-time offers at levels comparable to those they left are not terribly difficult to come by, as some of the more conflicted women feared before leaving their work. One reason is that employers are becoming accustomed to some women's preference to take a period of years totally away and no longer look askance at women who have done so; another is that women who have taken many years out—as did Ferraro, Day, and Barbara Black, dean of Columbia Law School—have shown that they return energetic, enthusiastic, with their intellectual capabilities fully intact, and able to meet the highest responsibilities in the country. These women have set outstanding precedents as have lesser-known names in corporations, law firms, schools, and hospitals throughout the land. It's now a known fact that mothers who return after years away do so with their professional priorities firmly established and that the jobs do not suffer!

As indicated above, level of reentry is protected in parts of the public sector, for example, for tenured government employees and in many states for teachers. In the private sector, whether a woman returns to a level comparable to the one she left is determined by a variety of factors: her profession, location, number of years away, contacts, and a host of other variables. A general rule of thumb among my sample was that when a woman reemphasized in a company *smaller* than the one she left, she usually returned at a *comparable* or *higher* level; when she returned to the same company, she usually did so in a *similar* or *sometimes higher position*; and when she returned to a substantially *larger* organization she usually began a notch or more *below* the level she had formerly occupied. A case in point is Sally Williams, who had been vice-president of a medium-sized West Coast advertising agency, resumed working full time in a much larger firm after six years away, and began a level below the vice-presidents:

"I wanted the larger company and couldn't expect to come in over heads at the VP level in the new organization. However, I came with the express understanding that if all went as well as I and my employer expected, I would be promoted to a level comparable to what I left in my former company within two years. I figured that I had six years completely away from work and that taking two years to build myself up to a position comparable to what I had left was not unrealistic. It seemed fair to me, and it worked out well. I was promoted within eighteen months."

If finding full-time positions again is not a major obstacle, and getting back in full time at comparable or near comparable title and salary level appears to be a distinct possibility for many women, why isn't full-time work the plan of choice for most sequencing women? What do the others want and do?

PART III

CAREER REEMPHASIS CHOICES

More than 90 percent of the women I interviewed who had already reemphasized careers either found, created, or negotiated changes in existing organizations, which enabled them to work part time, or they become entrepreneurs, setting their own schedules and other work conditions. Although most of these women say they plan to increase professional responsibilities as their children grow older, few of them speak of a return to full-time professionalism as they knew it in the past. Most of them articulated in one way or another that raising a child is far more than a few-year commitment, and in addition many say they have developed new self-perceptions and interests that extend far beyond their careers.

These are the women who are creating the first model of what sequencing is: first, full-time career; next, full-time raising children; and *then* reincorporation of career back into one's life so that a career complements the whole individual rather than dominates her life. Many of these women plan to spend more time on their careers as their children grow older; some will doubtless work again full time; but many women say that even when their children are grown, they don't ever again want to let their careers become the total focus of their lives. They want flexibility and are among those pioneering new ways for professionals to have it.

These sequencing women found the male career norm model on which Superwoman was based severely deficient and opted to mother their children on a full-time basis instead. It should come as no surprise that when they are ready to reincorporate careers back into their lives they seek alternatives to the Superwoman model and instead want to create more flexible ways in which to work. The reasons are twofold. First, once having broken out of the mold of total career dedication and priority, they have a different perspective on the role of work in their lives. Second, having invested the best of their time and energies in mothering their children, they are not doing a sudden about-face a few years later and choosing to leave them with latchkeys or in surrogate care.

In the words of a Manhattan literary agent who blends her work around her busy schedule with her two grade-schoolers, "Women today are being sold a romantic bill about babies . . . that somehow if you are home for a while with a baby, then it's all over. Well, it's only the beginning. Having a child to raise, to guide to maturity, to help overcome weaknesses, to encourage strengths, is a major life commitment." The prevailing view of sequencing mothers today appears to be that their children are, indeed, major life commitments. Rather than leaving their three- or five- or eight- or ten-year-olds once again to pursue full-time, nonstop careers, these women want to do *some* work again long before their families are grown, increasing the amount they do as their children get older. So the straight career/family/career model does not apply to them. Instead, they are seeking new ways to reincorporate work into their lives without compromising either the quantity or the quality of their mothering to do so. Their question goes far beyond merely, How can I get back in without losing professional ground? The question they now ask is, How can I reincorporate challenging professional activities into my life without diminishing my mothering? In deciding when and how to reincorporate their careers these women are choosing the roles they want their professions to play in their lives rather than expecting that a career will *be* their lives.

Once I realized that it is balance that they seek in their lives, I saw that for most women who leave careers the sequencing model is full-time career, then full-time mothering, followed by a gradual reintegration of career into total lifestyle so that it enhances without dominating. But, I wondered, does this desire for balance mean these women have lost their ambitions to succeed professionally? I might have jumped to that conclusion had I not been told by a young Wall Street attorney who left her firm, "Everybody I know is dissatisfied. My husband's cutting out of his hundred-hour-a-week investment banking job, too. He's going into his own business. My friends have had it, even the ones without children." Other sequencing women told me the same thing.

So I went beyond my sample of sequencing mothers and started researching work attitudes and motivations in the general population. I talked with women and with men who are working full time at their careers, to older executives, and to younger ones. I talked with the heads of some of the country's leading corporations, law firms, and management schools. I talked with career strategists and consultants throughout the country and with the country's leaders on new work options on both coasts.

From these conversations I came to recognize the full contextual framework for the responses of the sequencing women I've interviewed. It turns out that these women are in the forefront of exciting changes in this country with respect to work attitudes and options. I learned that they haven't lost their ambitions or motivations toward success, but rather that the entire definition of success is shifting dramatically among a generation of young professionals from emphasis on money, prestige, and power to developing total life balance. The new definition of success is the subject of books, studies, and articles. As John Naisbitt, author of *Megatrends* and *Reinventing the Corporation*, says, in the latter: "The definition of success is shifting so that balancing your life—rather than being very successful in business—is what constitutes success."

The editors of *Ms.* magazine concur. In their November 1985 spread on jobs women love they say: ". . . we [women] are transforming the work force with a changed definition of success. We measure it not just in dollars, but in the satisfaction we get from our jobs. Success is doing what we love—and getting paid for it."

Julia Kagan, in the October 1985 issue of *Working Woman* magazine, reports findings of the magazine's survey of eleven thousand respondents on "Who Succeeds and Who Doesn't": "Putting career success or making big bucks ahead of such priorities as a good family life or rewarding relationship does not produce greater work successes or satisfaction." If putting work ahead of all else doesn't even produce greater *work* success and satisfaction, it certainly cannot be expected to produce greater total lifestyle success or satisfaction either. Recognizing this, an increasing number of people simply refuse to put their work first.

It turns out that the sequencing women I've interviewed who have taken years away from their careers are saying the same things about work as are millions of other Americans who have stayed in the work force but whose agendas go beyond their professions: mothers who cannot or will not leave their work entirely but who want more time with their children; fathers who parent responsibly; persons who want to phase retirement over ten or fifteen years; individuals with meaningful avocations; men and women with major community commitments.

These people are all part of a growing revolution in this country of the new order of professionals, against the old: it is a revolution of those who enjoy the *substance* of their work but seek more appropriate *forms* for it than the old male career norm permits. They are overthrowing the old hierarchical structure with its rigid schedules, insistence on conformity, and military chain of command. They are establishing new flexible models and finding it thoroughly exciting.

For any revolution to succeed, the conditions have to be right. And they are. This workplace revolution comes at a time when the country is rapidly changing from an industrial to an information society. The old industrial models appropriate for the nineteenth and early twentieth centuries are obsolete as we enter the twenty-first. Technology has taken over many jobs at all levels and in turn created and expanded others. In addition, Naisbitt and others predict that by the 1990s there will be more jobs in many fields than there will be qualified people to fill them. Job specifications are changing with the new needs: the high-paid cog is out; creativity, ingenuity, and innovation are all part of the picture of the multidimensional new age professional.

THE NEW TERMS

Once I understood that women in my sample are part of a much larger constituency of professionals working to change marketplace conditions in this society, it didn't surprise me that when I asked them to rank order the terms upon which their second-time career decisions rest, *control over my own time* far outstrips every other factor. This choice cuts across profession, location, age, and socioeconomic lines as the factor women cite as most important in their second-time-around professional decisions. It is followed by *desire to do that which is intrinsically rewarding*, a factor listed again and again by women in various professions and expressed well by a former executive who said, "This time I'm going to have to know that I'm doing something of greater significance to society than managing blueberry waffles." Money comes in only third, with prestige, power, advancement, and security all ranked of lesser concern.

Here, again, these women are on target with the findings of researchers for the general population. The same October 1985 *Working Woman* magazine study lists "to be financially secure" as only fourth among women's work motivations. Last on the list is "to accumulate great wealth," below factors such as "to help others," "to be challenged," or "to improve myself." And this survey was conducted on women who have remained *in* the work force, not those who have left careers to mother.

The terms that sequencing women develop for making their new career decisions—control over their own time and doing work they consider intrinsically rewarding—are dramatically different from those the women say influenced their initial career decisions. Then, when they were fresh out of college or professional schools and eager to imitate the men in their fields, money, prestige, and advancement up a rigidly defined ladder took top spots in their career decisions.

Now, however, their new terms are influenced by their greater maturity and involvement with their families, to be sure, but beyond that, women say that time away from their work has enabled them to separate the substance of the work itself from the forms it has taken and the environments in which they previously did their work.

Whereas initially these women accepted the career-as-central norm upon which the old-style environments are based, the second time around they reject it and instead are creating—through their own actions—a new professional agenda.

THE NEW PROFESSIONAL AGENDA

The new agenda, which an increasing number of professionals are establishing, calls for emphasis on entrepreneuring, the continued creation of many more part-time professional opportunities, and flexiplace work options. That sequencing women are in the forefront among professionals seeking and creating these opportunities is not surprising. *They are unique in that they are the first large group of professionals from a wide diversity of fields who have ever voluntarily left their professions for a period of years to live another lifestyle and to reflect upon what they have given to and gotten from their work in the past and on what they want to bring to it and derive from it in the future.*

Entrepreneuring

When the huge industrial complexes swept our nation, Americans came to accord high stature to those who joined somebody else's organization, played by its rules, and rose as high as possible. Success was measured in the number of notches one climbed up somebody else's defined ladder. But those days are fast changing. Today it's the innovator, the creator, the person with the guts to do something different than following the leader in an already defined manner who is setting standards for what constitutes success. Self-employment is in, and from all projections it seems to be here to stay for a long time. The number of self-employed Americans nearly doubled between 1970 and 1985, bringing the total to close to 11 million, and according to the U.S. Department of Labor, women now own 30 percent of American businesses. No longer is one's worth determined by the imprint of somebody else's stationery—today and for the foreseeable future there's new stature in having one's own.

Entrepreneuring is the clear choice of *nearly all* sequencing mothers I interviewed who reincorporate careers back into their lives *while they still have preschoolers*, as well as for many women who resume professional activities once their children are all in school. It's not surprising. The personality profile fits. Sequencing women who become entrepreneurs are basically leaders rather than followers, independent persons who pride themselves on doing things their own way and have confidence in their own judgments. They are often highly innovative, creative people, stifled by hierarchical structures wherein the what, when, where, and how of their work is predetermined. Self-employment is clearly their preferred option because it enables them to work on their own terms and turf: it provides flexitime and flexiplace.

Entrepreneuring is the preferred choice of the mother who wants to phase back into her professional activities gradually; she can work two hours a week or ten and doesn't have to negotiate the why, when, or where of those hours with an employer. For the woman who wants to keep a hand in her field throughout her early mothering years, entre-preneuring is the number one choice because it offers flexibility.

Entrepreneuring works equally well for the mother of older children who wants to set her own schedule, determine her own standards, and be her own boss at all times. It's for the achiever at any stage of her life, who measures her growth and development by her own yardstick, who thrives on variety, change, and challenge.

Whereas switching from working for someone else to entrepreneuring can be a financial risk for the single person or the sole family breadwinner, it's an excellent option for the sequencing woman whose husband's salary provides the family a base income. She can then build a business, clientele, practice, or series of outlets for her work over a period of years while keeping mothering as her major time priority.

Some women view their private practices or businesses as temporary. They expect to spend five or ten years growing professionally and adding to their families' incomes while their children are growing, then join another organization. But others expect to and do continue as entrepreneurs, building practices or businesses into much larger commitments as their families grow older.

As will be thoroughly illustrated throughout Chapter 13, almost every woman who really wants to can adapt her background and skills, education, and professional or administrative experience to the entrepreneurial form that best suits her. Because of the wide range of choices, many sequencing women switching careers, as well as women returning to their former fields, embrace entrepreneuring in making their second-time career decisions.

Changing the System

Notwithstanding its attractiveness for some persons under some conditions, the whole world is not switching to one-woman and one-man shows. Many women return to existing organizations, but those who do are calling for changes that provide some of the same flexibility as does self-employment; and many organizations are responding. The most sought-after changes are flexiplace work options, particularly an increase in part-time professional, administrative, and managerial opportunities.

Flexiplace Options

The new generation of professionals recognizes that a great deal of work can be done within a variety of settings, on a variety of schedules, in contrast to the old norm, which assumes that work must be done within a centralized setting on a regimented schedule.

Flexitime work options, in which employees are on forty-hour-a-week worktime modules but can choose the module, be it 7 A.M. to 3 P.M. or 10 A.M. to 6 P.M., are now well established in many major institutions and organizations in the country. But *flexiplace*, a far more important breakthrough for professionals, is just coming into its own.

Flexiplace options—working in a variety of locations at various times—are modeled on the professional lifestyle of academicians rather than on that of corporate personnel. Academicians work on their own time in a variety of places: their offices, libraries, homes, or dentist offices while they wait for their children. Since they are considered competent, trustworthy adults by their employers, nobody takes attendance. Professors meet their classes, keep office hours, and attend department meetings—but beyond that they do their class preparation, grading, research, and writing for publications wherever it best suits them.

Corporate personnel, on the other hand, have traditionally punched in and out—at all levels from file clerks to executives. Male corporate culture was modeled upon the belief that people need to be in one central location, highly visible to coworkers, to do the job well. Yet women managers, executives, and attorneys, in organizations of all kinds, maintain that in most cases, in most fields, this inflexibility is unnecessary. A corporate attorney with a major law firm says, "The truth is that 85 percent of the work done in this office by me and by all of my colleagues could be done elsewhere . . . but the men don't want to believe it."

The men and women in many offices, however, are beginning to believe it. The office no longer is the sacrosanct place it once was. According to Jack Daley, manager for corporate telecommunications of Tymshare in Cupertino, California, who directly interacts with more than one hundred flexiplace employees, "Our people are paid for *what they do, not for where they do it.* Many of our employees work from their homes, some in teams which meet only occasionally. Technology is available to enable many people in various kinds of work to do much more in the way of working in a variety of situations than they actually do; it takes the marketplace a while to catch up. Many things make us feel 'there' when we are physically apart: electronic mail, voice mail, facsimile teleconferencing, personal computers, data networks, video teleconferencing, telephone callforwarding . . . It is not necessary to know where you are; it is what you *do* that matters."

Flexiplace options, when combined with part-time work, greatly enhance opportunities for the sequencing woman who can combine work done at home with work done in the office in a flexible manner. In some instances, she can work entirely from home.

Part-Time Professionalism

The major change an increasing number of professionals in this country seek today is a reduction in the amount of time they are expected to work. Professionals are hired to do a job until it's done, not by the hour. By definition a professional position is one in which the individual assumes responsibility to get the job done to the best of his or her ability. When the professional calls for the reduced work week, it's more than a reduction of total hours—it's a change in internal and external expectations within the profession of what doing the job involves. This call for a reduced work week is not a recommendation for lowering work standards; it means reducing the amount of work while maintaining the standards.

The reason such workload reduction in professional and managerial positions is possible is that every "full-time" professional job is but a series of "part-time" jobs—project after project, client after client, patient after patient, paragraph after paragraph, strung together to make work not only full time but often never-ending. In contrast, the new professional agenda insists that the quality of the work be absolutely first-rate but that the quantity can be reduced without harming—and often greatly enhancing—the quality. By reducing the load, professionals find they can give full energy, vitality, commitment, and intellectual capabilities to their work without work overtaking their lives or burning them out. Sometimes the load can be reduced by more efficient division and delegation, other times by dividing the position into two or even three parts. Each job is different, but when an employer wants to create a part-time position she or he can almost always devise a way to do so. Very frequently the impetus comes from the potential employee. Chapter 12 details strategies women in a wide variety of professions have used to sell employers on creating exciting part-time professional, administrative, and managerial positions with growth potential for them.

Companies in which part-time professionalism is already part of the corporate culture include Merck and Company, Control Data, Ameritrust Corporation, Levi Strauss, Kaiser Foundation Health Plan, Inc., and the Travelers Insurance companies. They are a few of the companies on an increasingly long list. But the list was not always long. Until recently negative myths about part-time work were perpetuated by those with nothing else in life but their work. These myths, however, are being demolished by a new generation of professionals who have much else to do, who work part time, and who have set standards of excellence.

An article in the August 1982 issue of *Money* magazine reports on the new view: "The traditional prejudice against part-timers—the feeling that they are basically unambitious—is diminishing as experience proves otherwise . . . part-timers are just as dedicated and often more productive than their full-time coworkers."

There are four reasons for the new positive attitude toward part-time professionalism. (1) Part-time professionals are known to bring freshness, enthusiasm, and innovation to their work without burning out *and* to get more done: they rarely take sick days, generally spend no work time socializing or doing personal business, are extraordinarily dependable and reliable, and produce top results. Like any minority, they have to be better! (2) There are a large number of talented professionals who want to work but insist on doing so without sacrificing their families or other priorities to do it. (3) An increasing number of enlightened executives, owners, and managers recognize that the only way to get and keep these professionals is to accommodate to their needs. (4) Organizations around the country such as New Ways to Work in San Francisco and the Association of Part-Time Professionals in McLean, Virginia, work consistently to encourage businesses, firms, and corporations to change. The groups also provide a network of information to professionals on current work options: part-time opportunities, including job-sharing, flexitime, and flexiplace.

The number of part-time professional positions has steadily increased for the past several years, indicating a definite trend toward a changed complexion of the world of work. The *Wall Street Journal*, as early as June 1982, reported that the rate of increase of part-time work had expanded 63 percent at the higher levels since 1976 and noted that "experts believe that the trend will spread further." The article recognized retention of valuable female executives as a major reason for the increased number.

Figures of the Association of Part-Time Professionals for 1984 indicate that 2,657,000 professionals chose to work part time; more than two-thirds of them are women with families. Of the total numbers, over one-half million fall into the executive, administrative, and managerial categories. Another half million are in the health diagnosing, assessment, and treating occupations, which include physicians, pharmacists, and nurses, with more than 200,000 in health support fields, as technologists and technicians. Another half million are teachers, *excluding* college and university faculty, who account for 141,000 more. There are 37,000 part-time attorneys and judges, 24,000 engineers, 15,000 math and computer scientists, 18,000 natural scientists, and 61,000 engineering technicians.

Progress in encouraging part-time work has come from both federal and state governments. The Federal Employee Part-Time Career Employment Act of 1978 dramatically increased career part-time employment opportunities throughout the federal government. More than thirty-five state governments followed suit; the state of Massachusetts, for example, has more than 1,600 permanent part-time employees. Employers in the private sector, spurred by the increasing number of women managers and executives, are increasingly making part-time arrangements.

What does all this mean for women who take years entirely out of the work force, then want to return on a part-time basis? It means that enlightened employers throughout the country are beginning to recognize their needs and abilities and to hire and rehire them. Charles Marcy, vice-president of retail marketing for Kitchens of Saralee in Deerfield, Illinois, is one such innovator. One M.B.A. whom he recently rehired was completely out of the organization while full-time mothering for eight years, during which time she had three children, all of them now in school. Last year she began working twenty hours a week, days and times of her choice, with six weeks entirely free during the summer.

"I think you have to be realistic," Marcy says. "Look at the marketing courses in business schools across the country; they are heavily populated by women. There are a large number of women among the marketing managers in major companies in the country—they are in the age twenty-five to thirty-five range, and many of them want to participate in the traditional aspects of the adult female experience, which includes having children. Children require an incredible amount of time and effort. A way that I can see to deal with this is for women to take leaves of absence, then slowly integrate back into the work force."

Marcy believes there is a real necessity to accommodate the needs of women who need time away from their professions to mother, then want to phase back slowly: "This is one way I see for companies to be able to retain high-quality personnel. If we don't accommodate those women we accelerate turnover. While there may be some disruption in the short term, long range we can build a more stable work force and actually minimize disruption. Companies who fail to accommodate these women will wake up one day, I fear, and see that they have a major gap."

Marcy's attitude is one held by an increasing number of employers—that the years a woman will be away from work are few in comparison to the total number of years she will be with the company: "I believe we are really building something long term; the kind and amount of loyalty you build doing this is staggering."

Like Marcy, Judy Corson, partner, Custom Research

Incorporated, and member of the Young Presidents Organization and the Committee of 200, runs her company with the philosophy that "you have to go through your employees' life cycles with them—women have babies, they're out for a while, they come back, some cut down, they come back. . . . Some need to work part time for an extended period, you go through it with them because if you don't there is a tremendous amount of good talent that you lose." Corson, like Marcy, believes this attitude helps build strong loyalty. "The commitment that you build, you get back many times over," Corson says.

Marcy, Corson, and others like them are leaders in the formation of a new corporate culture: a flexible environment built upon mutual integrity and trust, with the recognition throughout the organization that a person's work is a vital part of his or her life but not its entirety. The issue of corporate culture has become the hottest one around for professionals with families, for more and more of them choose an organization by the value system it holds. And more and more men and women alike now steer clear of those organizations that retain the old, inflexible norms. They are advised to do so by such authorities as Harvard Business School professor Joseph Auerbach, who says in the April 1985 *Harvard Business School Bulletin*, "Your work should fit your life. It's terribly important to make lifestyle the principal objective. . . . If you subordinate your career to your personal predilections invariably the career will fall into place. If you do the reverse you may never achieve the personal life you want." When such a recommendation comes from a chaired professor at the Harvard

Business School, where the ninety-hour work week was invented and for years perpetuated, one knows the world is changing fast!

In all regards this new professionalism is predicated upon a value system dramatically opposed to the old one in which the yardstick of success was the size of the paycheck and the length of the title. The new yardstick measures success in broader terms: the length and totality of one's life. The unit of measure is the minute rather than the dollar. The name of the game is use of these minutes to achieve success: control over one's own time—which is one's life—to enjoy a balanced, multidimensional lifetime.

How do mothers who have already implemented this new agenda make it work? They first determine how much of their lives they will allocate to their careers at a particular period, then carefully create or select the environments in which they work to create and maintain the balance they desire.

11

Controlling One's Own Time

WHEN TO RESUME WORKING

Overwhelmingly, sequencing women elect to reemphasize careers either by changing systems to accommodate their part-time work or by becoming entrepreneurs so they are in complete control of their own time schedules. In either case, their decisions dramatically change the question, What is the best time to return to a career?, asked by women ten and even five years ago, to, How much time can I most comfortably spend on professional activities at various periods in my life? Now that sequencing women are insisting on controlling the time they spend on their work, they can be much more flexible about when they resume working. Some women take a complete break from their work for five, ten, and more years; others work a few hours a week from home after only a year or less. Precisely when a woman works again depends upon a host of variables, including the couple's financial situation, the woman's profession, her personality, interests, number, and spacing of children, whether she will become an entrepreneur or work for others, and her motivation for working.

HOW MUCH TIME TO SPEND ON A CAREER

Although there is no one right time for all women to reintegrate careers, there is strong agreement on the part of women who have already done it that *certain amounts of time* work best for professional activities at a particular period in a mother's life.

There are two main phases in the life of a full-time mother. Phase I is when she has one or more preschoolers at home—a phase that lasts less than ten years in most families today. Phase II begins when the last child enters school and ends when he leaves home.

Mothers of preschoolers who want to reemphasize their work usually find they can do so comfortably during their "time for me" (the few hours a week they take for their own endeavors) so that professional activity doesn't take mothering time, provided they limit the work to well under ten hours a week, including preparation and transportation time.

Most mothers of *school-age children* find their lives the most balanced when they work primarily during their children's school hours. They are then able to maintain their full-time mothering standards, yet enjoy professional activities as well. This usually means that their work averages twenty to twenty-five hours a week with thirty a maximum.

The major problem cited by women who incorporate professional activities back into their lives in both phases is *overestimating the amount of time they have available to work*. Thus, when a mother of preschoolers tries to work twenty to twenty-five hours a week rather than less than ten she nearly always finds that work interferes tremendously with her mothering priorities. Yet when she waits until her children are all in school to work that same amount of time, it may take all her "time for me," but it nearly always enables her to continue full-time mothering as she wishes.

Similarly, when a mother of grade-schoolers attempts full-time work, she finds her mothering time is terribly squeezed, and she has most of the same problems she experienced as a full-time careerwoman-mother the first time around: not enough time for mothering or for herself. If she defers full-time work (if that is ultimately what she wants) for a few more years, working instead around twenty to twenty-five hours a week while she has school-age children, she can continue to enjoy her mothering, while also enjoying her work. If she works more than these hours, she inevitably finds that her career is crowding in, taking over her life in ways she finds detrimental.

If reincorporating work into her life pressures her, the problem is almost always a result of the woman's working ten to fifteen hours a week *more than would be optimal given the ages of her children*, yet the result is that the woman feels intensely frustrated that her priorities and values—interrupting a full-time career to raise a family— aren't matched by the realities. An understanding of the ramifications of the timing involved is critical to career reemphasis, for it is the underpinning of the methodology of a successful reincorporation of career back into a woman's life without conflict.

CAREER REEMPHASIS FOR
THE MOTHER OF PRESCHOOLERS

Women who reemphasize a few hours a week while they have preschoolers are primarily those who felt conflicts about leaving their work in the first place or who missed their work and were anxious to resume some aspects of it. In my sample, number of years away from one's career did not seem to correlate with ease or difficulty of resuming it. For women from such diverse fields as law, accounting, corporate work, advertising, public relations, various aspects of the media, pharmacy, interior design, photography, education, nursing, and many, many others, the major determinants of smooth career reintegration were the woman's creativity, motivation, and determination in designing a flexible situation.

In looking at the women who were away from their work for less than two years and at those who were away for more than five years, those factors were the determinants of ease of reintegration of their careers, not number of years away. (Since most of the physicians I interviewed did reemphasize within the first two years, often for only half a day or two part days a week, it is impossible to judge whether more years away would have affected their ease of reemphasis.)

The majority of women in my sample who reemphasized

while they still had preschoolers became entrepreneurs, consultants, freelancers, or private contractors so they were assured of reemphasizing on their own time, and they usually allocated their "time for me" to do it. They reported feeling little loss of personal time for they perceive a reemphasis of professional activities as more relevant to their personal needs than taking the time for unstructured activity or for community or avocational pursuits.

Whether reincorporating professional activity back into her life a few hours a week when she has preschoolers constitutes a career reemphasis or whether it's "keeping a hand in while out" is completely within the realm of the perception of the individual woman. Most women today who have been totally away from their work for a period of time see it as a return to career. For instance, a Chicago area psychiatrist who sees three or four patients one afternoon a week in a mental health clinic says, "This is definitely a return to practice after two years away. I am working full-time in that this is all the time I can give to patients right now. But when I am seeing my patients I am as totally involved with each of them as when I saw five or even ten times the number of cases a week."

A Boston area woman, formerly a product manager with a major food company, who took three years away from work entirely and recently began a marketing consultantship, says, "I see this as a definite career reemphasis because I'm beginning a business which I plan to expand as my time to do so increases. I definitely see it as growth potential, not just maintenance."

Many women find reincorporating careers into their lives,

or starting to work toward new ones a limited number of hours a week, while they still have preschoolers a wonderful way to reintegrate their professions back into their lives gradually so that career reemphasis is not a major life change. It's excellent for the woman who is worried about losing certain skills if she is many years away from returning to her career. It means that whatever the field, the woman will continue to grow professionally while her primary role is raising her family. A number of case histories of women who have reincorporated careers into their lives while they still have preschoolers will follow in Chapters 12 and 13. These examples are not intended to be paradigmatic for all sequencing mothers, however, because no one model fits all.

Just as some women find reemphasizing careers while they still have preschoolers highly appropriate, others much prefer to spend their children's early years entirely away from their careers. Many women feel strongly that they *will not* attempt any career reemphasis while they have small children because they do not want outside schedules and commitments. What they need and want least in life is for anybody to invade and dilute their sequencing choice by saying, Stay home but keep career-involved while you're there. For some women—particularly dedicated work-aholics—a drop of professional activity can escalate almost overnight to a whole bottle, so they choose to spend a period of years entirely away from their work. Others find trying to merge two paces unacceptable.

A woman who tried to return part time to her human resources post when her son was two years old, then left again within a few months, expresses the reason many mothers elect no Phase I career reemphasis when she says, "I found how different the rhythm of being in a workplace is from being with children. The more hours I worked away from home, the more convinced I became that trying to make both those rhythms work every day was a monumental task. When I don't have to continually be some place at a specific time my son has more of a sense that I have plenty of time for him. And I think that children need that sense of their importance in your life."

Other women, however, see their years at home with preschoolers as a period during which incorporating work back into their lives to a very limited extent does not detract from the rhythm of their mother-child relationship but can become part of that rhythm.

Women who elect to sequence are developing models that encompass both points of view. For *the definition of sequencing is leaving a career for full-time mothering, then reintegrating the career into one's life so that it complements rather than conflicts with one's other priorities.* Therefore, for some women the model is *full-time career, then full-time mothering, then career reemphasis while there are preschoolers and an increase in career activity when children enter school.* For other women the model is *full-time career, then full-time mothering, followed by career reemphasis when all children are in school and an increase in career activity as children grow older.* (The word "increase" is intended to provide option. For some women it means full-time work again, for others who prefer not to work full time it simply means more work but not necessarily forty, fifty, or sixty hours a week.) It is crucial that women contemplating the sequencing option, as well as those sequencing women presently in the process of deciding when to reintegrate careers into their lives, recognize that there is more than one way to do so.

I can identify from personal experience both with women who want to reintegrate careers while they have preschoolers as well as with those who very much want *not* to do so until their children are older. I was a Phase I mother for thirteen years. In my first seven mothering years—until Rachel, our second daughter, was four years old—the activities I enjoyed in addition to my little girls were community or avocational, and then in limited amounts.

Then, when I was expecting Rebecca, and forever after she was born, writing professionally—a new direction I took while home-based—also became part of my life. I managed to write during her naptimes or very quiet play times, when the older girls were gone, so that it would not encroach upon time with any of the children. For instance, every morning when the two older girls packed their lunchboxes, then left for school, Rebecca, emulating the "big kids," packed juice and crackers in a lunchbox and went to her "school," an area in one corner of the dining room where she had a table and chair, toys, and books. I sat next to her, my typewriter on the dining room table, writing and counting—for as her thirty-seventh book or toy went out the "window" of her "school," usually about thirty-seven minutes after she began to play there, I knew it was time to cover my typewriter. Then the rest of the day—exclusive of her abbreviated naptimes, when I'd edit what I'd written and make notes for the next morning's revisions—we were together. To some people thirty-seven minutes a day would be a frustrating way to write, think, or research, but it's actually less hectic and frequently less deadlined than a newsroom. That I wrote an entire book in two and one-half years at that pace was a tremendous learning experience for me. For I saw that I could create a large project with no externally imposed deadline, break it into small chunks, work at each piece, and, even in incredibly short time segments, complete a major task without blocking a year out of my life to do it.

I wholly enjoyed the period when Miriam and Rachel were preschoolers and I had no career considerations, and I equally but differently enjoyed the period when I wrote for a short while each day when Rebecca was young, then was with her (and the older girls when they came home) the rest of the time. I cannot say that one period was better than the other for me—I was happy in each in its own time. Nor can I say that I was any more or any less an involved mother when I wrote each day than when I did not. Had I been drawn to writing when Miriam and Rachel were preschoolers as I was later, I could certainly have spent a few hours a week at the typewriter with no detriment to them or to myself.

I wholly support the complete absence of career considerations when one's children are preschoolers, and simultaneously support a limited career reemphasis for women who want it during that period, because I know firsthand that it is possible if a woman moderates it carefully. Moderation is clearly the key. That sequencing mothers of preschoolers work less than ten hours a week is more than a suggestion from those of us who have tried it both ways: it's the golden rule of enjoying both one's children and one's work to the fullest while being pressured by neither.

CAREER REEMPHASIS FOR THE MOTHER OF SCHOOL-AGE CHILDREN

Whether or not they elect a career reemphasis while they have preschoolers, many women resume careers or begin serious reemphasis explorations when the last child begins to attend full days of school. Whereas the woman who initially left her work with certainty may wait until her youngest child is nine, ten, or older to reemphasize her career or explore a new direction, the woman who originally experienced greater conflict and who often remains more career-concerned throughout her preschoolers' years is sometimes out the door with her last child. In either case, a mother of school-age children has twenty to twenty-five discretionary hours a week, eight or nine months a year (exclusive of children's sick days) when her children are not with her.

This becomes a critical choice point, for most women who have not already reemphasized their careers consider doing so—or do so—at this juncture in their lives. Since her children are gone more than half the day, a woman has to decide whether she will be gone the total day to return to a full-time position outside the home and its concomitant scheduling demands. To do so is to face many of the same problems that she faced when she left her career in the first place: she will miss being with her children after school, on school release days and holidays, during winter, spring, and summer vacations, which total three to four months per year; she will have to take sick leave on their sick days or make contingency arrangements; and she will have to greet them each day by telephone rather than in person. In short, the price of a full-time career at this point is that a woman has to forgo participatory mothering as she has known it to become a managerial mother instead.

The vast majority of the mothers I interviewed are not willing to do this. Interestingly, many originally experienced great conflict; they had invested so much in their careers that they wondered how they could afford to leave their work. But now, having invested comparable time in their children, they value the close relationships they have developed with them. They feel that sharing after school and school vacation time with them is of prime importance, and in addition, knowing what a full-time career demands, they don't want to be so pressured by work that their children get short shrift.

Some mothers consider it as critical to be home with their grade-school and adolescent children after school as to be there during the day with babies and toddlers. Dr. Eleanor Paradise, a Cambridge, Massachusetts, clinical psychologist and mother of two grade-schoolers, builds her professional schedule around her children's school hours. Paradise says, "There comes a point when after school group care is simply unacceptable for a child. Leaving a child by himself means 'you have to stay inside, you can't go out and ride your bike, you can't have a friend over.'

It's not reasonable or fair; hiring a qualified substitute is very difficult; who else is going to really listen to your children, drive them to lessons, supervise their outdoor and indoor play with friends?"

Ruby Dorman, mother of a fifteen-year-old daughter and two preschoolers, who left her computer management position at great sacrifice to the family budget, says an adolescent has "a different kind of need but as important a need for a mother to be home as do preschoolers. An adolescent doesn't reach out to a parent all of the time—and so the times when they are willing, it's crucial that you are there to hear what they have to say, to respond, and to give advice. If you aren't available, are too preoccupied with your work, it's sure that they will reach out to somebody else, and who will that somebody be, what will their values be?"

An internationally known authority on child development, Harvard Medical School professor T. Berry Brazelton, makes the point even more bluntly. "Parents who don't supervise adolescents these days are out of their heads," he states in an October 1985 *U.S. News and World Report* interview.

The sequencing mother who holds similar views usually finds that working during times that basically correspond to her children's school hours can enable her to continue full-time mothering while reincorporating professional activities as well. It can theoretically provide a very balanced life. In actuality, however, I know from my own experience as well as from my interviews that if a woman tries to work during *all* of her children's school hours, as I have done from time to time during the past decade, she can lose almost as much balance as if she tried to work full time. I've found it's far better to work during many, even most, of their school hours—as I have moderated myself to do for the most part—but not during *all* of them. The difference is tremendously significant. That's because we are talking about more than just the allocation of a woman's physical presence and mental energies; we are talking also about the allocation of emotional energy. If every bit of one's emotional as well as physical energy goes into either work or mothering, the burnout potential is tremendous.

The reason is that when one becomes increasingly involved in professional activities one uses a great deal of mental and emotional energy, and, simultaneously, mothering begins to take an increasing amount of psychic energy as children (and mothers) get older. Mothering hours are different as children grow, but the hours don't diminish in number as much as one would think. Only the times change. Since a mothering day with school-age children doesn't begin in earnest until two or three in the afternoon, a mother often thinks she can easily pack all the morning and early afternoon hours with professional activity. But if she does that without realizing that mothering hours may extend until her own bedtime, she can become as tired, frustrated, and desirous of time away from work and family as does the career mother who works full time.

Because women who elect to work during their children's school hours largely select their own schedules, women in most professions find that they can as well work twenty hours a week as thirty if they establish that schedule from the first. Since they are effectively working part-time or reduced schedules anyway, the key is to recognize at the onset that they may not wish to fill all of their available hours with work.

TRANSITION TIME

The mother of school-age children can consider both her work and her family as "time for me" in the fullest sense if she allocates at least an hour of transition time for rest, exercise, reading a book, or having tea with a friend between her work and family time. This transition time is critical for the woman who is doing two jobs: mothering and working outside the home. The full-time careerwoman-mother desperately needs this time and rarely gets it because she generally must dash right home from the office to have dinner with her family. A major value of balancing one's life through working part time is having even a little transition "time for me" between work and the first child's rush through the front door.

A physician who works mornings in an HMO says, "I see patients and make hospital rounds mornings only. That is the beauty of a large organization—there are others to cover so I never have to feel guilty about my patients. I know they are seen when I cannot see them. My children are in school until three o'clock so I could work two-thirds time, but that would stretch me beyond what I can very comfortably do. This way I have time to come home and change hats, so to speak." A therapist with a busy practice and lecture schedule makes a similar point: "I see my last patient at one in the afternoon instead of two or three. One or another of my kids is home by 3:30 and I like to be there first, not only to greet him but to read the morning paper and unwind. Sometimes I take a walk. Whenever it is, I like at least an hour and preferably more, when I am not either seeing patients, dictating, or in the car, to relax myself before I'm with the family for the rest of the day."

From my own experience, I recognize that although the mother of school-age children who works part time often does not take time for lunch, she may want to try to arrange at least one coffee or tea "transition break" time with a friend each week. My greatest regret since my children have all been in school is that I've lost regular contact with dear friends who resumed working when their children began school. Now, when we are home we are all busy with our children and have no time in our days for the casual visits we used to have with one another during sandbox days. Many women I've interviewed told me the same thing. Though it's not possible to maintain every friendship, it's important to take pains to keep room in one's life for the friends who matter the very most. During the first or second year back working it may not seem too important, but five and ten years out one realizes that irreplaceable friendships need nurturing so they don't drift.

However a woman of school-age children structures her day when she reincorporates professional activities, most do so with the realization that their presence and participation in their children's lives is of as great importance to their grade-schoolers and adolescents as it is to their preschoolers.

Clearly, sequencing women want to be there when their

children are there; and clearly many of them so greatly value controlling their own time that they do not want to return to a situation in which their lives are dictated by somebody else's organizational schedule. Therefore, in re-emphasizing their careers, most of the sequencing women I interviewed create or negotiate flexible, less than full-time professional situations either through self-employment or by effecting changes in existing organizations. Because there are few role models, these women are setting new trends. The following two chapters will explore what they are doing and how they are doing it.

12

Changing the System

There is no guidebook telling women how to reincorporate careers flexibly into their lives after years of full-time mothering, so women who sequence are writing their own. The second time around they want a great deal from their work: challenge, growth potential, and personal satisfaction, in addition to money, all within a time frame that does not compromise time with their children.

In part, the strategies used by women who want to change the system to allow them to work more flexibly on a part-time basis are identical to those used by women who want to rejoin it and work full time. In both instances, the woman should *first* investigate a variety of possibilities by contacting former colleagues and employers, as well as friends she has made through professional organizations, alumni organization contacts, and others who might be helpful resources to let them know that she is available to work again and to see what opportunities they can suggest and what introductions they can make. *Second*, she should target the types of position she most wants. *Third*, she should tailor her résumé accordingly, highlighting those facets of her background that most apply to the work she now seeks. In addition to her education and career experience, she will include those activities she has been involved in while away from her work that apply: community participation, new interests, experiences that have direct bearing (a former executive with a leading food company gained new perspectives on food merchandising during the years she shopped with her children; a developmental psychologist returned to her career after seven years of full-time mothering with a broadened view on numerous theories of early childhood development, plus a number of her own). *Fourth*, before she begins interviewing, she should be certain she has current knowledge about the field by reading and talking extensively with others in the profession. *Finally*, before accepting a position, she should carefully examine the potential for continued growth and challenge, as well as the visibility it will provide in her field at large.

Initially, the woman who is willing to join an organization has a greater number of opportunities than the woman who wants to change it, for the woman who joins it simply has to convince the employer she is the best possible person to fill his present needs. If a woman has kept up with her field, in both contacts and information, securing a full-time job at a comparable level to that which she left is not much more difficult than changing jobs when one is working full time in the field.

As the illustrations throughout the rest of the book will

indicate, sequencing women in fields from administration to medicine have found that getting full-time job offers is far less difficult than getting part-time ones. In the words of Diane Rothberg, founder and director of the Association of Part-Time Professionals, a national organization based in McLean, Virginia, "It's more difficult to get a part-time position at a good level than full time, there's no question about it." Except in highly progressive organizations and certain locales, flexible job situations are simply not out there waiting. Because the vast majority of sequencing women want them, it's up to the woman herself to create the position through her own initiative, imagination, creativity, and motivation.

For the woman who wants to change a system, the process of getting a position she wants requires much more effort than if she were simply joining the system; but the women who have done it say that the extra effort is worthwhile. Not only will the woman who wants a part-time position need to take the five steps discussed above, which she would take if she were going back full-time, but, in addition, she needs to target organizations in which she believes she can either *adapt an existing position* or *create and sell a new one*. She can then gear her search strategies to them.

ADAPTING AN EXISTING POSITION

An increasing number of women reemphasize their careers by adapting an existing position to meet their needs. There are two main ways in which they do this: either by volun-

tarily paring down a full-time job to a part-time position
through an analysis and reshuffling of the components, or
by sharing a job with a partner.

Voluntary Job Paring

Forty-three-year-old Isobel Wilder sits with me in her spacious Evanston, Illinois, office, removes her red suit jacket,
and tells me how she launched an all-out search strategy for
the foundation directorship she now holds, a position that
she says "gives me autonomy, challenge, and flexibility."
A manager in a large Chicago manufacturing company
before she left when her first son was born, Wilder explains
that she wanted to return to comparable executive-level
work when her second son began school eight years later:
"I was happy at home while they were home all day, but
once they weren't there I was itching to get back to work.
The only thing is, as much as I wanted to work during their
school hours, I wanted even more to be home when they
came home in the afternoons. It seemed crazy to me to sit
around home all day to fill my time with stuff I didn't
really want to do in order to be home at three, rather than
working at a meaningful job. But the good jobs were all
full time. What was so frustrating was that I recognized that
with proper organization many of the positions *could* be
tailored to my hours and needs. I started searching for the
position which would offer me the most autonomy, so I
could pare it down. But that was not the only requisite. My
other requirements were visibility, challenge, and a chance
to make high-level contacts for future reference.

"I looked for over a year and was frequently discouraged. There were jobs which seemed so right but where they wouldn't cut the time; then there were more flexible jobs, but they weren't challenging enough. So I just doggedly kept at it and finally found this directorship, which is perfect for me. I waited until I had the offer in hand, then asked for a week to decide, during which time I told the board I would thoroughly investigate the inner workings of the organization, interview present and past staff, as well as talk with both contributors to the foundation and directors of the arts projects we fund. At the end of the week I accepted the position with one proviso: the former director had spent a lot of his time trying to educate the art groups to stay in the black. I proposed that instead of my doing it, I hire an educational director to work fifteen hours a week, report to me, and teach business techniques to these artists. I pointed out that I could then cut my hours down and use my return salary to fund the new post. I said I could be in the office early and leave every day before 2:30, that I'd sometimes attend evening functions presented by the groups we fund to get a feeling for what they really do with the money. So the board saw that I intended to take the position really seriously, not that I wanted just to punch in and out. I told them that alternatively I could keep my full salary and leave the office mid-afternoon anyway, using callforwarding and working the rest of the time from home, but that I much preferred officially paring the hours of the position and hiring the educational director.

"There was no real opposition to my proposal, other than that a couple of people on the board wanted to be sure if *they* needed me for any reason I'd be accessible. I assured them that I could always arrange to meet at their convenience but, in general, since most of my job would be spent dealing with people who want something from me badly that those people can fit their schedules to mine.

"I've been working a year and a half now and I frankly don't think anyone considers that I work 'part-time.' My secretary tells anyone who calls after I leave mid-afternoon that I'm out of the office and I'll get back to them the next day."

The strategy Wilder used—waiting until she had her offer firmly in hand before negotiating changes—is recommended by many career counselors. By that time the employer had settled on Wilder as the best person for the job, whereas if she had suggested those changes early in an interview, he might have been prejudiced against making her an offer.

Some career strategists contend, however, that even the time the job is offered is too soon to negotiate scheduling. They advocate taking the job full time, working for close to a year, then, once the woman has become an established, valuable insider, proposing ways to pare down the position. Career counselors who advocate this method have in mind the person who is currently working full time in the field and wants to switch jobs. For such people, an extra year of full-time work may not matter much, whereas for a sequencing mother who wants to maintain the continuity she has established with her children, a year of full-time work is a year too many, especially when there are no guarantees. If, after a year, the request to pare the job to part time is denied, the woman is stuck with either continuing to work full time or with searching for another job, which she would then propose paring down from the first. So for the sequencing mother, Wilder's method of paring at the beginning, even though it carries the risk of losing the job altogether, still seems the better approach.

Wilder's proposal is one of a variety of plans used by women who have pared positions. Others include doing the job in less time and leaving when it's done, which is often accomplished by maximum efficiency while there, working through lunch, and taking minimal other breaks; delegating pieces of the job to other personnel; or a combination. In these cases, as well as in the option Wilder chose, the most important factor in job paring is autonomy. The fewer people a woman reports to and the more she directs the way the organization runs, the freer she is to define the job's parameters and scheduling.

The concept of job paring, whether it's in a position one already holds or in negotiating a new position, falls under the heading of V-Time (voluntary reduced work time). This time-income trade-off arrangement allows employees to reduce work hours in exchange for some of their pay. According to Barbara Moonen and Barney Olmsted in their publication *V-Time: A New Way to Work*, the state of California passed the Reduced Time Act in 1980, which allows state employees to initiate V-Time. The state of New York has followed suit with a two-year project that permits state employees to elect reduced work schedules. This seems to be the beginning of a trend of states legislating for their employees what is already operative in various elements of the private sector: the voluntary trading of money back to the employer in exchange for time.

Job Sharing

Job sharing is far more than a strategy for getting a permanent professional position with growth potential, although it is that, too. Donald C. Lum, executive vice-president of Pfizer International, states in *The Complete Guide to Job Sharing* that job sharing is "a significant breakthrough in that it allows employers to think in terms of full-time positions without thereby precluding part-time opportunities for employees."

The notion of job sharing—two persons sharing the same position and splitting the hours and the responsibilities in a variety of ways—is not new. In the early 1970s it looked as if this was the way many women would combine their mothering and professional activities. But for years not much seemed to change. Now, however, it is clear that much has changed programmatically as well as individually, and job sharing has blossomed as a major way for a variety of Americans to merge personal and professional needs.

New Ways to Work in San Francisco is in large part responsible. This organization specializes in promoting job sharing to corporations, hospitals, and firms as well as in educating individuals on the best ways to approach and begin the shared position. Suzanne Smith and Barney Olmsted, founders and directors of New Ways to Work, are the authors of the now classic *Job Sharing Handbook* as well as excellent books on the how-tos of job sharing in education and health care. These books provide models of corporations, hospitals, and firms in which job sharing is already an established practice, model contracts between employers and job sharers, sample résumés, and advice to sharers on selecting and working with a mate. They show that job sharing is becoming paradigmatic profession by profession as in each it is viewed as a legitimate, acceptable, and sensible way for more and more people both to live and to work.

There is literally no field today in which job sharing is impossible. In many fields it's not only possible but actual. Practicing physicians across the country job share, as do apprentice physicians. Stanford Medical School innovated a shared internship program in 1978; Harvard followed with its shared residency program. Personnel directors and public relations and advertising personnel job share at all levels; many tax analysts, auditors, architects, managers at a variety of levels, and college and career counselors at all levels, are job sharers and have already paved the way for others.

Job sharing can be an excellent way for the woman who sequences to reincorporate her profession back into her life. Two mothers with children of different ages and needs can decide upon a schedule that suits them both and change that schedule as necessary. Another mother is not the only potential teammate. Frequently a mother teams with an older or a young person who wants to job share for a reason different from parenting.

An employment counselor job split in Connecticut is composed of two women—Anne Bennett, who at age fifty-eight is phasing into retirement, and Suzanne Plimpton, who at thirty-seven, after eight years out with two children, is phasing back into her counseling career. According to Plimpton, "This is perfect because by the time Anne is ready for retirement I may want the position full time. Or I may want to continue the present setup with a new partner. I feel I have a wonderful deal because it's the part-time situation I need now coupled with the certainty for more time or full time if I want it later."

On occasion a woman teams up with a spouse. There are a number of job-sharing professors in the country, including a wife-husband team of historians who came to the University of Minnesota on the condition that they share one position while their three children were small. Several years later each accepted a separate position in their department. A number of husband and wife therapist teams in the country job share, as do physician, attorney, and pharmacist couples. Job sharing has even hit the clergy, with a couple who are rabbis in California.

The post of city attorney in Palo Alto, California, is currently shared by two women. New York City recently instituted a pilot program in which more than a dozen attorneys pair to share positions. Public health nurses, staff nurses, and head nurses across the country job share, as do educators teaching in all fields and grade levels from kindergarten through doctoral programs.

I was first exposed to the job split at close range nearly a decade ago by the first grade teachers at our neighborhood school. Pioneering the idea of job splitting in the system, these women were both experienced teachers. One had school-age children and wanted to teach mornings, then jog home, relax, and be refreshed when her children got home from school in mid-afternoon. The other wanted to teach while her son was in an afternoon nursery school.

One taught from 8:30 to 11:30; the other came at 11:30 and taught from 12:00 to 3:00 after meeting with her teammate for half an hour while the children were at lunch. Teaching only three hours at a time rather than six meant that neither woman was exhausted at the end of the day. Each taught her own special areas of interest and expertise: for one it was reading, which she taught during her morning time. For the other it was science, and her innovative science projects were a highlight of each afternoon's activities.

Although employers still generally perceive that they need employees in single positions, it is now common for a team of two to seek to fill a position, with a joint résumé listing combined education, positions held, and functions performed. In many cases, there is no way that a single applicant can compete with a team that has done twice as much, had twice the experience, and possesses twice the expertise. Thus employers are becoming more and more open to hiring a duo, recognizing that they can nearly always count on greater depth and breadth of experience, productivity, and reliability (literally no absenteeism because they cover for each other) than from a single employee. Therefore, a growing number of employers are finding it worthwhile to make whatever limited managerial accommodations might be necessary to hire the pair, includin prorating benefits, which is routinely done in job-sharing positions across the country.

Although job sharing is best suited to the person who can work well as a team member, no woman who wants to reincorporate her career back into her life should disregard that avenue without a thorough investigation of its possibilities for her. She can read the general publications as well as those pertaining to her field, visit or telephone one of the organizations that promotes job sharing, and talk to people who are doing it to gain understanding of both the benefits and the pitfalls. That way she can get ideas from those who are already involved in the job-sharing process and develop a few new ones besides. Job sharing, like any other work arrangement, carries its own set of potential problems (such as competition between partners, need to share equally in both praise and criticism, and need to stay abreast of the other's work so that colleagues don't feel there is buck-passing). But job sharing is the only part-time strategy to date that guarantees one committed to working limited hours access to any full-time position available in the field.

DESIGNING AND SELLING A NEW POSITION

Designing and selling a new position is extremely popular today among women who sequence; it requires that the woman herself define what she would do for a particular organization, then show it that it needs her to do it. This is a form of intrapreneuring, the fastest-growing form of decentralized management in firms around the country today. It provides a woman with the flexibility she would have as an entrepreneur along with the added advantage of a guaranteed salary and usually prorated benefits as well.

To design and sell a position, a woman has to define clearly her objectives and evaluate thoroughly her own areas of strength. Otherwise, she tends to look solely at what she did before as *the* way to work, thereby severely limiting her range of options. Carol Kanarek, founder and partner in Kanarek and Shaw Consulting Services of Manhattan, an attorney who counsels other attorneys on career options and author of a book for the American Bar Association on part-time work, finds the concept of recognizing a wide variety of options one of the hardest to teach people: "I try to counsel people who want flexible working conditions out of litigation, an area in which there are already too many lawyers, and into areas such as tax, ERISA, immigration, probate, specialties where there isn't already an oversupply.

"Law is a fabulous degree to have because of the many available options other than the direct practice of law," Kanarek says, "but people don't hand it to you. You have to figure out *how your law background will benefit somebody else and sell it to them.* It can be a tremendously flexible degree if people see it that way; but too often they're locked into the notion of equating a law degree with practicing law within a huge organization. The truth is that only 5 percent of lawyers practice in major firms, although the articles you read always make it seem as if everyone is."

What Kanarek finds true of law, women in most other fields find true of their own specialties: medicine is more than practicing in a large group; management is more than filling a slot in a tremendous hierarchical system. Whatever her field, a woman who wants to work under conditions that contribute to a balanced lifestyle needs to recognize a multiplicity of possible courses of action so that she can create the most desirable position for herself.

Once she examines all her options, she can use one of three strategies for selling a new position for herself: (1) return to a former company in a new position, (2) sell skills she gained in a large company to a smaller one, and (3) sell from the strength of a specialty.

Gretchen Nyman, Angela Judapher, and Jennifer Markek are among the new breed of corporate sequencers who sold the new positions they wanted to existing organizations. Each wanted a challenging position in which she would have control over her own time; none was willing to settle for "just a job"—each wanted to grow professionally.

Each of these women had previously worked for a large company for more than five years, and each was well on her way up the ladder within her respective organization when she left it to raise her family. Each has returned to a position of her choice through the strategy of targeting her abilities to needs she knew existed in her former organization.

Returning to a Former Organization
in a New Capacity

Gretchen Nyman radiates energy. At three in the afternoon she sits in her kitchen, *Wall Street Journal* spread out on the table, talking with me, as she waits for the school bus to deposit her three sons, ages six through nine. Nyman has already gotten her children off to school, spent four hours in her office, and now has a busy afternoon ahead umpiring a softball game in which her oldest boys are playing.

Nyman left an executive-level position with a Minneapolis-based Fortune 500 company in 1975 without thought of her eventual return, yet in 1984 she was back with the company in what she terms "a very favorable spot." Nyman created that spot through careful research of the company's present needs, coupled with an evaluation of the type and amount of work she felt she could best do at this stage in her life. "When I left to have my first baby I was at a management level that necessitated sixty to seventy hours a week on the job. The rule was either you come back full time or you don't come back. But now the younger executives have replaced the old guard and are progressive thinkers; they realize that time out to raise a family is the way women are going, and they are going with us." Nyman, one of the University of Minnesota's first female M.B.A.'s in the early 1970s, is as astute as she is energetic. She kept contact with two of her former colleagues throughout her years away. Both of them are now in the upper echelons of management. "We'd talk now and again," she says, "get together with spouses occasionally, once in a while meet for lunch. Whenever we did they'd always ask 'Are you ready to come back yet?' and my stock answer given in corporate language was 'I'm happy in my present position right now; it's a highly responsible post in which I've invested a tremendous amount and I'm not ready to move from it.'

"But as my youngest son was nearing school age I saw that when he began I could keep my present position and add to it besides. So whenever I talked with my former colleagues I felt them out on new directions they'd like to see the company take, what kinds of changes they wanted to make. When I was ready to return to work I called one of them and asked to meet with him. I told him that I'd deduced from conversations that he had several major projects on the back burner but nobody in the company at a high enough level with enough free time to tackle them. I told him I felt that I was the perfect person to take on those projects because I knew the company, knew him and many of the other executives, and I could work well with them. I explained that I was excited about the projects and wanted to work—but on my own time. He was enthusiastic. We talked at length several times to work out details. What we arrived at is that I am special projects director reporting directly to him and one of the three senior vice-presidents. My work is interesting and challenging because it takes me into all divisions of the company. Because of my flexible schedule, I feel I've got exactly the balance I want in my life."

For Nyman, the balance means being able to continue full-time mothering. "I leave home after my children leave for school, and I'm always home before they are in the afternoon, which is a great advantage of my situation. If one of them has a problem when he comes in from school he doesn't have to wait until seven at night to make an appointment to talk with me.

"My life is very full now, but it's not impossible. I am

certainly glad that I waited until my kids were in school. If I'd have done this five or even three years ago it wouldn't have been fun at all—I'd have given up a tremendous amount with my boys, work would have been a pressure and a rush every day."

Even now, Nyman says that adding a twenty-hour work week outside the family to her life means she is "economizing my energies in other areas. Although I've preserved my time with the children, I've cut out my volunteer activities except those that pertain to the children, I stopped the piano lessons I so enjoyed, and I see fewer friends."

The economizing of energies of which Nyman speaks is the trade-off she is willing to make so she can work again. She will not trade time with her children. She will, however, trade most of her community activities, an avocation she enjoyed, and even some of her friendships. But Nyman feels the trades are well worth it. "Professionally I'm just where I want to be right now. Personally, I feel I have the best of both worlds. I have a challenging job with growth potential. I don't know what the future will bring, but I have some very definite plans in mind, and because I've always been a first, I am not too worried about implementing them. My plan is to continue to do an excellent job on the special projects I'm assigned, as well as those I'm beginning to generate. Then, in a few years, I plan to design a management segment for myself—based on what I'm learning now—with my own budget and personnel. Since I'll be in charge I'll be able to continue working on my own time. I can only suspect that a dozen years from now, when my children are all in college, if there still is line management

I will be in a very favorable place, one I'll probably achieve as a result of my contributions from this, or another, staff position. If it's all intrapreneurial—which I suspect it will be—then I'll run a top division. The main thing is that I am now utilizing my professional skills, all of which came back as if I'd only been gone for a short vacation, 'like riding a bike.' I'm working within the corporate environment and doing it on my own time schedule. Nine years ago I would not have believed such a thing was possible."

Nyman's situation is exciting, but it is not unique. I interviewed other women who, like her, returned to their former organizations in new capacities, essentially through using Nyman's type of strategy of creating a new niche. Angela Judapher, a research and development scientist who returned to her former pharmaceutical manufacturing company after three years away, initially came back several times a year, for a couple of weeks each, for peak projects, began suggesting project ideas to her employer, and ultimately became a permanent employee on her own terms: she works five hours a day and selects her own projects. Jen Markek, a former product manager, moved back into a large food manufacturing firm in a new role, through researching the competition and coming to see former colleagues there with a new marketing proposal. They asked her first to direct and implement that project, then another, and after seventeen months rehired her for the new product planning team, a permanent part-time post created for and by her, and she is in line for potential promotion to the director of product planning spot.

Nyman, Judapher, Markek, and many others across the

country have created these situations because they have the imagination and innovative abilities to see a career as more than merely a path up one single hill. They have been able to look ahead rather than behind to design a career course for themselves that enables them to live whole, balanced lives.

Selling Skills Learned in a Large Organization to a Smaller One

Irma Fredericks, vice-president of finance for a small Boston area manufacturing company, custom designed her career reemphasis using a strategy which Manhattan-based career counselor Carol Kanarek recommends to the attorneys she advises: "Take the skills you learn with a large, inflexible firm, then sell them to a smaller firm where you will have more control." Fredericks, who left her post as a financial analyst for a major corporation six years ago to mother her two children, decided that now that her children are six and eight, she wanted to work again but not for her former company. "I wasn't about to sell my soul a second time."

Her search strategy was to assess her most salable skills, then target the companies that needed them. Fredericks's prime skill was financial management; she searched for small and medium-sized companies without financial divisions, then wrote to presidents of nine companies for which she felt she could implement and run a financial divsion that would increase profits. She attached an extensive functional résumé to her letter and called each president the following week. Six agreed to interview her. "I bypassed personnel departments, which are set up to hire existing positions, and went directly to the top, where I knew if they were interested at all that I would get an audience for my new ideas," Frederick says. "In the end, I had two firm opportunities and selected the one which appeared to me to offer not only the most flexibility but also the best growth and visibility in my field so that if I'm not permanently satisfied I'll be in good position to make a move later on.

"I work every day from nine to two, meeting with bank people, with my staff, once a week meeting with the company president, dictating to my secretary, seeing anybody else who needs to be seen. I have such latitude in scheduling because I'm in a position not only of much greater autonomy than I was before but, as importantly, I'm not constantly interrupted with employee problems because in this size company, I have fewer people reporting to me.

"My new post changed the operating policy of the entire company in that they never had a part-time person at the executive level, though they have subsequently hired another. I am very happy with my arrangement—the work is challenging and dovetails very well with the rest of my life. I'm home from the office every day well before the children are. My husband and I both sing in a community choir one night a week; this is something which, had I gone back to work full time, I would have felt necessary to give up. If I didn't get home until after six, I wouldn't leave again at seven for choir practice or that would be a day where I would never see the children. But this way I'm retaining not only my family time but also some time for me."

Nobody handed Fredericks her position; it never would have appeared in the want ads. Rather, Fredericks constructed her own new career course. She used her experience with the large, inflexible organization in which she worked before leaving for mothering as a valuable apprenticeship rather than a path to which she felt bound to return. She took what was most valuable to her from that experience—the managment and problem-solving techniques learned from top-flight colleagues and supervisors. She left behind what she found detrimental—the inflexibility of management and its concomitant expectations for long hours and work done on site, which were unacceptable to her mothering priorities. She parlayed the valuable assets she gained with her former company coupled with her own abilities into a package which she offered a smaller, more flexible firm: she would design and run a finance department that would enable the entire company to increase profits. She designed the job specifications to provide her with maximum autonomy so that she can work a limited number of hours a week, can work either in the company office or in her home, and reports only to the company president. Fredericks accomplished this by clearly defining her background, abilities, and skills. Then she targeted the form of organization she believed would be most receptive to them and launched an extensive search for a company that would offer her the challenge and flexibility she wanted. She was sure that she would have a highly autonomous situation with growth potential before signing on.

Margaret Perkins used a similar strategy. She parlayed

skills she developed in a major New York public relations firm into a flexible position with a smaller company to which she sold the need for an in-house public relations department with herself as the twenty-five-hour-a-week director. Lillian Mead, a human resource specialist who headed the personnel department of a major firm before leaving seven years ago to mother her two children, sold the skills and techniques she'd developed to a small "head-hunting" firm when she decided to resume her career on a limited time basis to correspond with her children's school hours. In each of these instances, the woman carefully assessed her skills, targeted companies that she believed needed those resources, then sold a company on what she could do for it—on her own time schedule.

As the following illustration will indicate, the strategies of selling a new position are not limited to women in business but apply equally well to women in a variety of professions. What's important is that a woman clearly delineate her own strengths and as clearly define what form of organization would best profit from them. Then she can approach an organization with the thesis that she sees it needs a job done and she is uniquely qualified to do it.

When selling the idea for a new or special position to a firm or organization, a woman can make a strong case for working fifteen, twenty, or twenty-five hours a week. Since the position is new and possibly experimental, less time is often easier to sell. It's important that when a woman initially tries to sell the idea of the new post she show very clearly how she can do the job within the time frame of the hours she suggests, what the cost to the firm would be for her salary, prorated benefits, need for support staff, and so on, and what the payoff would be to the organization. Her challenge is selling the firm on its need for *her* to do a *particular job*.

Selling from Specialty Strength

Whatever a woman's general field, having a specialty can help immeasurably in selling a new position. Pamela Jacobs, a Los Angeles area internist, found a full-time career incompatible with her mothering values, and after two years of full-time mothering she found that not working at all was incompatible with her professional needs. She sold a new position from the strength of her subspecialty to effect what she terms "an ideal situation for my life. But it took nearly a year to do," she says.

Jacobs, now a mother of two grade-schoolers, says, "When I was going through medical school in the early seventies, women doctors just assumed that we would not let marriage and children 'get in the way' of our careers. So I worked full time after my first daughter was born. However, I saw I was missing too much so I took off work entirely when the second one came.

"I was home virtually full time for a couple of years, helping out a day here or there in an office with overload as as needed. Then I began to feel the need to see patients on a regular basis. I looked for a permanent part-time situation, but I came up against a tremendous amount of resistance, even from partnerships and firms which had asked me to help out, where it was clear to all of us that they needed more help. But their mind-sets were toward full time. Finally, I convinced a group of internists that I could benefit their practice through my subspecialty of hematology and joined them. I worked only two half days per week by choice until my children began school. Now I work an additional full day besides. I am in the office fifteen or sixteen hours a week and spend another few hours on the rounds I make when I have patients in the hospital. I make university grand rounds once a week, I'm on call one weekend a month and one night a week. My husband is always home at these times so that he covers the family while I cover the practice.

"Now that my children are full time in school, I could conceivably take on a larger patient load and be in the office more, every day until three o'clock, for instance. But I like to keep up with the journals, and that takes time, and I have community interests outside medicine which are very important to me, and I want to continue them."

Jacobs does not feel that her career has suffered because of working less than full time. "I am the doctor that I would be whether I have twenty or two hundred patients," she says. "I get referrals from other doctors in all branches of medicine, and four years ago I became a full partner in our group through a strategy similar to the one I used in convincing them to take me in the first place. I called a meeting with my associates, told them what I felt I'd contributed to the practice; drew up a list of patients whom I had brought into the practice through my subspecialty and who I felt would follow me if I left; showed them which and how many of their own patients I saw for them from time to time;

pointed out in black and white what I felt I was worth to the practice. I gave them a month to think it over, to get additional data from me, and to compile their own, and then suggested we meet again. Before the month was over they told me they agreed that I should be a partner. Of course, I draw a much smaller percentage of the total because I am spending far less total time, but I consider that completely fair all around."

Jacobs effected her initial arrangement nearly a decade ago, when there was high resistance to part-time work. Now, however, a limited-time practice is becoming the way of the present and future for women physicians with families. I also interviewed an anesthesiologist and mother of four who works two days a week; an ophthalmologist who practices mornings while her two children are in school; and three psychiatrists who returned to practice on schedules of their own designs so that they can continue full-time mothering. Like Jacobs, these women knew what they wanted to do and what environment they wanted, then proceeded to create the places they now fill. Many medical specialties lend themselves to a woman adapting to her family needs. Male physicians began freeing themselves from twenty-four-hour-a-day practices three or more decades ago when they began forming group practices, covering calls, and working alternate weekends, so the model is already there. In a myriad of other fields—advertising, public relations, counseling, business from cost and corporate accounting to marketing, and computer science—women are now establishing more flexible models. For example, in Chicago, women have spearheaded the formation of the

PART III

Part-Time Lawyers Network, and women are also founders and leaders of LAWS (Lawyers for Alternative Work Schedules), a national organization directed toward educating the legal community on new work options for attorneys.

Clearly, women with imagination and innovative ability custom create positions for themselves in a variety of fields. In most cases, the field is not the determinant. What counts is the imagination of the women to see precisely what needs to be done and her innovative ability to present a plan to a potential employer for the new position that will benefit him, his organization, and its constituents.

For instance, Miriam Werner sold a Chicago advertising firm on her strengths in creating advertising campaigns for companies selling children's products—toys, clothes, and equipment. "I was in general advertising for eight years prior to leaving when my first son was born five years ago," Werner says. "When I wanted to return to work, I could get full-time offers but nothing which suited my needs for part time. Then I began assessing what I could do differently and better . . . what strength I had which would really give me some bargaining power. I was dissatisfied with much of the print advertising to parents for children's products; I felt I could provide more creative approaches to reach the educated parents who would buy the higher-priced upscale toys and clothes. I designed a couple of trial campaigns for products I knew my present company is handling. I went to them and said that I thought I could do something that they weren't but should be doing. My strength was my years of expertise in the field coupled with my knowledge—as an intelligent parent—of a certain market segment. They hired me for two days a week, which is what I specified, on a trial basis for six months, then made the position which I've held for three years permanent."

Another example of a woman who sold from strength is Carlotta Parks, an experienced social worker who did not want to return to the pressures of hospital teaching once her three children were in school but did want to use her professional abilities constructively. She custom designed a community center counseling position for herself, then sold it to the center to which she and her family had gone for years, where she knew intimately the needs for professional counseling of some of the members, particularly the elderly and adolescents. Parks first developed a counseling position on a half-time, one-year trial basis, projecting that the demands for more counseling, seminars, and workshops would exceed the half-time availabilities. In her plan for the second year, she developed a permanent counseling center with herself as the director. Before the first year was up, she was asked to continue working permanently as the full-time counseling director. She elected, however, to handle the directorship as a half-time position and has hired a psychiatric social worker and clinical psychologist, each working quarter time, to do the additional work needed to diversify the program. Parks, like Nyman, Judapher, Markek, Perkins, Fredericks, Mead, Werner, and Jacobs, is among thousands of innovative sequencing mothers throughout the country today who have custom created part-time professional positions for themselves that enable them to grow professionally as their children grow and to have whole lives instead of fragmented parts. In nearly every case, the posi-

PART III

tion can be expanded to full time should the women wish it
as their families grow older or a financial need arises that
requires it. In nearly every case, the woman creates a niche
that makes her visible enough to her general professional
community so that should she want to make a switch in later
years, she is mobile.

Whether a woman custom designs a position and then
sells it to an organization or whether she takes an existing
post, then adapts it to her needs, the woman who does it
must be imaginative and innovative. She has to have the
vision to view her own background, abilities, and expertise
as a highly salable package, to assess her comparative advantage over others in the field, and to sell the package with
its advantage to the organization she has targeted. This
takes perseverance, research, patience, and motivation. But
the rewards to the woman who wants a whole life are enormous: she can continue as a full-time participatory mother
yet can develop professionally by controlling her own time,
working a limited number of hours, and having her career
as an important component rather than the sole focus of
her life. For the person who wants a whole life and is creative enough to find ways to bend her career to her total
lifestyle, the part-time professional position is without question the wave of the future.

DEALING WITH FULL-TIME COWORKERS

Part-time work carries with it some occupational hazards
which women just beginning can try to avoid if they are
forewarned. These include being left out by colleagues and

jealousy on the part of coworkers. Because part-time professionals usually work through lunch and coffee breaks, they are often left out of organizational networking. To avoid this, it's worthwhile for a woman to try to build a lunch once a week with a colleague into her schedule so that she feels she has friends in the organization, knows what's going on behind the scenes in other divisions, and feels at home. Sometimes being left out is part of a larger problem: jealousy on the part of the full-timers, who like to maintain the fiction that because they log more hours they are the "real" personnel.

Most part-time personnel who have dealt with coworker jealousy effectively have done so by initiating conversations about it with those they sense are potentially resentful. It almost always turns out that the resentment comes when the full-timer considers herself exploited by management. Rarely does the person working a straight forty hours a week feel jealous of the woman who works twenty hours a week at half her pay. The problems arise when the full-timer is jealous because the part-timer is working "half time" at "half pay"—which means twenty hours a week—while she, the full-timer, is working "full time"—which means sixty or more hours a week: three times the hours of the part-time person at only twice the salary.

Mass recognition of this discrepancy will lead, I am sure, to the "unionization" of the executive suite. For the past several decades organizations of all kinds have milked their upper-echelon employees of life outside work by dangling the carrot of success: more money, a higher title, and with it the chance to work all the time. People who played the game accepted those rules. But now a new generation of professionals is changing the rules and the game. Whereas in earlier days those who sought part-time opportunities were considered lazy or uninterested in their careers or were dismissed as dead-ended, the picture has changed and continues to change dramatically. Suddenly, persons who are working not only full time but *all* the time are questioning their own motivations, and with those questions the old definition of professionalism—"doing the job until it is done"—is changing. For "doing the job until it is done," in situations when it is literally *never* done, is no longer acceptable to the person who sits alongside someone who is doing a *piece of the job until it is done*, then going home to another life.

The first response on the part of the person who is working all the time is, quite naturally, jealousy. But competent, successful, part-time professionals are pointing the way for their coworkers to turn that jealousy into constructive changes in their own lives. Suddenly, the person working all the time has to look in the mirror and take stock: why is she doing it? Is she slugging for promotion and believes this is the route? Is she simply not as effective because she is over-immersed? Is she inefficient? Or is she a fool?

Sometimes it's the latter, and sequencing mothers give their sixty-hour-a-week coworkers helpful advice. For instance, at a college where the half-time (twenty-hour-a-week) counselors—all mothers working during their children's school hours—outnumbered the full-timers three to one, the full-timers worked many more than forty hours per week at peak seasons, and of course they received no additional pay because professional positions don't include over-time. So the part-time people confronted the full-timers with the inequities and suggested to the full-timers that they keep track of the time they spent "working overtime" and take that time off during the summers and other slack peri-ods. Both full- and part-time personnel say this open dis-cussion not only markedly decreased hostilities on the part of the full-timers but made them realize their jealousy was totally inappropriate to the situation. They were the ones who had a problem because the changed marketplace con-ditions exploited them. Their jealousy turned to construc-tive implementation of new ways to do their work. They drew up a letter to the administration stating that they were willing to continue working overtime at peak periods but would keep track of that time and take time off at less busy periods to compensate for it. This proposal was accepted without complaint.

Most part-time personnel who have experienced col-league resentment say that the best way to deal with it is to expose the issue, not bury it, and to discuss with colleagues why they feel resentful. Do they feel they have an unfair workload? Are they jealous of the underlying personal situa-tion that enables the part-time professional to work fewer hours than they do? Suggest comp time to full-time profes-sionals as the college counselors did; persons who cannot work less time can at least be financially compensated for putting in more time. Ultimately, recognize that the burden of proof is not yours: the part-time professional who is con-scientiously doing an excellent job during the hours she works, then leaves for other commitments, has nothing to apologize for. There will always be workaholics and also less efficient, less competent people who take longer to get the same job done; there will always be people who must work full time. This is not the problem of the part-time professional. Her charge is to do her work well, to pride herself on work well accomplished, and never to appear apologetic that she is not doing what she is not paid to do, is not expected by the terms of her agreement with her employer to do, and does not herself expect to do.

As the number of high echelon part-timers continues to grow each year, coworker resentment is fast becoming a problem for management to solve. Dealing with coworkers' feelings is but one of the difficulties in the first stage in a long process of change which organizations are going through because of the changing social norms that underlie part-time work. The second stage, which we are now beginning to see, is that others in the organization that offers some people part-time options are now requesting and getting changes in their situations, too: either they are demanding more money for more work, in effect "overtime," or, more frequently, they are negotiating scheduling changes—working fewer total hours a day, spending less time in the office, and taking more days entirely away from work.

A further complication which employers are facing is that, until recently, convention dictated that part-timers could not be promoted to managerial positions. That, too, is changing even though full-timers are often angry when a part-timer is advanced over them. An executive of a large midwestern chain told me he is currently having to decide whether to promote a part-time female manager at one of his stores who is his clear choice for the job and risk the wrath of several full-timers at her present level, or to promote someone he deems less competent. He is inclined, he says, to promote the part-timer: "She'll get more done," he says. "She is just plain better than any of the others."

Part of the reason part-time professionals are better is that so many of them are women who are creative thinkers. Creativity—and leadership and vision, which are part of it —is in prime demand today and will continue to be in the future. Cogs—even high-level ones—who merely keep the wheels going twelve hours a day are not valued as much as the creative person who comes in a third of the time but has a strong impact on the organization with her insights and ideas. I recently attended a Young Presidents Organization meeting at which the questions men and women who become presidents of multimillion-dollar businesses asked business school leaders weren't about managment. They were asking about leadership: How do you train executive thinking? How does a company become a leader in the industry? The answer, of course, is in the persons that company attracts. If it attracts followers, it cannot lead. To attract creative thinkers companies will have to become more and more accommodating to part-time professionals. Many women in professional schools and later in their professions have proven themselves highly creative thinkers. Increasingly, women opt for part-time positions. Organizations cannot afford to lose these women permanently or they will lose many of their most forward thinkers. An executive of a Fortune 500 company told me, in lowered tones, "At the risk of sex-stereotyping, we've found, hands down, that women are among our most creative thinkers, and they've got highly developed people skills besides. But we're finding we're having to accommodate to them or they'll go where somebody else will." Because women have proven their ability to think creatively, because they're known for their interpersonal skills, because most become mothers, and because many of them insist on working part time—whether leaving for a period of years and then working again or staying in the work force throughout their mothering but cutting back their time—the die is cast. All that's left is that more and more parents and others with agendas outside their work insist that they, too, must have challenging part-time options.

13

Beyond the System

Nicole Lizst developed a one-woman ethnic dance company in Denver; Michelle Broderick established a Manhattan literary agency; Marge Stewart is a pharmacological consultant in rural Wisconsin. Each left a mainstream career to mother full time, then reincorporated professional activities into her life in a unique way so that her work serves her. Each is highly enthusiastic about her success.

These and scores of other women like them all over the country custom design careers to work for them by going beyond existing organizations to work when, where, and how they want to. In so doing, many of them are creating wholly satisfying lifestyles by combining the best of traditional mothering with the best of feminist philosophy. Before the emergence of modern feminism, many women gave up their chances for careers to raise families, then when their children were grown found there was nothing left for themselves. Feminism taught women instead to maintain full-time careers throughout all stages of their lives so that they would always have their work. Neither extreme was healthy. Today, sequencing mothers are creating a happy medium by developing a whole spectrum of successful reintegrations of entrepreneurial careers into their personal and family lives.

In a sense, this is nothing new. Throughout my mothering years, which began in 1963, there were those of us who made mothering a primary commitment and yet made ways to do the work we wanted to do, or had to do, besides. But there were never so many as now. Nor were so many women trained in such a diversity of professions with as much previous work experience, expertise, and confidence in their fields. Thus I look with respect and amazement at today's sequencing women who reemphasize their careers as entrepreneurs. I am certain that they are trendsetters leading the way the majority of women will both mother and work during the coming decades. What to me is so wonderful about what these women are doing is that each of them, regardless of location or profession, is innovating ways to reincorporate her work into her life so that she is independent. Therefore, she is able to reemphasize the work she loves to do, or needs to do, on a gradual basis without diminishing her mothering. It is essential, however, that the women who follow this lead don't misunderstand the concept and abuse it, for too much entrepreneuring too soon will create a new and potentially more dangerous breed of Superwoman than the one we've recently buried.

PHASED CAREER REEMPHASIS

At this time, the women I've interviewed and observed are being extremely careful to phase their work back into their lives in ways that will preserve their mothering. They are still reeling from the Superwoman norm and thus realize how critical it is that they don't let their work come into their lives and homes only to let it absorb them there. Each has a definite goal in mind: to make her work enhance her total lifestyle without conflicting with her mothering. Many of these women begin phasing careers back into their lives while their children are small, working a very few hours a week, building their practices and businesses gradually over a period of years as their children grow.

The means through which these independents phase their work back into their lives impress me greatly. For what each has done is to extract from her work the core substance, that which she truly enjoys about it, and then give that substance new form. She is able to do this through a very flexible outlook on life. Many of the women I interviewed are in areas that have traditionally lent themselves to entrepreneuring such as law, medicine, accounting, social work, writing, and photography. But scores of others have broken new ground. In selecting case histories to illustrate how women have accomplished the merger of entrepreneuring and mothering, I have tried to show those women who are typical in their methods and outlooks of most of the women to whom I've spoken. I have selected some from professions that are not generally considered fields in which independents can work to illustrate that if a woman really wants to be a full-time mother and genuinely wants to reincorporate work back into her life, she can almost always find a way to do it as an independent by retaining the substance but changing the form of her work.

RETAINING THE SUBSTANCE, CHANGING THE FORM OF ONE'S WORK

Nicole Lizst gave the substance of her work new form when she left a prestigious West Coast dance company fifteen years ago during the first of her three pregnancies. Lizst greets me in her Denver dance studio, straightens her black leotard, sits down next to me, back straight, chin high, and reminisces: "In the early years, while I was having the children, my primary professional concern was to keep myself physically maintained so that when I was ready to perform again I would be in shape to do it. I left home at 6:30 every morning, sometimes right after nursing a new baby, and went to practice at a nearby studio. The night watchman let me in, and I worked out until eight while my husband was still home with the children. Some mornings I had to argue myself into going to practice—it was so tempting just to roll over and sleep. But I always felt better once I did, and in the long run, of course, it was the only way I could have stayed in condition.

"Later, when the last baby was about three, I began to really want to perform for an audience again but recognized that I couldn't work on anyone else's schedule, so I tried to figure out what I could do as a one-woman show that would be unique. I decided to specialize in ethnic dancing. First, I went into French and Germanic dances because that's my own origin; then I began seeing the similarities and differences with other cultures, gradually researched and learned other dances from countries, including Spain, Poland, and Czechoslovakia. Since I dance with my mind as well as my body, I have learned the folklore, the development of each kind of dance so when I perform it's more than a show; it's a whole history lesson.

"When I first began, I did only a few performances a year. My invitations were strictly by word of mouth; then, when all my children were in school, I began to market myself more aggressively through various church groups, schools, community centers, and civic organizations. Now I am very busy performing frequently. I also teach a course I developed in a dance institute, and I write reviews for dance journals. I practice, write, teach, and do some performing all during the hours the children are in school. When I perform evenings or weekends the family comes to cheer me on.

"But this has all evolved. When I began, I did so with only one thought in mind: that I would never stop dancing. It's like breathing to me."

Fifteen years later, where does Lizst believe she would be now if she had continued to dance with the company? "Without a family life," she says, "and in all likelihood I would not have developed professionally to anywhere near the degree that I have as an independent. Dancers, like ice skaters, gymnasts, athletes of all kinds, live in fear of the day that they have to slow down, that they can no longer physically keep up the pace. Since I've developed intellectually as well as physically, I am doing what a lot of company dancers past forty or forty-five wish they could. Besides dancing, I write, teach, and am looked on as an authority in the field instead of a has-been dancer, as too often happens as company dancers get older."

When Lizst decided to leave the company to mother her children, she could have sacrificed her performing career to do it, for on its face, dancing seems to be a field in which one either dances with a company, teaches it, or doesn't do it. But because of her determination to be a full-time mother yet not let go of the essence of the work she loved, Lizst has succeeded in making a reputation for herself as a performing artist and as a dance authority *without* leaving her children to do it.

Lizst accomplished the mothering part of this balancing act through carefully moderating how much she danced at a particular period in her life. During the years she had preschoolers, she danced only an hour and a half early in the morning; she did not try to dance three or four hours a day or to incorporate performances into her life. To have done so would be to have added pressures, deadlines, and heavy practice sessions which would have conflicted with her mothering priorities.

She accomplished the professional part of the balance through differentiating between the form and the substance of her work. The substance was dancing itself. She changed the form from dancing with a professional company on its schedules to becoming a one-woman show on her own.

This ability to cut through to the core of what it is that she really loves about her work, then to retain the core substance while changing the form, is not limited to any one profession. Although Nicole Lizst is a dancer, the adaptation she made is one which artists in scores of other areas can and do make as well. Vocalists and instrumentalists who love their music but want their independence go solo while raising their families. So do writers and photographers who once worked on newspapers or on magazines, then became freelancers. But retaining the substance of one's work while changing the form is not limited to those in the arts. Even a banker can do it.

Barbara Stanton, who formerly managed the personal loan division of a large New Jersey bank, found while at home with two small children that she needed to earn some money. In analyzing how she could do so without leaving home, she thought about what it was she most enjoyed about her previous work at the bank. She found what she liked the best and missed the most was helping other people. After some thought, research, and discussion with former colleagues, she decided to begin a personal investment consultantship. "From my experience with individuals who needed bank loans I knew that some people are thoroughly disorganized about their personal finances and need help. I directed my abilities toward that market. I love what I am doing because it's much more than working with people's budgets; by helping them work through how they want to spend their money I am helping them decide how they want to spend their lives." Because her children are still preschoolers, Stanton moderates her business so that she meets with clients one or two evenings a week, when her husband is with the children, and does preparation work on their accounts Saturday mornings, when he is home with them.

Through giving new form to the substance of what she most enjoyed about her work—helping people—Stanton has reemphasized the role of her career in her life in a new way.

Like Lizst, who phased back into her career over a fifteen-year period, Stanton is phasing into hers gradually. "I have more calls now than I can handle given my other priorities," she says. "But in a couple of years, when my youngest is in school, I plan to expand my business. In fact, I envision expanding manifold, perhaps hiring other consultants as well."

Like Nicole Lizst and Barbara Stanton, Marge Stewart phased back into a field that didn't appear to lend itself to entrepreneuring. She did it by delineating what it was she most enjoyed about pharmacy and then creating new forms to express it. Stewart was clear about her professional goals from the time her youngest child was two and she wanted to resume working only a few hours a week. "I love the intellectual part of pharmacy, but I didn't like standing behind a counter and filling prescriptions. I wanted to do something more exciting and creative."

Stewart innovated a plan for improving pharmacological services for the only nursing home in her small town, approached the director, and suggested that she consult for the home. "She turned me down flat," Steward recalls. "But it didn't stop me. I told her I'd work for her as a volunteer, setting up programs I believed the hospital needed to follow. I went in a couple times a week, viewed patient charts, made sure that all drugs were current, destroyed those which had expired, talked with patients about possible side effects when I saw something on the chart to make me suspicious.

After a few months, I wrote a report on what I'd done and met again with the director. By then she realized the usefulness of the program I'd established, so she funded me. I have worked twenty hours a month as a paid consultant for them for the last four years."

Stewart expanded her consulting services last year when her youngest child began school. "In addition to the nursing home I'm working as a consumer adviser to a pharmacy two mornings a week, counseling patients on drug interactions, cost of generic versus brand name drugs, and other of their pharmaceutical needs. I also consult on interactions to the local general hospital regular pharmacy staff and give monthly seminars on drug reactions to the medical staff."

Stewart is pleased with her consultantship for several reasons: "I love the diversity of working different places and the variety of the situations. Think where I'd be if I hadn't developed this consulting practice—filling prescriptions. This way I have really grown in my profession in all new ways. I'm able to work around my children's hours, which is a major goal, and I've opened a new area. Doctors and lawyers always set up their own practices, but the pharmacists didn't do this . . . I've charted a new course."

Stewart's excitement about her success is characteristic of the entrepreneur who starts with her own background, a good idea, and immense determination—then creates the rest. It's particularly rewarding for the sequencing woman who finds that her own innovative efforts enable her to reincorporate work she loves into her life on her own timetable while mothering according to her own standards.

PART III

A FLEXIBLE OUTLOOK

Sequencing women turned entrepreneurs are characterized by a highly flexible outlook on life, which enables them to leave jobs, change jobs, change locations, to sequence in the first place, and to reemphasize their careers innovatively: to take a chance on themselves.

Michelle Broderick is illustrative of this flexibility, though at first I didn't recognize it. When I began talking with her it seemed to me that she sequenced more by accident than design and that she established her literary agency through a quirk of fate.

On closer examination, however, I recognized that Broderick is a shrewd and sensitive woman who has led a richly varied life precisely because she doesn't get locked into thinking in one vein. She took advantage of each unpredicted opportunity in her life and, as a result, developed her own workable lifestyle in which she has made what she terms "a happy mix of career and family considerations."

In 1972, at age thirty, Broderick was on her way up the editorial ladder in a Manhattan publishing house when her husband's firm offered him the opportunity to work in the Middle East for four years. Broderick, who was then pregnant for the first time, says, "I couldn't see that kind of separation from him. Nor could I see both of us losing the chance to live abroad, to travel, to grow in so many ways that staying in New York would simply never give us." So Broderick resigned, lived and traveled abroad, and returned to New York four years later with her husband, two young children, no job, and some nonsupportive former colleagues.

"Everybody was telling me, 'The industry has changed so much you'll never get back in.' Actually, it had changed very little; at least the changes seemed minimal to me compared to the kinds of eye-opening changes I'd experienced, as a mother and living in a totally different culture to boot. One of the main changes in myself was that I was no longer one-track career-oriented. For years I'd aspired to a major position in a big publishing house. Not for the money, nobody makes real money in publishing—at least not the kind you can make in many other industries—but for the challenge, the excitement, the power, the stimulation. But when I returned, my world had expanded tremendously. Although I was pretty sure that I no longer wanted to go the organizational route, I needed to check myself out. So I called my contacts, talked with people in several houses, and got an excellent offer which showed me I could go right back on the old track again if I wanted to. I really thought it through and found that I didn't. I'd been on my own too long to go back to an organizational setting. I wanted to stay independent.

"I did want to get back into publishing, however. It's in my blood—I delight in the machinations of the industry, and I love getting my hands on a terrific manuscript. But I saw that in order to continue my kind of mothering I'd have to create my own niche in the industry rather than go to work for somebody else. While I was exploring what that niche might be, a friend brought me a manuscript which I showed to a publisher friend, who grabbed it, loved it, and asked, 'Who's the agent on this book?' 'I brought it in; I'm the agent,' I said. The book won a major award for new

PART III

fiction that year. The author was launched and so was I! I opened my own literary agency and worked very limited at-home hours for four years until the kids were both in school. Then I began expanding my literary services to include not only acquisition of American authors but scouting coming titles for foreign publishers and new books for movie producers."

Broderick says that although money was never her central reason for working, "Oddly enough it's coming in to the point that I consider my business a financial as well as a personal lifestyle success." Broderick now works two days a week from her Manhattan office and three days from her Connecticut home, "until the kids come in around three."

Broderick, like Lizst, Stanton, and Stewart, carefully moderated the amount of work she did at particular periods in her life so that she wouldn't become a new breed of Superwoman. She began her agency in a limited way when her children were still preschoolers. "The other women around me who were not working saw me as very ambitious because I spent five or sometimes even ten hours a week working," Broderick said. "But my colleagues barely considered me in the game. When the children began school, then I began building a clientele in earnest, and it wasn't until several years later, until they were very busy with their own after-school activities and rarely home with illnesses anymore, that I started dealing with the foreign publishers."

Broderick's remark that her friends who were not working thought she was doing much whereas her colleagues barely considered her working at all, is typical of the response to sequencing mothers who gradually reintegrate work into their lives through entrepreneuring. The mother with two children in diapers, who can hardly find a moment to read the newspaper, sometimes looks at her as a traitor to the cause of full-time mothering. Can she really be caring for her children or is she putting them behind the television and doing her own thing? The executive who's logging fifty or sixty hours or more at work looks at the woman working five hours a week from home and snorts, "She calls *that* working?"

The woman who slowly reincorporates her work back into her life is frequently caught between these two sets of peers and has to remind herself that their perceptions of what she is doing are their problem, not hers. It's well for the woman with her children still in diapers to recognize that in a few years she, too, may well want to begin working again a limited number of hours and for the full-time career-woman to recognize that in a few years she may want to have children and spend most of her time at home with them. She will also see, in a few years, that the mother who begins gradually, while her children are small, is indeed "in the game" once they are older—a game she plays by her own rules. For Broderick the rules are a total lifestyle design that gives her opportunities for continual professional growth, to mother according to her own standards, time for her husband and friends, and even time for playing the clarinet, which she sometimes does "to relax" in her home office, interspersed with reading manuscripts and waiting for transatlantic calls regarding foreign rights. "I'm glad that I've taken each opportunity in my life as a chance to change; it makes life more exciting than going one direction all the way."

It's this ability to incorporate new circumstances into her life and change with them that is characteristic of many of the sequencing women I meet. These are the women who saw raising their children not as a career deterrent but as a new life challenge. Rather than trying to cram their children into an existing pattern, these women enlarged and altered the pattern to accommodate their children. It's not surprising that given this flexibility they are less resistant to change in other ways, too, than women who stay on one career ladder through their adult lives. Once having made the decision to leave their work, they don't feel terribly constrained by location—they'll move as Broderick did when her husband had a transfer opportunity abroad. Or as Andrea Marth did when she and her husband decided that instead of dreaming about living in the country they'd leave Los Angeles and do it. Marth, her husband, and two children settled in a small New Mexico community where they have lots of land, a huge garden, and "space for the children to run." Although her husband has a thriving medical practice, "the price I paid for this lifestyle choice— and it is definitely as much or more my choice than his —is that there is no lab or university setting within 150 miles in which I could use my biochemistry background as I did before. So I have had to totally redirect my training."

Marth retained the substance of her work—she remained in the area of science—but by having a flexible attitude, she changed the form completely to serve her new needs.

She switched from working within a university research setting, where she did research in one limited scientific area, to general teaching and writing on a variety of scientific topics on a freelance basis. She teaches a series of science courses for laypersons that she has developed and gives through the town community education center. She writes a column based on the courses for her local paper and a series of articles for a small specialty publication. "Next, I plan a book for teens," she says. "I realize that for a book what I have to do is read and think ahead, see what the hot issues will be eighteen months and two years hence, then research and work up my writing on a particular issue accordingly."

Just as flexibility of attitude enables women like Broderick and Marth to change location and to give new entrepreneurial form to the substance of their work, it also enables women to change the course of their careers entirely.

When tall, blonde Alicia Maldon, a former sportswear buyer for a major New York department store, left her position seven years ago, she fully expected to return to a similar post when her children were older. But now that both of her sons are in school full days she feels differently. "I had an excellent offer from a small, prestigious store; management was impressed by my experience, by the way I've kept up with fashion merchandising and trends, and I think, quite frankly, by my appearance. They want a chic merchandise manager who is visible to certain wealthy customers: somebody past forty who looks terrific, who can wear the kind of clothes the store specializes in.

"I sat on their offer for a couple of months, but I am not going to take it because I want to try something new. I began designing and making my own things four years ago as a kind of odd-hours hobby, really. Some of my friends in the industry have been wild about them. One of them, a buyer for an avant-garde shop, has told me that if I will design a line, she will try my stuff, and now that I have the time to seriously give it a try, I'm going to do it. I love women's fashions but I don't want to select clothes anymore; I want to create them. I know it's a highly competitive market, but I feel that if I don't give it a real try I'll always feel I shortchanged myself."

Maldon's flexible attitude allows her to take a chance on herself rather than returning to the work area in which she has already done well. Maldon has, in effect, phased her career reemphasis. She began designing and making her clothes as an avocation while home full time with her children, and now that her children are in school full days, she is meeting the new challenge of turning that avocation into a vocation. She is retaining the substance of her work—fashion—but switching the form entirely from fashion acquisition to fashion designing.

ENTREPRENEURIAL FORMS

The three most popular entrepreneurial forms among sequencing women are consulting, freelancing a product of the woman's own design, and running a service-oriented business. These definitions are based on the ways in which the women themselves express what they do. The consultant is one who sells expertise in the form of advice, information, or special projects to others. A freelancer of products of her own creation is the writer, artist, artisan, dancer, or musician who produces (or performs) artistically and then markets what she produces, whether it's a book, an oil painting, a song, or a dance. The service business (as distinct from the retail business in which one sells goods, the manufacturing business in which one mass produces goods, and the wholesale business in which one serves as a middle-woman selling goods) is a business in which a women sells a service, whether it's a literary agency or a family day care center. These three entrepreneurial forms are the most popular with sequencing mothers because they lend themselves most easily to a gradual career reemphasis and flexible scheduling.

Consulting

Women like Barbara Stanton and Marge Stewart demonstrate that the consultantship is an excellent means for a woman to phase back into professional commitments on a flexible schedule of her own design. Among the advantages of a consultantship particular to the sequencing mother are flexibility of timing, variety of work and contacts, and the opportunities continually to add new clients to her résumé for future work. Consulting keeps open her options so that as her children grow older she can either continue as a soloist increasing her client base as Margie Stewart has done with her pharmacological consultantship, take in associates and become an administrator and potential major contractor as investment counselor Barbara Stanton envisions, or take her client base with her into an already existing organization as several attorneys, accountants, and counselors I interviewed whose children are now older have done. They have joined firms, bringing clients with them as their bargaining chips.

Consultants are increasingly in demand by individuals who need their expertise and institutions and organizations that want to purchase a selected service or get advice or expertise on a particular problem or project.

"Consulting has to be a win/win," says Gail McClure, head of the University of Minnesota Communications Resource Division. McClure, who innovated a communications consultant pool two years ago at the university, says, "Benefits to the institution are that we don't have the same thinkers doing all the thinking, we can hire new perspectives and talents, and we don't have to pay salaries when not needed for specific tasks. Benefits to the consultant include flexible work opportunities and to the emerging entrepreneur the U of M credential for future work with other clients."

Consultantships work well in a tremendous range of fields. Health care professionals, including physicians, consult in many specialties, as do nutritionists and pharmacists; speech, hearing, and reading therapists; mental health professionals in all fields—social workers, psychologists, and psychiatrists; attorneys in nearly all subspecialties, including corporate law, tax, investments, and estate planning; women in a multiplicity of areas of business from accounting to stocks and bonds; statisticians; computer programmers; print, television, and film editors; and advertising and public relations specialists. The list is endless. And where the list of people who have already established consultantships stops, imaginative women begin.

Freelancing: Creating and Marketing One's Own Product

Freelancing a product of her own creation is the clear career reemphasis choice for the sequencing mother who writes, is a visual artist or photographer, sculpts, or is a musician or artisan. The reasons are obvious. She can usually learn to work around her children's hours very conveniently —a few minutes or an hour a day while the baby is napping, or after the bedtime of her preschoolers, or early in the morning before anybody else is awake, or during hours when they are in school. If she is flexible about when she does her work, her *creativity* need not be diminished during her sequencing years. For a time, her *productivity* will be, however, for clearly the mother of babies and preschoolers doesn't have the time to devote to her other creative endeavors that she did before they were born or that she will have when they are all in school. The mother of school-age children still won't have all day, every day, free to work, but if she disciplines herself she can make nearly as much time as most other working artists or writers spend on their work.

PART III

Running a Service Business

Service businesses lend themselves more easily to the career reemphasis of the woman who wants to maintain her mothering priorities than do retail, wholesale, or manufacturing businesses because a service business can be far more flexible. Also, selling a service generally requires far less capital than other types of businesses, especially if a woman begins from her home and thus has no overhead expenses: she may need only business cards, perhaps a brochure, a business phone, and an answering machine. Even if she rents office space and hires secretarial help she has less total investment than if she rents a storefront and requires an inventory. Also, she may have much more flexibility of time and place if she sells services than if she retails goods and thus gets locked into definite store hours.

Some women use prior backgrounds to begin service businesses as did Michelle Broderick in developing her literary agency; others begin anew. Women throughout the country with no background either in the field or in business have successfully developed baby-sitting agencies, housecleaning agencies, and catering services for which they don't do the hands-on work but rather act as a broker matching the service provider with the buyer.

Women with word processing, typing, and other secretarial skills run service businesses. Three of the women who have typed for me over the years were mothers, each of whom developed a service business out of her home when her children were young. One was a former office manager and mother of preschoolers, who worked several evenings a week after the children were in bed. She supplemented her husband's income sufficiently that she could remain at home with her children until they were well into grade school. Another ran a typing service from her apartment while her children slept at night and her student husband studied. She expanded her business when her children began school and hires other students and student wives to do the typing while she manages the business. The third worked from home when her children were in preschool and later left her service business to become administrative assistant to the president of a college.

Mothers often develop delightfully creative services for other mothers and their children. A Connecticut mother founded a party planning business specifically for children's birthday parties. She plans all details from theme, to invitations, to menu, with the birthday child and parents, then she (often with her children) caters the affair. Two Los Angeles mothers teamed on a balloons-for-all-occasions business. Many of their clients are parents of birthday children, and they have also done balloon centerpiece arrangements for dances and balloon decorations for corporate extravaganzas.

A Chicago area mother runs a customized travel service from her home for selected clients who pay her directly to arrange the details of their vacations. An upstate New York woman, who formerly worked with a major real estate agency, developed her own business and after three years handles most of the houses that change hands in her own neighborhood. A Midwest mother of four grown children developed a premium tour-guide service in her city for visitors to the area's corporations. She gives guests custom tours of the area tailored to their particular interests, arranges their social schedules, and frequently attends the social events with them. As these examples illustrate, the list of possible service businesses is as limitless as a woman's imagination and creative abilities.

GETTING STARTED

Whether a woman is a consultant, creator and freelancer of a talent or product, or runs a service business, it's important that she begins by targeting her market precisely and then going after that market. There are various no- or low-cost ways of doing so, including contact referrals, volunteering one's services, and speaking publicly to various organizations.

Contact Referrals

Referral from contacts, friends, or satisfied clients is the chief means most of the entrepreneurs I talked with cited for getting started.

Barbara Stanton began her personal investment consultantship by printing business cards, writing a piece for her businesswomen's organization, and getting former colleagues excited about it. They generated her first clients because they know her work and thought she had a great idea.

Many other entrepreneurs say their referrals come through personal contacts or word of mouth, as well. Anne Wilson, a social worker who began a family therapy practice two years ago, received most of her early referrals from her gynecologist, a woman who took several years for full-time mothering and who empathized with Wilson's situation. Corrine Marshall, who began a personal law practice after eight years out of the field, found her early referrals through persons who had heard her speak at board meetings of various community organizations on which she served during those years. Stanton, Wilson, and Marshall all knew their markets existed so getting started was not too difficult. However, when a woman is certain a market exists but the market itself doesn't feel the need for her or her services, she has to prove that need. Pharmacist Marge Stewart did so by beginning as a volunteer.

Volunteering

The idea of volunteering a professional service smacks to some women of exploitation. In Stewart's case, however, the purposeful volunteering of her professional services at a nursing home for a limited period proved the point she wanted to make, got her the work she wanted to get, and paid off in the end. Had things not worked out as she wanted, she would still have had the nursing home work credential when seeking clients later, or, if she had not been able to establish her own practice, she could have cited the experience on her résumé when looking for a job. In either case, the time would not have been all lost.

Volunteering one's professional expertise is not appropriate for all women at all times, but on occasion it can benefit the woman who wants to reemphasize her career or the woman who wants to change career directions. Linda Marks, client program manager of New Ways to Work in San Francisco, often recommends volunteering as a way in the door because it worked so well for her. Marks had been working full time when she cut down to part time and sought a career switch. She went into New Ways to Work one day for some resources and, Marks said, "knew from the minute I walked in that door that I had to be a part of it but there were no openings." So Marks worked there one day a week without salary for nearly a year until a vacancy arose. "There were over sixty applicants, many of whom were exceptionally qualified, but my foot was already firmly in the door, and I got the job I most wanted," she says.

There is obviously a point when, for some women under some circumstances, volunteering their professional services is the best thing they can do for their long-range plans. In Marks's case it enabled her to do work she found very rewarding in the environment she wanted and gave her an inside track for the paying job that eventually arose. In Marge Stewart's case, she not only proved the need to the nursing home for her services, she proved that she believed in her ability to fill it strongly enough to gamble her time. That gamble was the foundation for the innovative consulting practice she has now established.

Public Speaking Engagements

Visibility is essential to the entrepreneur who wants to increase the volume of her clients. So speaking, appearing on panels, radio, television, or anywhere one is able to publicize her expertise helps.

POTENTIAL PROBLEMS

Although consulting, freelancing, or running service businesses can be terrific for sequencing women who want to maintain their mothering priorities, there are two major problem areas which women contemplating any form of entrepreneuring can anticipate and try to correct in advance to save themselves time, energy, and potential trouble. These areas are allocation of money and management of time.

Managing Money

Money management can be a major problem area, particularly for the entrepreneur who lacks a business background. The psychiatrist or attorney who opens a private practice, or the artist or writer who freelances, may do the actual work extremely well but lack previous business orientation or experience.

Therefore, consultants to small businesses often recommend that the person who wants to establish her own consultantship, service, or other business hire an accountant to help establish a recordkeeping system appropriate to the business, follow those directions on a daily basis, and have the accountant do the annual tax work—it often saves money in the end.

It's important to select an accountant who deals routinely with small businesses and more helpful still for entrepreneurs without previous business background to find one who speaks in easily understandable terms. Tax and accounting specialist Sharon LaColla, writing in the *Women's Home Business* summer 1985 newsletter, recommends that an accountant who specializes in small business can be of great assistance with questions on insurance requirements, whether or not to incorporate, getting the best tax advantages, and so forth.

Part of money management is total office management. Often consultants, freelancers, and small businesswomen are loath to hire secretarial or bookkeeping help, feeling either that the cost would cut into profits or that when one is working restricted hours it's more trouble than it's worth to supervise help.

Dr. Ruth Roberts, a clinical psychologist and mother of two grade-schoolers, began developing her private practice when they were preschoolers and now sees patients fifteen hours a week. "I still hate the office work," Roberts says. "I must devote at least two hours a week to records for taxes, billing, correspondence, that kind of thing. It's boring and you don't get paid for doing it; but you also don't get paid if you don't do it." Roberts, however, does not want to hire a part-time secretary to keep records and send bills because she doesn't want to invest the money and the training time.

Although this is Roberts's personal management style (some women find it easier to do it themselves than to manage others), many women find doing the management and bookkeeping can be so tedious and time-consuming that it diminishes the enjoyment of actual work.

A case in point is Martha Williams, a former art educator who began her graphic art business when her last child was ten and thought she had everything under control. "I had help with the housework, left the office in enough time to have some transition time before the children got home— did everything the book tells you. Yet after a couple of years I developed an ulcer, and my mother and mother-in-law each said independently of the other, 'I told you so; you shouldn't be working.' I consulted two doctors—an internist and a psychiatrist. They both took careful histories and both gave essentially the same diagnosis: by all means continue working, but hire office help to take over all the details you hate so you can do the creative work you enjoy. I took the advice, and within six months of the time I hired help the ulcer cleared and has not returned."

Most women don't need an ulcer to convince them to hire help when they need it. In fact, many entrepreneurs say their career reemphasis is successful because they hire both enough secretarial help at the office and enough household help at home to ensure that their professional time is not siphoned off by officekeeping chores and their family and personal time is not taken by housekeeping.

Managing Time

Entrepreneuring is not by definition synonymous with part-time work. Entrepreneuring can be 5 hours a week, but it can be 150 hours, too. For the mother of preschoolers, working less than 10 hours a week, and for the mother of gradeschoolers, working 20 to 25 hours weekly, is as appropriate for the entrepreneur as for the woman working for someone else. However, working for oneself can be as or more difficult to monitor. Leaving the office behind can be a problem to the sequencing mother who works at home, as most do, at least at first. The advantages of a home office are proximity to one's children, no wasted time commuting, no extra overhead expenses, and tax breaks. Yet if an entrepreneur does not turn work off and the answering machine on, she becomes the very Simon Legree she would leave in a minute if the boss were anyone else. In fact, she can become the antithesis of what she wanted and feel herself a Superwoman in disguise. As Michelle Broderick cautions, "When you are mentally preoccupied you can't be there for your children any more than when you are physically absent. You have to inject some real flexibility in your work."

It's sometimes difficult to create this flexibility because the volume of work is often highly unpredictable. After the usual slow start, many entrepreneurs, male and female, complain of what a male statistical analyst calls "the bunching of work; it's either feast or famine, and I can't predict it." The sequencing mother has the volume control problem in spades, for she needs to generate clientele on one hand yet restrict it on the other. Usually the former is easier than the latter.

Michelle Broderick opened her literary agency when her children were both preschoolers. She worked "a limited number of hours a week from home. I didn't really start to hustle until they were both in school." Marge Stewart consulted on pharmaceutical matters at the nursing home five hours a week until her children began school, and she expanded her market.

Anne Wilson began a family therapy practice two years ago on an "on-call" basis, found it too intrusive on the family, and "quickly established regular office hours." Wilson, who sees clients no more than six hours a week, says, "With two preschoolers, working a total of six hours divided into two sets of office hours a week is a full caseload. Sometimes I have too many calls, sometimes not enough to fill the time I've set aside. I handle it by always keeping Tuesday afternoon office hours, when my children are with a sitter, and Wednesday evenings, when my husband is home with them, as my working hours. People have standing appointments during those times, yet when somebody is finished with therapy, it may be weeks before their slot is filled again. However, sometimes all my slots are filled, and then I get several new calls in a week and cannot schedule them without opening up more space. I constantly resist the temptation to make more and more new time slots in order to avoid losing a new client—pretty soon I could be working all of the time. Instead of doing that, I have a wait-list. If I see that I cannot accommodate a new client within my existing time frame beginning within a few weeks of when they first called, I refer them on. When my children are older I expect to expand my practice, but right now this is perfect for me."

Wilson restricts clientele by her decision that some weeks

she may see fewer cases than she can accommodate, so that she will not ever take on more cases than she can comfortably accept at any time. Corrine Marshall, who waited until all of her children were in school to resume her law practice, restricts clients by taking only those she can accommodate during her regular nine-to-three hours. "I make clear that their work will always be done well, thoroughly, and on time, but not after three in the afternoon." Marshall closes the door to her rented office, where she shares support staff with several other attorneys, every afternoon at that time to "beat the school bus home" and doesn't schedule clients on school release days, during her children's vacations, or during the month of July.

Marshall says her practice is growing "in spite of these restrictions or perhaps because of them. My work is good, and people respect it. That's really the bottom line. Since I restrict my clientele, in the end I am actually serving each client's needs more quickly than I did when I worked sixty hours a week in a large firm where we were so overloaded that sometimes a client had to wait for weeks." Like Wilson, Marshall plans to expand her practice as her children grow. "Right now money is not my prime motivation for working; I'm doing it because I enjoy it and I am building for the future. As the kids get older, I'll add more work time so that I can contribute heavily to their college educations. They'll be gone from home then and I'll devote more time to my career. But right now the balance is super."

Broderick, Stewart, Wilson, Marshall, and many others like them demonstrate that it is possible for the mother-entrepreneur to establish a schedule that best serves her needs and stick to it. The temptation to increase work when it comes one's way is always there. Developing strict guidelines and sticking to them is the only way for the entrepreneur to realize both mothering and professional priorities without one set conflicting with the other.

For the freelance artist or writer the situation of monitoring her time differs from that of consultants and service business operators in two important respects. First, because she works alone, the freelancer may be able to work in short snatches of time, and second, because of the nature of her work, she does well to avoid externally imposed deadlines at least while the children are small.

Since she works alone, the writer or artist can take advantage of naptimes. The prime requisite to doing this is to have a private place within earshot of the children where all supplies are stored and where a project can remain in process well out of reach of small children.

Deadlines, however, can be extremely difficult for the woman who freelances a product of her own creation, more so than for one who offers a consulting service, who usually can estimate fairly accurately from prior experience the time a project will take. The writer or visual artist has to make the product she creates correspond to the image in her mind—and that sometimes takes an incredible amount of time, thought, practice, vision, and revision. Doing it can be tremendously rewarding if one has the time to work the clay, the words, or the canvas, over and over again until the image and the reality correspond, but enormously frustrating if somebody else's deadline prevents one from bringing the creation to its fullest fruition.

SHARING OUR WORK WITH OUR CHILDREN

A major advantage of working independently is that one often can share one's work with one's children; this blurs the lines between family and work time. In fact, often for some time each day or week the two are inseparable, as in the now reemerging small family cottage industries. This can be delightful for parent and child so long as the tasks and timing are realistic for the age and interests of the child.

Many of my interviewees have expressed what I've found —that sharing work with one's children adds another dimension to their work because it's much more fun when their children can be a part of it. Jane Peters, who formerly headed the photography department of a regional magazine, left when her first child was born, then began freelancing when the younger was three. She worked limited hours until both children were in school full days, "then tripled my output.

"My eight-year-old son helps me if there's something I'm anxious to do in the darkroom after school or at night. I take both him and my six-year-old daughter with me if there is something I have to do after school. They each have cameras, and they often shoot the same things alongside me. Then we compare and contrast what we did and why we did it.

"One of the most rewarding parts of my work is that I can share this part of me with them. They see firsthand the real tough discipline of my work and yet at the same time the fun of it. When I was on the magazine it would have been wholly unprofessional to talk about work as being fun, but I now see that one's profession should not be such a straight-lipped, serious business. It should be fun, and sharing it with your kids can make it so."

Although writing is fundamentally a solitary business, my girls have long helped me with it, talking over ideas I'm working on, doing library research for or with me, and reading and commenting on draft after manuscript draft. When I teach as an artist in residence for a week every summer, the whole family comes along and helps. Dick is our marketing consultant, and I introduce my daughters from the beginning as my assistants. They read manuscripts along with me, call my attention to points I would miss, give suggestions, and sometimes help counsel my students on ways to change or improve their writing. Each of my girls has excellent writing and research skills, and rather than credit either their native abilities or the schools they've attended, I prefer to think they've developed them from their early and consistent exposure with me to the work and the fun of writing.

The whole family has been part of the promotion side of my writing, too. When the first book was published, Miriam and Rachel stayed out of school sharing autograph parties and television shows with me (sometimes, when shows were local, bringing the entire class along). After the second book the whole family appeared with me on "Donahue." By the third book we were such veterans that book promotion no longer meant everybody stopped everything else. Instead, Miriam, Rachel, and Rebecca took turns coming with me for television, radio, and personal appearances, often joining me on a program or a platform. These are the shared activities one doesn't plan when starting a business, developing a consultantship, or freelancing a product of one's own creation. But they are extras, which when they do come along are delightful to share with one's children at the time and make for wonderful deposits in the joint memory bank later.

Although entrepreneuring can often enable one to merge work with family life, it's important to moderate the amount of time spent on the merger so that it remains fun for everyone involved. That is easiest done when the time spent working together is flexible enough so that neither mother nor child feels tied to it so much of the time that the younger child's attention span wears thin. Mother and the older children need to discuss what parts of the joint work are strictly when the child is "helping out," and when it's reasonable and right for the child to be on salary for efforts performed.

Anita Edwards became a family day care provider rather than return to nursing work when her children were all in school, so she could be home in the afternoon when her children arrived or were out of school ill. Edwards includes her three children in her work. "We're a small family so my children wouldn't otherwise learn the child care techniques which children used to acquire automatically in the larger families of my great grandmother's day," she says. "The day care children can hardly wait for my own to come home to play with them, and mine like playing with them, too. I hire additional help, though, so that when mine first come I have time to talk with each of them, then I pay my children to help me during the last hour before the parent pick-ups."

Even when one's children are not directly involved in her work, they are often an integral part of professional aspects of the independent's life. Attorney Corrine Marshall says, "I don't schedule work on my children's school release or vacation days. I've told a client, 'No, I can't meet with you Wednesday because I'm taking my children to the zoo.' I say this deliberately because I think it's important that professionals who are parents make the rest of society aware of the needs, existence, and primacy of children. If I told a client I'm booked solid, even that I'm having some heavy dental work done that day, the client would automatically understand. We're programmed to understand. So why can't 'I'm taking the children to the zoo' be programmed into our understanding of other priorities, too?"

Marshall's point is frequently echoed by other independents who believe children must be recognized segments of society with special needs. Another self-employed attorney says, "I've never yet lost a client because I've said, 'Not then, I'm taking my daughter to a birthday party,' but I feel I've gained respect for having said so."

This transmission of the priorities of children is a prerogative of the independent; and as the number of independents in our society continues to skyrocket we can expect more and more of them not only to schedule work around the needs of their children but to educate the rest of society to respect those needs.

Conclusion

World of Our Daughters

Every woman who elects to sequence is pioneering a new way of life for herself today and for our daughters tomorrow. From traditional mothering she brings the desire to spend a large quantity of high-quality time with her children; from feminism she brings the charge to become trained and experienced in the career of her choice. Each sequencing woman merges these two values in a unique way to chart a heretofore unknown lifestyle. In so doing she creates a new model for the mothers of tomorrow.

The efforts of today's sequencing mothers will have a profound impact on our daughters and our sons as well. For as women professionals validate the needs of mothers and children to spend some years of their lives together by leaving their careers to take that time with their children, we as a society begin to view children in an entirely different light. We are coming to recognize them for exactly what they are: our future. And as we come to value our children as our most important natural resource we see the necessity for them to receive the best possible care. We are coming to recognize that care means much more than supervision and stimulation. It also means the day-in, day-out, consistent involvement of the child with someone who truly loves her and cares deeply for her future.

Bibliography

Alter, Joanne. *A Part-Time Career for a Full-Time You.* Boston: Houghton Mifflin, 1982.

Barko, Naomi. "The Part-Time Path." *Working Mother*, April 1985.

Barry, Thomas E., Mary C. Gilly, and Lindley E. Doran. "Advertising to Women with Different Career Orientations." *Journal of Advertising Research*, April/May 1985.

Bolles, Richard Nelson. *What Color Is Your Parachute?* Berkeley: Ten Speed Press, 1972, 1975, 1976, 1977.

Bowlby, John. *Attachment.* Attachment and Loss Series, Vol. 1. New York: Basic Books, 1969.

————. *Loss: Sadness and Depression.* Attachment and Loss Series, Vol. 3. New York: Basic Books, 1980.

————. *Separation: Anxiety and Anger.* Attachment and Loss Series, Vol. 2. New York: Basic Books, 1973.

Brazelton, T. B. "The Early Mother-Infant Adjustment." *Pediatrics* 32 (1963).

————. *Infants and Mothers.* New York: Delacorte Press/Seymour Lawrence, 1969.

————. *Neonatal Behavioral Assessment Scale.* Clinics in Developmental Medicine, No. 50. Philadelphia: Spastics International Medical Publications, Lippincott, 1973.

————, B. Koslowski, and M. Main. "The Origins of Reciprocity: The Early Mother-Infant Interaction." In *The Effects of the Infant on His Caregiver*, ed. M. Lewis and L. Rosenblum. New York: John Wiley & Son, 1974.

Chin, Kathy. "Home Is Where the Job Is." *InfoWorld*, April 23, 1984.

Churchman, Deborah. "Group Supports At-Home Mothers." *Christian Science Monitor*, May 25, 1983.

Collins, Glenn. "Changes in a Marriage When a Baby Is Born." *New York Times*, January 6, 1985.

————. "Day Care: Mother's Positive View." *New York Times*, November 25, 1984.

Bibliography

————. "Experts Debate Impact of Day Care on Children and on Society." *New York Times*, September 4, 1984.

Cook, Barbara, and Diane Rothberg. *A Part-Timer's Guide to Federal Part-Time Employment*. 2d ed. McLean, Va.: Association for Part-Time Professionals, 1983.

Cosell, Hillary. *Women on a Seesaw*. New York: Putnam, 1985.

Cox, Meg. "Many Professional Women Apply Career Lessons to Job of Childbirth." *Wall Street Journal*, August 17, 1984.

Day, Nancy. "Dual Career Marriages: Making Them Work." *Harvard Business School Bulletin*, April 1985.

Dizard, Wilson P., Jr. *The Coming Information Age*. New York: Annenberg/Longman Communication Books, 1982.

Dullea, Georgia. "Ranks of American Nannies Are Growing." *New York Times*, January 18, 1985.

Elder, Janet. "New Programs Offer Assistance for Latchkey Children." *New York Times*, September 5, 1985.

Fader, Shirley Sloan. "A Guide to Part-Time Work." *Ladies' Home Journal*, October 1984.

Fallows, Deborah. *A Mother's Work*. Boston: Houghton Mifflin, 1985.

Ferraro, Geraldine A. *Ferraro: My Story*. New York: Bantam Books, 1985.

Foegen, J. H. "A New View towards Part-Timers." *Administrative Management*, July 1984.

"For Love and Money." *Ms.*, November 1985.

Fraiberg, Selma. *Every Child's Birthright: In Defense of Mothering*. New York: Basic Books, 1977.

Freeman, Marsha A. "Women in the Legal Profession." *Bench & Bar of Minnesota*, September 1984.

Freudenberger, Herbert J., and Gail North. *Women's Burnout*. New York: Doubleday, 1985.

Friedan, Betty. *The Feminine Mystique*. New York: Norton, 1963.

————. *The Second Stage*. New York: Summit Books, 1981.

Gallese, Liz Romano. *Women Like Us*. New York: Morrow, 1985.

Garland, Anne Witte. "The Surprising Boom of Women Entrepreneurs: If You Need an Employer, Why Not Become One?" *Ms.*, July 1985.

Gillis, Phyllis. *Entrepreneurial Mothers*. New York: Rawson Associates, 1984.

Hall, Trish. "Many Women Decide They Want Careers Rather Than Children." *Wall Street Journal*, October 10, 1984.

Bibliography

Hayghe, Howard. "Working Mothers Reach Record Number in 1984." Research Summaries Division, *Monthly Labor Review*, December 1984.

Hirsch, Stuart A. "In Support of Stay-at-Home Mothers." *Baltimore Sun*, January 25, 1984.

Hitchings, Bradley. "Today's Choices in Child Care." *Business Week*, April 1, 1985.

Hodges, Jill R. "Homemakers Get Champion at Last." *Washington Post*, January 10, 1984.

Josefowitz, Natasha. *Paths to Power*. Reading, Mass.: Addison-Wesley, 1980.

Kagan, Julia. "Who Succeeds and Who Doesn't." *Working Woman*, October 1985.

Kanter, Rosebeth Moss. *The Change Masters*. New York: Simon & Schuster, 1983.

Kantrowitz, Barbara. "A Mother's Choice." *Newsweek*, March 31, 1986.

Keller, Bill. "Of Health and Home, and the Right to Work." *New York Times*, November 11, 1984.

Kennedy, Marilyn Moats. "Can You Afford to Take Time Out from Your Career?" *Glamour*, June 1985.

Klemesrud, Judy. "Mothers Who Shift Back from Jobs to Homemaking." *New York Times*, January 19, 1983.

Larsen, Dave. "Professor of Motherhood Offers Advice." Los Angeles Times Service, *Minneapolis Star and Tribune*, January 6, 1985.

Larsen, Erik. "Working at Home: Is It Freedom or a Life of Flabby Loneliness?" *Wall Street Journal*, February 13, 1985.

Lee, Patricia. *The Complete Guide to Job-Sharing*. New York: Walker & Company, 1983.

Lindsay, Robert. "Increased Demand for Day Care Prompts a Debate on Regulation." *New York Times*, September 2, 1984.

Lublin, Joanna S. "More Managers Are Working Part Time; Some Like It, But Others Have No Choice." *Wall Street Journal*, July 2, 1982.

————. "Mutual Aid: Firms and Job-Seekers Discover More Benefits of Part-Time Positions." *Wall Street Journal*, October 4, 1978.

————. "Running a Firm from Home Gives Women More Flexibility." *Wall Street Journal*, December 31, 1984.

Bibliography

Lueck, Thomas J. "A Boom in Temporary Work." *New York Times*, October 24, 1985.

Margolick, David. "Columbia to Pick Woman as Law School Dean." *New York Times*, January 2, 1986.

Marie, Joan S. "Her Honor: The Rancher's Daughter (Sandra Day O'Connor)." *Saturday Evening Post*, September 1985.

Moorman, Barbara, and Barney Olmsted. "V-Time: A New Way to Work." San Francisco: New Ways to Work, 1985.

Morse, Susan. "Careers: Is Part-Time Working?" *The Washington Post*, July 2, 1984.

Naisbitt, John, and Patricia Aburdene. *Reinventing the Corporation.* New York: Warner Books, 1985.

New Ways to Work Staff. *Job Sharing in Health Care.* San Francisco: New Ways to Work, 1984.

———. *Job Sharing in the Schools.* San Francisco: New Ways to Work, 1980.

New Ways to Work—Karyn Feiden and Linda Marks. *Negotiating Time: New Scheduling Options in the Legal Profession.* San Francisco: New Ways to Work, 1986.

"Number of Working Mothers Now at Record Levels." *News*, July 26, 1984, U.S. Department of Labor, Bureau of Labor Statistics, Washington, D.C.

Olmsted, Barney, and Suzanne Smith. *The Job Sharing Handbook.* Harmondsworth, England: Penguin Books, 1983.

Part-Time Employment in America, McLean, Va.: Association of Part-Time Professionals, April 1984.

Peterson, Karen S. "Putting a Career on Hold to Raise Kids." *USA Today*, January 8, 1985.

Pokela, Barbara. "Women Entrepreneurs Learn from One Another." *Minneapolis Star and Tribune*, September 20, 1985.

Ricks, Thomas E. "New Minority of Mothers at Home Finds Support in Family Centers." *Wall Street Journal*, October 25, 1985.

Rogan, Helen. "Executive Women Find It Difficult to Balance Demands of Job, Home." *Wall Street Journal*, October 30, 1984.

Rotchford, Nancy L., and Karlene M. Roberts. "Part Time Workers as Missing Persons in Organizational Research." *Academy of Management Review*, 1982.

Rothberg, Diane S., and Barbara Ensor Cook. *Part Time Professional.* Washington, D.C.: Acropolis Books, 1985.

Bibliography

Rubin, Lillian B. *Just Friends: The Role of Friendship in Our Lives.* New York: Harper & Row, 1985.

Scarr, Sandra. "A Child-Care Checklist." *Ms.,* January 1985.

Scheele, Adele. "Freelancing Is for Those Who Don't Seek Guarantees." *Minneapolis Star and Tribune,* November 6, 1984.

Steinem, Gloria. "Good News: Here Come the New Megatrends." *Ms.,* July 1985.

Stern, Carol Simpson, Jesse M. Choper, Mary W. Gray, and Robert J. Wolfson. "The Status of Part Time Faculty." *Academe,* February/March 1981.

Traywick, Robin. "Magazine for Mothers at Home." *Richmond Times Dispatch,* February 21, 1984.

Wagner, Barbara, and Robert Grant. "The New One Paycheck Family." *Ladies' Home Journal,* September 1984.

Walsh, Mary Williams. "Career Women Rely on Day Care Nannies to Meet Child Care Needs." *Wall Street Journal,* September 25, 1984.

Walter, Stephanie K., and Sherli Evans. "Telecommuting: An Idea Whose Time Has Almost Come." *Management Technology,* January 1984.

"What the Boom in Part-Time Work Means for Management." *International Management,* May 1984.

Important Resources

BOOKS

Woman at Home (originally published by Doubleday in 1976). So many women have asked me how to obtain copies of *Woman at Home*, my first book on the issue of home-based mothering, that I have recently made it available through Woman at Home Workshops: 1955 East River Parkway, Minneapolis, Minnesota 55414. $8.95 per copy plus $1.50 postage and handling.

CAREER OPTIONS

The Association of Part-Time Professionals in McLean, Virginia, and **New Ways to Work** in San Francisco, California, are major forces in humanizing today's workplace. Both organizations publish valuable books (as listed in the bibliography under the organization or author names: Diane Rothberg and Barbara Cook of the Association of Part-Time Professionals; Barney Olmsted and Suzanne Smith of New Ways to Work). For an annual fee, each organization provides members with periodic newsletters, updates on current corporate changes, and a variety of other information pertinent to those interested in alternatives to traditional work patterns. New Ways to Work is located at 149 Ninth Street, San Francisco, California 94103; the telephone number is (415) 552-1000.

The Association of Part-Time Professionals' address is Flow

General Building, 7655 Old Springhouse Road, McLean, Virginia 22102; its telephone number is (703) 734-7975.

ORGANIZATIONS

FEMALE is a Chicago-based national organization of formerly employed, currently home-based mothers. For membership and monthly newsletter information, contact FEMALE, P.O. Box 31, Elmhurst, Illinois 60126.

Mothers at Home More, an advocacy group headed by Amy Stewart Stillman, helps parents, their employers, and communities work together to make it easier for parents who want to be at home more to do so. The group maintains a speaker's bureau and functions as a clearing house, collecting and disseminating information about organizations and individuals with similar goals. Their address is P.O. Box 74, Rowayton, Connecticut 06853.